The
Innocent
Man

John Grisham

The Innocent Man

MURDER AND INJUSTICE
IN A SMALL TOWN

C̅

Century · London

Published by Century in 2006

3 5 7 9 10 8 6 4 2

*Grateful acknowledgment is given to the following for permission
to reprint the photos in the insert:*
Courtesy of the Williamson family: page 1, all photos; page 2, bottom right;
page 4, bottom left; page 8, all photos.
Courtesy of the *Ada Evening News*: page 3, middle; page 4, top and bottom right;
page 5, top and middle; page 6, middle; page 7, all photos.
Courtesy of Murl Bowen: page 2, middle.
© John Donovan: page 2, bottom.
Courtesy of the Carter family: page 3, top.
Courtesy of the Wilhoit family: page 5, bottom.
Courtesy of Frank Seay: page 6, top.

First published in Great Britain in 2006 by Century
The Random House Group Limited
20 Vauxhall Bridge Road, London, SW1V 2SA

www.randomhouse.co.uk

Addresses for companies within The Random House Group Limited can be found at:
www.randomhouse.co.uk/offices.htm

The Random House Group Limited Reg. No. 954009

A CIP catalogue record for this book is available from the British Library

Papers used by Random House are
natural, recyclable products made from wood grown in
sustainable forests. The manufacturing processes conform to
the environmental regulations of the country of origin

ISBN (hardback) 1 8441 3790 2
ISBN (hardback) 9781844137909
ISBN (air TPB) 1 8460 5038 3
ISBN (air TPB) 9781846050381
ISBN (UK TPB) 1846051487
ISBN (UK TPB) 9781846051487

Printed and bound in Great Britain by
Mackays of Chatham Plc, Chatham, Kent

Dedicated to
Annette Hudson and Renee Simmons
and to the memory of their brother

The
Innocent
Man

CHAPTER 1

The rolling hills of southeast Oklahoma stretch from Norman across to Arkansas and show little evidence of the vast deposits of crude oil that were once beneath them. Some old rigs dot the countryside; the active ones churn on, pumping out a few gallons with each slow turn and prompting a passerby to ask if the effort is really worth it. Many have simply given up, and sit motionless amid the fields as corroding reminders of the glory days of gushers and wildcatters and instant fortunes.

There are rigs scattered through the farmland around Ada, an old oil town of sixteen thousand with a college and a county courthouse. The rigs are idle, though—the oil is gone. Money is now made in Ada by the hour in factories and feed mills and on pecan farms.

Downtown Ada is a busy place. There are no empty or boarded-up buildings on Main Street. The merchants survive, though much of their business has moved to the edge of town. The cafés are crowded at lunch.

The Pontotoc County Courthouse is old and cramped and full of lawyers and their clients. Around it is the usual hodgepodge of county buildings and law offices. The jail, a squat, windowless bomb shelter, was for some forgotten reason built on the courthouse lawn. The methamphetamine scourge keeps it full.

Main Street ends at the campus of East Central University, home to four thousand students, many of them commuters. The school pumps life into the community with a fresh supply of young people and a faculty that adds some diversity to southeastern Oklahoma.

Few things escape the attention of the *Ada Evening News*, a lively daily that covers the region and works hard to compete with *The Oklahoman*, the state's largest paper. There's usually world and national news on the front page, then state and regional, then the important items— high school sports, local politics, community calendars, and obituaries.

The people of Ada and Pontotoc County are a pleasant blend of small-town southerners and independent westerners. The accent could be from east Texas or Arkansas, with flat *i*'s and other long vowels. It's Chickasaw country. Oklahoma has more Native Americans than any other state, and after a hundred years of mixing many of the white folks have Indian blood. The stigma is fading fast; indeed, there is now pride in the heritage.

The Bible Belt runs hard through Ada. The town has fifty churches from a dozen strains of Christianity. They are active places, and not just on Sundays. There is one Catholic church, and one for the Episcopalians, but no temple or synagogue. Most folks are Christians, or claim to be, and belonging to a church is rather expected. A person's social status is often determined by religious affiliation.

With sixteen thousand people, Ada is considered large for rural Oklahoma, and it attracts factories and discount stores. Workers and shoppers make the drive from several counties. It is eighty miles south and east of Oklahoma City, and three hours north of Dallas. Everybody knows somebody working or living in Texas.

The biggest source of local pride is the quarter-horse "bidness." Some of the best horses are bred by Ada ranchers. And when the Ada

High Cougars win another state title in football, the town struts for years.

It's a friendly place, filled with people who speak to strangers and always to each other and are anxious to help anyone in need. Kids play on shaded front lawns. Doors are left open during the day. Teenagers cruise through the night causing little trouble.

Had it not been for two notorious murders in the early 1980s, Ada would have gone unnoticed by the world. And that would have been just fine with the good folks of Pontotoc County.

As IF by some unwritten city ordinance, most of the nightclubs and watering holes in Ada were on the periphery of the town, banished to the edges to keep the riffraff and their mischief away from the better folks. The Coachlight was one such place, a cavernous metal building with bad lighting, cheap beer, jukeboxes, a weekend band, a dance floor, and outside a sprawling gravel parking lot where dusty pickups greatly outnumbered sedans. Its regulars were what you would expect—factory workers looking for a drink before heading home, country boys looking for fun, late-night twenty-somethings, and the dance and party crowd there to listen to live music. Vince Gill and Randy Travis passed through early in their careers.

It was a popular and busy place, employing many part-time bartenders and bouncers and cocktail waitresses. One was Debbie Carter, a twenty-one-year-old local girl who'd graduated from Ada High School a few years earlier and was enjoying the single life. She held two other part-time jobs and also worked occasionally as a babysitter. Debbie had her own car and lived by herself in a three-room apartment above a garage on Eighth Street, near East Central University. She was a pretty girl, dark-haired, slender, athletic, popular with the boys, and very independent.

Her mother, Peggy Stillwell, worried that she was spending too much time at the Coachlight and other clubs. She had not raised her daughter to live such a life; in fact, Debbie had been raised in the church. After high school, though, she began partying and keeping later hours. Peggy objected and they fought occasionally over the new lifestyle. Debbie became determined to have her independence. She found an apartment, left home, but remained very close to her mother.

On the night of December 7, 1982, Debbie was working at the Coachlight, serving drinks and watching the clock. It was a slow night, and she asked her boss if she could go off-duty and hang out with some friends. He did not object, and she was soon sitting at a table having a drink with Gina Vietta, a close friend from high school, and some others. Another friend from high school, Glen Gore, stopped by and asked Debbie to dance. She did, but halfway through the song she suddenly stopped and angrily walked away from Gore. Later, in the ladies' restroom, she said she would feel safer if one of her girlfriends would spend the night at her place, but she did not say what worried her.

The Coachlight began closing early, around 12:30 a.m., and Gina Vietta invited several of their group to have another drink at her apartment. Most said yes; Debbie, though, was tired and hungry and just wanted to go home. They drifted out of the club, in no particular hurry.

Several people saw Debbie in the parking lot chatting with Glen Gore as the Coachlight was shutting down. Tommy Glover knew Debbie well because he worked with her at a local glass company. He also knew Gore. As he was getting in his pickup truck to leave, he saw Debbie open the driver's door of her car. Gore appeared from nowhere, they talked for a few seconds, then she pushed him away.

Mike and Terri Carpenter both worked at the Coachlight, he as a bouncer, she as a waitress. As they were walking to their car, they passed Debbie's. She was in the driver's seat, talking to Glen Gore, who was standing beside her door. The Carpenters waved good-bye and kept walking. A month earlier Debbie had told Mike that she was afraid of Gore because of his temper.

Toni Ramsey worked at the club as a shoe-shine girl. The oil business was still booming in Oklahoma in 1982. There were plenty of nice boots being worn around Ada. Someone had to shine them, and Toni picked up some much-needed cash. She knew Gore well. As Toni left that night, she saw Debbie sitting behind the wheel of her car. Gore was on the passenger's side, crouching by the open door, outside the car. They were talking in what seemed to be a civilized manner. Nothing appeared to be wrong.

Gore, who didn't own a car, had bummed a ride to the Coachlight with an acquaintance named Ron West, arriving there around 11:30. West ordered beers and settled in to relax while Gore made the rounds. He seemed to know everyone. When last call was announced, West grabbed Gore and asked him if he still needed a ride. Yes, Gore said, so West went to the parking lot and waited for him. A few minutes passed, then Gore appeared in a rush and got in.

They decided they were hungry, so West drove to a downtown café called the Waffler, where they ordered a quick breakfast. West paid for the meal, just as he'd paid for the drinks at the Coachlight. He had started the night at Harold's, another club where he'd gone looking for some business associates. Instead, he bumped into Gore, who worked there as an occasional bartender and disc jockey. The two hardly knew each other, but when Gore asked for a ride to the Coachlight, West couldn't say no.

West was a happily married father with two young daughters and didn't routinely keep late hours in bars. He wanted to go home but was stuck with Gore, who was becoming more expensive by the hour. When they left the café, West asked his passenger where he wanted to go. To his mother's house, Gore said, on Oak Street, just a few blocks to the north. West knew the town well and headed that way, but before they made it to Oak Street, Gore suddenly changed his mind. After riding around with West for several hours, Gore wanted to walk. The temperature was frigid and falling, with a raw wind. A cold front was moving in.

They stopped near the Oak Avenue Baptist Church, not far from where Gore said his mother lived. He jumped out, said thanks for everything, and began walking west.

The Oak Avenue Baptist Church was about a mile from Debbie Carter's apartment.

Gore's mother actually lived on the other side of town, nowhere near the church.

Around 2:30 a.m., Gina Vietta was in her apartment with some friends when she received two unusual phone calls, both from Debbie Carter. In the first call, Debbie asked Gina to drive over and pick her up because someone, a visitor, was in her apartment and he was making her feel uncomfortable. Gina asked who it was, who was there? The conversation was cut short by muffled voices and the sounds of a struggle over the use of the phone. Gina was rightfully worried and thought the request strange. Debbie had her own car, a 1975 Oldsmobile, and could certainly drive herself anywhere. As Gina was hurriedly leaving her apartment, the phone rang again. It was Debbie, saying that she had changed her mind, things were fine on her end, don't bother. Gina again asked who the visitor was, but Debbie changed the subject and would not give his name. She asked Gina to call her in the morning, to wake her so she wouldn't be late for work. It was an odd request, one Debbie had never made before.

Gina started to drive over anyway, but had second thoughts. She had guests in her apartment. It was very late. Debbie Carter could take care of herself, and besides, if she had a guy in her room, Gina didn't want to intrude. Gina went to bed and forgot to call Debbie a few hours later.

Around 11:00 a.m. on December 8, Donna Johnson stopped by to say hello to Debbie. The two had been close in high school before Donna moved to Shawnee, an hour away. She was in town for the day to see her parents and catch up with some friends. As she bounced up the narrow outdoor staircase to Debbie's garage apartment, she slowed when she realized she was stepping on broken glass. The small window in the door was broken. For some reason, her first thought was that Debbie had locked her keys inside and been forced to break a window to get in. Donna knocked on the door. There was no answer. Then she heard music from a radio inside. When she turned the knob, she realized the door was not locked. One step inside, and she knew something was wrong.

The small den was a wreck—sofa cushions thrown on the floor, clothing scattered about. Across the wall to the right someone had scrawled, with some type of reddish liquid, the words "Jim Smith next will die."

Donna yelled Debbie's name; no response. She had been in the apartment once before, so she moved quickly to the bedroom, still calling for her friend. The bed had been moved, yanked out of place, all the covers pulled off. She saw a foot, then on the floor on the other side of the bed she saw Debbie—facedown, nude, bloody, with something written on her back.

Donna froze in horror, unable to step forward, instead staring at her friend and waiting for her to breathe. Maybe it was just a dream, she thought.

She backed away and stepped into the kitchen, where, on a small white table, she saw more words scribbled and left behind by the killer. He could still be there, she suddenly thought, then ran from the apartment to her car. She sped down the street to a convenience store where she found a phone and called Debbie's mother.

Peggy Stillwell heard the words, but could not believe them. Her daughter was lying on the floor nude, bloodied, not moving. She made Donna repeat what she had said, then ran to her car. The battery was dead. Numb with fear, she ran back inside and called Charlie Carter, Debbie's father and her ex-husband. The divorce a few years earlier had not been amicable, and the two rarely spoke.

No one answered at Charlie Carter's. A friend named Carol Edwards lived across the street from Debbie. Peggy called her, told her something was terribly wrong, and asked her to run and check on her daughter. Then Peggy waited and waited. Finally she called Charlie again, and he answered the phone.

Carol Edwards ran down the street to the apartment, noticed the same broken glass and the open front door. She stepped inside and saw the body.

Charlie Carter was a thick-chested brick mason who occasionally worked as a bouncer at the Coachlight. He jumped in his pickup and raced toward his daughter's apartment, along the way thinking every horrible thought a father could have. The scene was worse than anything he could have imagined.

When he saw her body, he called her name twice. He knelt beside her, gently lifted her shoulder so he could see her face. A bloody wash-cloth was stuck in her mouth. He was certain his daughter was dead, but he waited anyway, hoping for some sign of life. When there was none, he stood slowly and looked around. The bed had been moved, shoved away from the wall, the covers were missing, the room was in disarray. Obviously, there had been a struggle. He walked to the den and saw the words on the wall, then he went to the kitchen and looked around. It was a crime scene now. Charlie stuffed his hands in his pockets and left.

Donna Johnson and Carol Edwards were on the landing outside the front door, crying and waiting. They heard Charlie say good-bye to his daughter and tell her how sorry he was for what had happened to her. When he stumbled outside, he was crying, too.

"Should I call an ambulance?" Donna asked.

"No," he said. "Ambulance won't do no good. Call the police."

THE paramedics arrived first, two of them. They hustled up the stairs, into the apartment, and within seconds one was back outside, on the landing, vomiting.

When Detective Dennis Smith arrived at the apartment, the scene outside was busy with street cops, paramedics, onlookers, and even two of the local prosecutors. When he realized it was a potential homicide, he secured the area and sealed it off from the neighbors.

A captain and seventeen-year veteran of the Ada Police Department, Smith knew what to do. He cleared the apartment of everyone but himself and another detective, then he sent the other cops throughout the neighborhood, knocking on doors, looking for witnesses. Smith was fuming and fighting his emotions. He knew Debbie well; his daughter and Debbie's youngest sister were friends. He knew Charlie Carter and Peggy Stillwell and couldn't believe that their child was lying dead on the floor of her own bedroom. When the crime scene was under control, he began an examination of the apartment.

The glass on the landing came from a broken pane in the front door, and it was shattered both to the inside and to the outside. In the den there was a sofa to the left, and its cushions had been thrown around the room. In front of it he found a new flannel nightgown, a Wal-Mart tag still attached to it. On the wall across the room he examined the message, which he immediately knew had been written in nail polish. "Jim Smith next will die."

He knew Jim Smith.

In the kitchen, on a small white square table he saw another message, apparently written in catsup—"Don't look fore us or ealse." On the floor by the table he saw some jeans and a pair of boots. He would soon learn that Debbie had been wearing them the night before at the Coachlight.

He walked to the bedroom, where the bed was partially blocking the door. The windows were open, the curtains pulled back, and the room was very cold. A mighty struggle had preceded death; the floor was covered with clothing, sheets, blankets, stuffed animals. Nothing appeared to be in place. When Detective Smith knelt by Debbie's body, he noticed the third message left by the killer. On her back, in what appeared to be dried catsup, were the words "Duke Gram."

He knew Duke Graham.

Under her body was an electrical cord and a Western-style belt with a large silver buckle. The name "Debbie" was engraved in the center of it.

As Officer Mike Kieswetter, also of the Ada Police Department, was photographing the scene, Smith began gathering evidence. He found hair on the body, the floor, the bed, on the stuffed animals. He methodically picked up each hair and placed it in a sheet of folded paper, a "bindle," then recorded exactly where he found it.

He carefully removed, tagged and bagged the bedsheets, pillowcases, blankets, the electrical cord and belt, a pair of torn panties he found on the floor of the bathroom, some of her stuffed animals, a package of Marlboro cigarettes, an empty 7-Up can, a plastic shampoo bottle, cigarette butts, a drinking glass from the kitchen, the telephone, and some hair found under the body. Wrapped in a bedsheet and found near Debbie was a Del Monte catsup bottle. It, too, was carefully bagged for examination by the state crime lab. Its cap was missing, but would later be found by the medical examiner.

When he finished gathering evidence, Detective Smith began the fingerprinting process, something he'd done many times at many crime scenes. He dusted both sides of the front door, the casings around the windows, all wooden surfaces in the bedroom, the kitchen table, the larger pieces of broken glass, the telephone, the areas of painted trim around the doors and windows, even Debbie's car parked outside.

Gary Rogers was an agent with the Oklahoma State Bureau of Investigation, or OSBI, who lived in Ada. When he arrived at the apartment, around 12:30, he was briefed by Dennis Smith. The two were friends and had worked many crimes together.

In the bedroom, Rogers noticed what appeared to be a small bloodstain near the bottom of the south wall, just above the baseboard and close to an electrical outlet. Later, after the body was removed, he asked Officer Rick Carson to cut out a four-inch square section of the Sheetrock and preserve the bloody print.

Dennis Smith and Gary Rogers shared the initial impression that there was more than one killer. The chaos of the scene, the absence of bind marks on Debbie's ankles and wrists, the extensive trauma to her head, the washcloth stuffed deep in her mouth, the bruises on her sides and arms, the likely use of the cord and belt—it just seemed like too much violence for one killer. Debbie was not small—five feet eight inches tall, 130 pounds. She was feisty and would certainly have fought valiantly to save her life.

Dr. Larry Cartmell, the local medical examiner, arrived for a brief inspection. His initial opinion was that the cause of death was strangulation. He authorized the removal of the body and released it to Tom Criswell, owner of the local funeral home. It was taken in a Criswell hearse to the state medical examiner's office in Oklahoma City, where it arrived at 6:25 p.m. and was placed in a refrigerated unit.

DETECTIVE Smith and Agent Rogers returned to the Ada Police Department and spent time with the family of Debbie Carter. As they tried to console them, they also gathered names. Friends, boyfriends, co-workers, enemies, ex-bosses, anybody who knew Debbie and might know something about her death. As the list grew, Smith and Rogers began calling her male acquaintances. Their request was simple: Please come down to the police department and provide us with fingerprints and samples of saliva and head and pubic hair.

No one refused. Mike Carpenter, the bouncer at the Coachlight who'd seen Debbie in the parking lot with Glen Gore around 12:30 that morning, was one of the first to volunteer evidence. Tommy Glover, another witness to Debbie's encounter with Gore, was quick to provide samples.

Around 7:30 p.m., December 8, Glen Gore showed up at Harold's Club, where he was scheduled to spin records and tend bar. The place was practically empty, and when he asked why the crowd was so thin, someone told him about the murder. Many of the customers, and even some of Harold's employees, were down at the police station answering questions and getting fingerprinted.

Gore hustled over to the station, where he was interviewed by Gary Rogers and D. W. Barrett, an Ada policeman. He told them that he had known Debbie Carter since high school and had seen her at the Coachlight the night before.

The entire police report of Gore's interview reads as follows:

Glen Gore works at Harold's Club as a disc jockey. Susie Johnson told Glen about Debbie at Harold's Club about 7:30 PM, 12–8–82. Glen went to school with Debbie. Glen saw her Monday Dec 6th at Harold's Club. Glen saw her 12–7–82 at the Coachlight. They talked about painting Debbie's car. Never said anything to Glen about having problems with anyone. Glen went to the Coachlight about 10:30 PM with Ron West. Left with Ron about 1:15 AM. Glen has never been to Debbie's apt.

The report was prepared by D. W. Barrett, witnessed by Gary Rogers, and filed away with dozens of others.

Gore would later change this story and claim that he'd seen a man named Ron Williamson pestering Debbie at the club on the night of December 7. This revised version would be verified by no one. Many of those present actually knew Ron Williamson, a somewhat notorious carouser with a loud mouth. None remembered seeing him at the Coachlight; in fact, most of those interviewed stated emphatically that he was not there.

When Ron Williamson was in a bar, everyone knew it.

Oddly enough, in the midst of all the fingerprinting and hair clipping on December 8, Gore fell through the cracks. He either slipped away, or was simply neglected. Whatever the reason, he was not fingerprinted, nor did he give saliva and hair samples.

Over three and a half years would pass before the Ada police finally took samples from Gore, the last person seen with Debbie Carter before her murder.

AT 3:00 the following afternoon, December 9, Dr. Fred Jordan, a state medical examiner and forensic pathologist, performed an autopsy. Present were Agent Gary Rogers and Jerry Peters, also with the OSBI.

Dr. Jordan, a veteran of thousands of autopsies, first observed that it was the body of a young white female, nude except for a pair of white socks. Rigor mortis was complete, meaning she had been dead for at least twenty-four hours. Across her chest, written in what appeared to be red fingernail polish, was the word "die." Another red substance, probably catsup, was smeared over her body, and on her back, also in catsup, were the words "Duke Gram."

There were several small bruises on her arms, chest, and face. He noticed small cuts inside her lips, and shoved deep into the back of her throat and extruding out through her mouth was a blood-soaked greenish washcloth, which he carefully removed. There were abrasions and bruises across her neck, in a semicircle. Her vagina was bruised. Her rectum was quite dilated. Upon examining it, Dr. Jordan found and removed a small, metal, screw-type bottle cap.

His internal examination revealed nothing unexpected—collapsed lungs, dilated heart, a few small bruises along the scalp but no underlying brain injury.

All injuries had been inflicted while she was still alive.

There was no indication of binding on her wrists and ankles. A series of small bruises on her forearms were probably defensive wounds. Her blood alcohol content at the time of death was low, .04. Swabs were taken from her mouth, vagina, and anus. Microscopic examinations would later reveal the presence of spermatozoa in her vagina and anus but not in her mouth.

To preserve evidence, Dr. Jordan clipped her fingernails, scraped off a sample of the catsup and nail polish, combed out the loose pubic hairs, and also cut a portion of hair from her head.

The cause of death was asphyxiation, which was caused by the combination of the washcloth choking her and either the belt or the electrical cord strangling her.

When Dr. Jordan finished the autopsy, Jerry Peters photographed the body and collected a complete set of finger and palm prints.

PEGGY STILLWELL was distraught to the point of being unable to function and make decisions. She didn't care who planned the funeral, or what was planned, because she would not attend. She couldn't eat and she couldn't bathe, and she certainly could not accept the fact that her daughter was dead. A sister, Glenna Lucas, stayed with her and slowly took control. Services were planned, and Peggy was politely informed by her family that she would be expected to attend.

On Saturday, December 11, Debbie's funeral was held in the chapel at Criswell Funeral Home. Glenna bathed and dressed Peggy, then drove her to the service and held her hand throughout the ordeal.

In rural Oklahoma, virtually all funerals take place with the casket open and positioned just below the pulpit, so that the deceased is in view of the mourners. The reasons for this are unclear and forgotten, but the effect is to add an extra layer of agony to the suffering.

With the casket open, it was obvious that Debbie had been beaten. Her face was bruised and swollen, but a high-collared, lacy blouse hid the strangulation wounds. She was also buried in her favorite jeans and boots, with a wide-buckled cowboy belt and a diamond horseshoe ring that her mother had already bought her for Christmas.

The Reverend Rick Summers conducted the service before a large crowd. Afterward, with a light snow falling, Debbie was buried in Rosedale Cemetery. She was survived by her parents, two sisters, two of her four grandparents, and two nephews. She was a member of a small Baptist church, where she had been baptized at the age of six.

The murder rocked Ada. Though the town had a rich history of violence and killings, the victims had usually been cowpokes and drifters and such, men who, if they hadn't taken a bullet, would've probably discharged their share in due time. But such a brutal rape and murder of a young woman was terrifying, and the town seethed with gossip, speculation, and fear. Windows and doors were locked at night. Strict curfews were laid down for teenagers. Young mothers hovered near their children as they played on the shaded front lawns.

And in the honky-tonks there was talk of little else. Since Debbie had made the rounds, many of the regulars knew her. She'd had her share of boyfriends, and in the days following her death the police interviewed them. Names were passed along, more friends, more acquaintances, more boyfriends. Dozens of interviews produced more names, but no real suspects. She was a very popular girl, well liked and sociable, and it was hard to believe anyone would want to harm her.

The police put together a list of twenty-three people who were at the Coachlight on December 7, and interviewed most of them. No one recalled seeing Ron Williamson, though most knew him.

Tips and stories and recollections of strange characters poured into the police department. A young lady named Angelia Nail contacted Dennis Smith and told him of an encounter with Glen Gore. She and Debbie Carter were close friends, and Debbie had been convinced Gore had stolen the windshield wipers from her car. It had become a running dispute. She had known Gore since high school and was afraid of him. A week or so before the murder, Angelia drove Debbie to the house where Gore was living for a confrontation. Debbie disappeared inside the house and had a chat with Gore. When she returned to the car, she was angry and convinced he had taken the wipers. They drove to the police station and talked to an officer, but no formal report was prepared.

BOTH Duke Graham and Jim Smith were well known to the Ada police. Graham, along with his wife, Johnnie, ran his own nightclub, a fairly civilized place where they tolerated little trouble. Altercations were rare, but there had been a particularly ugly one with Jim Smith, a local thug and small-time criminal. Smith was drunk and causing trouble, and when he refused to leave, Duke whipped out a shotgun and ran him off. Threats were exchanged, and for a few days things were tense around the club. Smith was the type who might return with his own shotgun and start blasting away.

Glen Gore had been a regular at Duke's place until he spent too much time flirting with Johnnie. When he became a bit too aggressive, she stiff-armed him and Duke took charge. Gore was banished from the place.

Whoever killed Debbie Carter tried awkwardly to pin the murder on Duke Graham and scare away Jim Smith at the same time. Smith was already put away; he was serving time in a state prison. Duke Graham drove to the police station and provided a solid alibi.

DEBBIE'S family was informed that the apartment she'd been renting needed to be vacated. Her mother was still not functioning. Her aunt Glenna Lucas volunteered for the unpleasant task.

A policeman unlocked the apartment, and Glenna entered slowly. Nothing had been moved since the murder, and her first reaction was one of raw anger. There had obviously been a brawl. Her niece had fought desperately for her life. How could anyone inflict such violence on such a sweet, pretty girl?

The apartment was cold, with an offensive smell, one she could not identify. The words "Jim Smith next will die" were still on the wall. Glenna gawked in disbelief at the killer's badly scrawled message. It took time, she thought. He was here for a long time. Her niece had finally died after a brutal ordeal. In the bedroom, the mattress was against a wall and nothing was in place. In the closet, not a single dress or blouse was still on a hanger. Why would the killer strip all the clothing from the hangers?

The small kitchen was disorganized but showed no signs of a struggle. Debbie's last meal had included frozen potatoes—Tater Tots—and the leftovers sat untouched on a paper plate with catsup. A saltshaker was next to the plate, which was on the small white table she used for her meals. Near the plate was another crude message—"Don't look fore us or ealse." Glenna knew that the killer had used catsup for some of his writings. She was struck by the misspelled words.

Glenna managed to block out the terrible thoughts and begin packing. It took two hours to collect and box the clothing and dishes and towels and such. The bloody bedspread had not been taken by the police. There was still blood on the floor.

Glenna had not planned to clean the apartment, just to gather Debbie's belongings and get out as soon as possible. It was strange, though, leaving behind the killer's words written in Debbie's fingernail polish. And there was something wrong with leaving her bloodstains on the floor for someone else to clean up.

She thought about scrubbing the place, every inch of it, to remove every remaining trace of the murder. But Glenna had seen enough. She was as close to the death as she cared to be.

THE ROUNDUP of the usual suspects continued in the days following the murder. A total of twenty-one men gave fingerprints and samples of either hair or saliva. On December 16, Detective Smith and Agent Rogers drove to the OSBI crime lab in Oklahoma City and delivered the evidence taken from the murder scene, along with samples taken from seventeen of the men.

The four-inch square of Sheetrock was the most promising piece of evidence. If the bloody print had indeed been left on the wall during the struggle and murder, and if it did not belong to Debbie Carter, then the police would have a solid lead that would eventually take them to the killer. OSBI agent Jerry Peters examined the Sheetrock and carefully compared its markings with the prints he'd taken from Debbie during her autopsy. His first impression was that the prints did not belong to Debbie Carter, but he wanted to review his analysis.

On January 4, 1983, Dennis Smith submitted more fingerprints. On the same day, the hair samples from Debbie Carter and from the crime scene were given to Susan Land, an OSBI hair analyst. Two weeks later, more crime scene samples landed on her desk. These were cataloged, added to the others, and placed in a long line to someday be examined and analyzed by Land, who was overworked and fighting a backlog of cases. Like most crime labs, Oklahoma's was underfunded, understaffed, and under enormous pressure to solve crimes.

While they waited on results from the OSBI, Smith and Rogers plowed ahead, chasing leads. The murder was still the hottest news in Ada, and folks wanted it solved. But after talking to all the bartenders and bouncers and boyfriends and late-night characters, the investigation was quickly settling into drudgery. There was no clear suspect; there were no clear leads.

On March 7, 1983, Gary Rogers interviewed Robert Gene Deatherage, a local. Deatherage had just completed a short stint in the Pontotoc County jail for drunk driving. He had shared a cell with one Ron Williamson, also locked up for a DUI. The jailhouse chatter about the Carter murder was rampant, with plenty of wild theories about what happened and no shortage of claims of inside knowledge. The cell mates talked about the killing on several occasions, and, according to Deatherage, such talk seemed to bother Williamson. They argued often and even exchanged blows. Williamson was soon moved to another cell. Deatherage developed the vague opinion that Ron was somehow involved in the murder, and suggested to Gary Rogers that the police concentrate on Williamson as a suspect.

It was the first time Ron Williamson's name had been mentioned in the investigation.

Two days later, the police interviewed Noel Clement, one of the first men to volunteer fingerprints and hair samples. Clement told the story of how Ron Williamson had recently visited his apartment, supposedly looking for someone else. Williamson walked in without knocking, saw a guitar, picked it up, and began discussing the Carter murder with Clement. During the conversation, Williamson said that when he saw police cars in his neighborhood the morning of the murder, he figured

the cops were after him. He'd had some trouble in Tulsa, he said, and he
was trying to avoid more of it in Ada.

IT WAS inevitable that the police would find their way to Ron Williamson; indeed, it was odd that it took them three months to question him.
A few, including Rick Carson, had grown up with him, and most of the
cops remembered Ron from his high school baseball days. In 1983 he
was still the highest draft pick Ada had ever produced. When he signed
with the Oakland A's in 1971, many people, certainly including Williamson himself, thought he just might be the next Mickey Mantle, the next
great one from Oklahoma.

But the baseball was long gone, and the police now knew him as an
unemployed guitar picker who lived with his mother, drank too much,
and acted strange.

He had a couple of DUIs, one arrest for public drunkenness, and
a bad reputation from Tulsa.

CHAPTER 2

R on Williamson was born in Ada on February 3, 1953, the only son
and last child of Juanita and Roy Williamson. Roy worked as a
door-to-door salesman for the Rawleigh home products company. He
was a fixture in Ada, trudging down the sidewalks in coat and tie with
his heavy sample case filled with food supplements, spices, and kitchen
products. He always carried a pocketful of candy for the kids who ea-
gerly greeted him. It was a hard way to make a living, physically grueling
and with long hours of paperwork at night. His commissions were modest, and soon after Ronnie was born, Juanita took a job with the hospital
in Ada.

With both parents working, Ronnie naturally fell into the lap of his
twelve-year-old sister, Annette, and she could not have been happier. She
fed him, cleaned him, played with him, pampered and spoiled him—he
was a wonderful little plaything she'd been lucky enough to inherit.
When Annette wasn't in school, she was babysitting her brother, as well
as cleaning the house and preparing dinner.

Renee, the middle child, was five when Ron was born, and though she had no desire to care for him, she soon became his playmate. Annette bossed her around, too, and as they grew older, Renee and Ronnie often tag-teamed against their motherlike guardian.

Juanita was a devout Christian, a headstrong woman who had her family in church every Sunday and Wednesday and whenever other services were offered. The children never missed Sunday school, vacation Bible school, summer camp, revivals, church socials, even a few weddings and funerals. Roy was less devout, but nonetheless adhered to a disciplined lifestyle: a faithful church attendance, absolutely no alcohol, gambling, swearing, card playing, or dancing; and complete devotion to his family. He was strict with his rules and quick to yank off his belt and deliver bold threats or an actual lick or two, usually to the backside of his only son.

The family worshipped at the First Pentecostal Holiness Church, an energetic, full-gospel congregation. As Pentecostals, they believed in a fervent prayer life, the constant nurturing of a personal relationship with Christ, faithfulness to the church and all aspects of its work, diligent study of the Bible, and a loving embrace of other members. Worship was not for the timid, with vibrant music, fiery sermons, and emotional participation from the congregation, which often included the speaking of unknown tongues, on-the-spot healing, or "laying on of hands," and a general openness in expressing, loudly, whatever emotion the Spirit was pulling forth.

Young children were taught the colorful stories of the Old Testament and were prompted to memorize the more popular Bible verses. They were encouraged to "accept Christ" at an early age—to confess sin, ask the Holy Spirit to enter their lives for eternity, and follow the example of Christ with a public baptism. Ronnie accepted Christ at the age of six and was baptized in the Blue River, south of town, at the end of a long spring revival.

The Williamsons lived quietly in a small house on Fourth Street, on the east side of Ada, near the college. For relaxation, they visited relatives in the area, stayed busy with church work, and camped occasionally at a nearby state park. They had little interest in sports, but that changed dramatically when Ronnie discovered baseball. He started playing with the other boys on the street, pickup games of a dozen varieties and endless rule changes. From the beginning it was obvious that his arm was strong and his hands were quick. He swung the bat from the left side of the plate. He was hooked on the game from day one, and was soon bugging his father to buy him a glove and a bat. Spare money was scarce around the house, but Roy took the kid shopping. An annual rite was born—the early springtime trip to Haynes Hardware for the selection of a new glove. And it was usually the most expensive one in the store.

When he wasn't using the glove, he kept it in a corner of his bedroom where he erected a shrine to Mickey Mantle, the greatest Yankee and the greatest Oklahoman in the major leagues. Mantle was idolized by kids throughout the country, but in Oklahoma he was godlike. Every Little Leaguer in the state dreamed of being the next Mickey, including Ronnie, who taped photos and baseball cards of the Mick to a poster board in the corner of his room. By the age of six he could recite every Mantle statistic, as well as those of many other players.

When he wasn't playing in the streets, Ronnie was in the living room, swinging the bat with all the force he could muster. The house was very small, the furnishings modest but irreplaceable, and whenever his mother caught him flailing away and barely missing a lamp or a chair, she ran him outside. Minutes later, he was back. To Juanita, her little boy was special. Though somewhat spoiled, he could do nothing wrong.

He was also very confusing. He could be sweet and sensitive, unafraid to show his affection to his mother and sisters, and, a moment later, bratty and selfish, making demands of the entire family. His mood swings were noticed early in life but were the cause of no particular alarm. Ronnie was simply a difficult child at times. Perhaps it was because he was the youngest and had a houseful of women doting on him.

IN EVERY small town there is a Little League coach who loves the game so much that he is constantly on the prowl for fresh talent, even that of an eight-year-old. In Ada, the guy was Dewayne Sanders, coach of the Police Eagles. He worked at a corner service station not far from the Williamson home on Fourth Street. Word reached Coach Sanders about the Williamson kid, and he was soon signed up.

Even at such an early age, it was obvious Ronnie could play the game. And it was odd because his father knew very little about baseball. Ronnie had picked it up on the streets.

In the summer months, baseball began early in the day as the boys gathered and talked about the Yankee game the day before. Only the Yankees. They studied the box score, talked about Mickey Mantle, tossed the ball around as they waited for more players. A small group meant a game in the street, dodging the occasional car, breaking the occasional window. When more kids showed up, the street ball was abandoned and they headed for a vacant lot for serious games that would last all day. Late in the afternoon they would drift back home, just in time to clean up, eat a bite, put on a uniform, and hurry over to Kiwanis Park for a real game.

The Police Eagles were usually in first place, a testament to the dedication of Dewayne Sanders. The team's star was Ronnie Williamson. His name first appeared in the *Ada Evening News* when he was just nine years old—"The Police Eagles used 12 hits, including 2 homers by Ron Williamson, who also had 2 doubles."

Roy Williamson was at every game, watching quietly from the bleachers. He never yelled at an umpire or a coach, nor did he yell at his own son. Occasionally, after a bad game, he would offer fatherly advice, usually about life in general. Roy had never played baseball and was still learning the game. His young son was years ahead of him.

When Ronnie was eleven, he moved up to the Ada Kids League and was the top draft pick of the Yankees, sponsored by the Oklahoma State Bank. He led the team to an undefeated season.

When he was twelve, still playing for the Yankees, the Ada paper followed the team's season: "Oklahoma State Bank scored 15 runs in the bottom of the first inning . . . Ronnie Williamson had 2 triples" (June 9, 1965); "The Yankees went to bat only three times . . . but the booming bats of Roy Haney, Ron Williamson and James Lamb told the story. Williamson tripled" (June 11, 1965); "The Oklahoma State Bank Yankees scored twice in the opening inning . . . Ron Williamson and Carl Tilley got two of the four hits . . . each being a double" (July 13, 1965); "Meanwhile the Bank team bounced into the second place nest . . . Ronnie Williamson had two doubles and a single" (July 15, 1965).

In the 1960s, Byng High School was about eight miles north and east of the Ada city limits. It was considered a country school, much smaller than the sprawling Ada High School. Though the neighborhood kids could attend Ada High if they chose, and if they were willing to make the drive, virtually all opted for the smaller school, primarily because the Byng bus ran through the east side of town and the Ada bus did not. Most of the kids on Ron's street chose Byng.

At Byng Junior High School, Ronnie was elected secretary of the seventh-grade class, and the following year he was voted president and a class favorite of the eighth grade.

He entered the ninth grade at Byng High School in 1967, one of sixty freshman.

Byng did not play football—that was unofficially reserved for Ada, whose powerful teams annually competed for the state title. Byng was a basketball school, and Ronnie picked up the game his freshman year and absorbed it as quickly as he had baseball.

Though never a bookworm, he did enjoy reading and made As and Bs. Math was his favorite subject. When he was bored with textbooks, he plowed through dictionaries and encyclopedias. He grew obsessive with certain topics. In the midst of a dictionary binge, he would pepper his friends with words they'd never heard of, chiding them if they did not know the meanings. He studied every American president, memorized countless details about each one, then for months talked of nothing else. Though he was steadily growing away from his church, he still knew dozens of verses of Scripture, which he often used to his advantage, and more often used to challenge those around him. At times, his obsessions wore thin with his friends and family.

But Ronnie was a gifted athlete, and thus very popular in school. He was elected vice president of his freshman class. The girls noticed him, liked him, wanted to date him, and he certainly was not shy around them. He became very particular about his appearance and fussy about his wardrobe. He wanted nicer clothes than his parents could afford, but he pushed hard for them anyway. Roy began quietly buying himself secondhand clothes so his son could wear better ones.

Annette had married and was living in Ada. In 1969, she and her mother opened the Beauty Casa, a hair salon, on the ground floor of the old Julienne Hotel in downtown Ada. They worked hard and soon built a brisk business, one that included several call girls who used the upper floors of the hotel. These ladies of the evening had been a fixture in the town for decades, and had taken their toll on a few marriages. Juanita could barely tolerate them.

Annette's lifelong inability to say no to her little brother came back to haunt her as he constantly wheedled money out of her for clothes and girls. When he somehow discovered that she had a charge account at a local clothing store, he began adding to it. And he never thought of buying the cheap stuff. Sometimes he would ask permission; often he would not. Annette would explode, they'd argue, then he would con her into paying the bill. She adored him too much to say no, and she wanted her little brother to have the best of everything. In the middle of every fight, he always managed to tell her how much he loved her. And there was no doubt that he did.

Both Renee and Annette worried that their brother was growing too spoiled and putting too much pressure on their parents. At times they lashed out at him; some of the fights were memorable, but Ronnie prevailed. He would cry and apologize and make everybody smile and laugh. The sisters often found themselves sneaking him money to help buy things their parents couldn't afford. He could be self-absorbed, demanding, egocentric, downright childish—the obvious baby of the family—and then, with a burst of his oversized personality, he would have the entire family eating out of his hand.

They loved him dearly, and he loved them right back. And even in the midst of their bickering they knew he would get whatever he wanted.

THE SUMMER after Ronnie's ninth grade, a few of the luckier boys planned to attend a baseball camp at a nearby college. Ronnie wanted to go, too, but Roy and Juanita simply couldn't afford it. He persisted; it was a rare opportunity to improve his game and maybe get noticed by college coaches. For weeks he talked of nothing else and pouted when things looked hopeless. Roy finally acquiesced and borrowed the money from a bank.

Ron's next project was the purchase of a motorbike, something Roy and Juanita were opposed to. They went through the usual series of denials and lectures and claims that it was something they simply couldn't afford and too dangerous anyway, so Ronnie announced he would pay for it himself. He found his first job, an afternoon paper route, and began saving every penny. When he had enough for the down payment, he bought the motorbike and arranged monthly payments with the dealer.

The repayment plan was derailed when a tent revival came to town. The Bud Chambers Crusade hit Ada—big crowds, lots of music, charismatic sermons, something to do at night. Ronnie went to the first service, was deeply moved, and returned the next night with most of his savings. When they passed the offering plate, he emptied his pockets. But Brother Bud needed more, so Ronnie returned the next night with the rest of his money. The next day he scraped up all the loose cash he could find or borrow and hustled back to the tent that night for another rowdy service and another hard-earned donation. For the entire week, Ronnie somehow managed to give and give, and when the crusade finally left town, he was flat broke.

Then he quit the paper route because it interfered with baseball. Roy scraped together the money and paid off the motorbike.

With both sisters out of the house, Ronnie demanded all the attention. A less beguiling child might have been intolerable, but he had developed an immense talent for charm. Warm, outgoing, and generous himself, he had no problem expecting unwarranted generosity from his family.

As Ronnie was entering the tenth grade, the football coach at Ada High approached Roy and suggested that his son enroll in the larger school. The kid was a natural athlete; by then everybody in town knew Ronnie was an outstanding basketball and baseball player. But Oklahoma is football country, and the coach assured Roy that the lights were brighter playing on the gridiron for the Ada Cougars. With his size, speed, and arm, he could quickly develop into a top player, possibly a recruit. The coach offered to stop by the house each morning and give the kid a ride to school.

The decision was Ronnie's, and he stuck with Byng, for two more years anyway.

THE RURAL community of Asher sits almost unnoticed on Highway 177 twenty miles north of Ada. It has few people—fewer than five hundred—no downtown to speak of, a couple of churches, a water tower, and a few paved streets with some aging homes scattered about. Its pride is a beautiful baseball field, just past its tiny, Class-B high school on Division Street.

Like most very small towns, Asher seems an unlikely place for anything noteworthy, but for forty years it had the winningest high school baseball team in the nation. In fact, no high school in history, public or private, has won as many games as the Asher Indians.

It all began in 1959 when a young coach named Murl Bowen arrived and inherited a long-neglected program—the 1958 team did not win a game. Things changed quickly. Within three years Asher had its first state title. Dozens would follow.

For reasons that are unlikely to ever become clear, Oklahoma sanctions varsity baseball in the fall, but only for those schools too small for football. During his career at Asher, it was not unusual for Coach Bowen's teams to win a state title in the fall, then follow it up with another in the spring. During one remarkable stretch, Asher qualified for the state finals sixty straight times—thirty years in a row, fall and spring.

In forty years, Coach Bowen's teams won 2,115 games, lost only 349, hauled home forty-three state championship trophies, and sent dozens of players to college and minor-league baseball. In 1975, Bowen was named the national high school coach of the year, and the town rewarded him by upgrading Bowen Field. In 1995, he received the same award again.

"It wasn't me," he says modestly, looking back. "It was the kids. I never scored a run."

Maybe not, but he certainly produced enough. Beginning each August, when temperatures in Oklahoma often reach a hundred degrees, Coach Bowen would gather his small group of players and plan the next assault on the state play-offs. His rosters were always slim—each graduating class at Asher had about twenty kids, half girls—and it was not unusual to have a squad of only a dozen players, including an occasional eighth grader with promise. To make sure no one quit, his first order of business was to pass out the uniforms. Every kid made the team.

Then he worked them, beginning with three-a-day practices. The workouts were beyond rigorous—hours of conditioning, sprinting, running bases, drilling in the fundamentals. He preached hard work, strong legs, dedication, and, above all, sportsmanship. No Asher player ever argued with an umpire, threw a helmet in frustration, or did anything to show up an opponent. If at all possible, no Asher team ever ran up the score against a weaker school.

Coach Bowen tried to avoid weak opponents, especially in the spring, when the season was longer and he had more flexibility with the schedule. Asher became famous for taking on the big schools and beating them. They routinely thrashed Ada, Norman, and the 4A and 5A giants from Oklahoma City and Tulsa. As the legend grew, these teams preferred to travel to Asher, to play on the pristine field that Coach Bowen maintained himself. More often than not, they left on a quiet bus.

His teams were highly disciplined and, some critics said, very well recruited. Asher became a magnet for serious baseball players with big dreams, and it was inevitable that Ronnie Williamson would find his way to the school. During the summer leagues, he met and became close to Bruce Leba, an Asher boy and probably the second-best player in the area, a step or two behind Ronnie. They became inseparable and soon were talking of playing their senior year together at Asher. There were more scouts, both college and professional, hanging around Bowen Field. And there was an excellent chance of winning the state titles in the fall of 1970 and the spring of 1971. Ron's visibility would be much higher just up the road.

Changing schools meant renting a place in Asher, a huge sacrifice for his parents. Money was always tight, and Roy and Juanita would have to commute back and forth to Ada. But Ronnie was determined. He was convinced, as were most baseball coaches and scouts in the area, that he could be a high draft pick the summer after his senior year. His dream of playing professionally was within reach; he just needed an extra push.

There were whispers that he just might be the next Mickey Mantle, and Ronnie heard them.

With covert help from some baseball boosters, the Williamsons rented a small house two blocks from Asher High School, and Ronnie reported in August to Coach Bowen's boot camp. At first, he was overwhelmed by the level of conditioning, the sheer time spent running and running and running. The coach had to explain several times to his new star that iron legs are crucial to hitting, pitching, baserunning, making long throws from the outfield, and surviving the late innings of the second game of a doubleheader with a thin roster. Ronnie was slow to see things this way, but he was soon influenced by the fierce work ethic of his pal Bruce Leba and the other Asher players. He fell in line and was soon in great shape. One of only four seniors on the team, he was soon an unofficial captain and, with Leba, a leader.

Murl Bowen loved his size, speed, and rocket throws from center field. He had a cannon for an arm and a big power swing from the left side. Some of his batting-practice shots over the right field wall were remarkable. When the fall season started, the scouts were back and soon taking serious notes on Ron Williamson and Bruce Leba. With its schedule loaded with small non-football schools, Asher lost only one game and walked through the play-offs for another title. Ron hit .468 with six home runs. Bruce, his friendly rival, hit .444 with six homers. They pushed each other, both certain they were headed for the major leagues.

And they began playing hard off the field as well. They drank beer on the weekends and discovered marijuana. They chased the girls, who were easy to catch because Asher loved its heroes. Partying became a routine, and the clubs and honky-tonks around Ada proved irresistible. If they got too drunk and were afraid of driving back to Asher, they would land at Annette's, where they would wake her up and usually want something to eat, apologizing profusely the entire time. Ronnie would beg her not to tell their parents.

They were careful, though, and managed to avoid trouble with the police. They lived in fear of Murl Bowen, plus the spring of 1971 held such great promise.

Basketball at Asher was little more than a good way for the baseball team to stay in shape. Ron started at forward and led the team in scoring. There was some interest from a couple of small colleges, but none from him. As the season was winding down, he began receiving letters from pro-baseball scouts saying hello, promising to watch him in just a few weeks, requesting schedules, asking him to attend tryout camps during the summer. Bruce Leba was getting letters, too, and they had a grand time comparing their correspondence. Phillies and Cubs one week, Angels and Athletics the next.

When the basketball season ended in late February, it was showtime in Asher.

The team warmed up nicely with a few walkovers, then hit full stride when the big schools came to town. Ron began with a hot bat and never cooled off. The scouts were buzzing, the team was winning, life was good at Asher High. Since they usually faced the ace of their opponent's staff, Coach Bowen's players saw great pitching every week. With more scouts in the bleachers, Ron proved with each game that he could handle anybody's pitching. He hit .500 for the season, with five home runs and forty-six RBIs. He rarely struck out and walked a lot because teams tried to pitch around him. The scouts liked his power and discipline at the plate, his speed to first base, and, of course, his arm.

In late April, he was nominated for the Jim Thorpe Award, for the outstanding high school athlete in the state of Oklahoma.

Asher won twenty-six, lost five, and on May 1, 1971, defeated Glenpool 5-0 to win another state championship.

Coach Bowen nominated Ron and Bruce Leba for all-state consideration. They certainly deserved it, but almost took themselves out of consideration.

A few days before their graduation, with a drastic change in life facing them, they realized that Asher baseball would soon be behind them. They would never be as close as they had been during the past year. A celebration was needed, a particularly memorable night of hell-raising.

At the time, Oklahoma City had three strip clubs. They selected a fine one called the Red Dog, and before heading out, they took a fifth of whiskey and a six-pack of beer from the Leba kitchen. They left Asher with the loot, and by the time they arrived at the Red Dog, they were drunk. They ordered more beer and watched the strippers, who grew prettier by the minute. Lap dances were called for, and the two boys began burning through their cash. Bruce's father had laid down a strict

1:00 a.m. curfew, but the lap dances and the booze kept pushing it back. They finally staggered out around 12:30 a.m., two hours from home. Bruce, driving his new souped-up Camaro, sped away, but stopped suddenly when Ron said something that upset him. They began cursing each other and decided to settle the matter then and there. They spilled out of the Camaro and began fist-fighting in the middle of Tenth Street.

After a few minutes of slugging and kicking, both grew weary and agreed on a quick truce. They got back in the car and resumed their drive home. Neither could remember the cause of the fight; it was just one of the night's details forever lost in a fog.

Bruce missed an exit, took a wrong turn, then, very lost, decided to make a long loop on some unknown country roads, heading back, he thought, in the general direction of Asher. With the curfew blown, he was flying across the countryside. His cohort was comatose in the backseat. Things were very dark until Bruce saw red lights approaching rapidly from the rear.

He remembered stopping in front of the Williams Meat Packing company, but wasn't sure what town was nearby. Wasn't sure of the county, either.

Bruce got out of the car. The state trooper was very nice and asked if he'd been drinking. Yes, sir.

Did you realize you were speeding?

Yes, sir.

They chatted and the officer seemed to have little interest in writing a ticket or making an arrest. Bruce had convinced him that he could drive safely home, when suddenly Ron stuck his head out the back window and yelled something incomprehensible in a thick, slurry voice. Who's that? the officer asked.

Just a friend.

The friend yelled something else, and the state trooper told Ron to get out of the car. For some reason, Ron opened the door away from the highway, and when he did, he fell into a deep ditch.

Both were arrested and taken to jail, a cold, damp place with a shortage of beds. A jailer threw two mattresses on the floor of a tiny cell, and there they spent the night, shivering, terrified, still drunk. They knew better than to call their fathers.

For Ron, it was the first of many nights behind bars.

The next morning the jailer brought them coffee and bacon and advised them to call home. Both did with great hesitation, and two hours later they were released. Bruce drove his Camaro home, alone, while Ron, for some reason, was forced to ride in the car with Mr. Leba and Mr. Williamson. It was a very long two-hour ride, made even longer by the prospect of facing Coach Bowen.

Both fathers insisted that the boys go straight to their coach and tell the truth, which they did. Murl gave them the silent treatment, but did not withdraw their nominations for postseason honors.

They made it to graduation without further incident. Bruce, the class salutatorian, gave a well-honed speech. The commencement address was delivered by the Honorable Frank H. Seay, a popular district court judge from next door in Seminole County.

The Asher High class of 1971 had seventeen students, and for all of them graduation was a significant event, a milestone cherished with their proud families. Very few of their parents had the opportunity to attend college; some had not finished high school. But to Ron and Bruce the ceremony meant little. They were still basking in the glory of state titles and, much more important, dreaming of the major-league draft. Their lives would not end in rural Oklahoma.

A month later, both were named all-state, and Ron was runner-up for Oklahoma player of the year. In the annual state all-star game, they played before a packed house, which included scouts from every major-league team and many colleges. After the game, two scouts, one for the Phillies and one for the Oakland A's, pulled the two aside and made them off-the-record offers. If they would agree to a bonus of $18,000 each, the Phillies would draft Bruce, and the A's would take Ron. Ron thought the offer was too low and declined. Bruce was beginning to worry about his knees, and he, too, thought the money was low. He tried to squeeze the scout by saying he was planning to play for two years at Seminole Junior College. More money might persuade him, but the offer stood.

A month later, Ron was selected by the Oakland Athletics in the second round of the free-agent draft, the forty-first player chosen out of eight hundred, and the first picked from Oklahoma. The Phillies did not draft Bruce but did offer him a contract. Again he declined and headed to junior college. Their dream of playing together professionally began to fade.

Oakland's first official offer was insulting. The Williamsons had no agent or lawyer, but they knew the A's were trying to sign Ron on the cheap.

He traveled alone to Oakland and met with team executives. Their discussions were not productive, and Ron returned to Ada without a contract. They soon called him back, and on his second visit he met with Dick Williams, the manager, and several of the players. The A's second baseman was Dick Green, a friendly sort who showed Ron around the clubhouse and field. They bumped into Reggie Jackson, the unabashed superstar, Mr. Oakland himself, and when Reggie learned that Ron was the team's second-round pick, he asked what position he played.

Dick Green needled Reggie a bit by replying, "Ron's a right fielder." Reggie, of course, owned right field. "Man, you're gonna die in the minors," he said as he walked away. And with that the conversation was over.

Oakland was reluctant to pay a large bonus because they projected Ron as a catcher but had yet to see him catch. Negotiations dragged on with little money being offered.

There were discussions at the dinner table about going to college. Ron had verbally committed to accept a scholarship from the University of Oklahoma, and his parents pushed him to consider that option. It was his one chance for a college education, something that could never be taken away. Ron understood that, but he argued that he could always do college later. When Oakland suddenly offered him $50,000 as a signing bonus, Ron just as suddenly grabbed the money and forgot about college.

It was big news in Asher and Ada. Ron was the highest draft pick ever from the area, and for a brief period the attention had a humbling effect on him. His dream was coming true. He was now a professional baseball player. The sacrifices by his family were paying off. He felt led by the Holy Spirit to get things right with God. He went back to church and in a Sunday night service walked to the altar and prayed with the preacher. Then he addressed the congregation, and thanked his brothers and sisters in Christ for their love and support. God had blessed him; he indeed felt lucky. As he fought back tears, he promised to use his money and talents solely for the glory of the Lord.

He bought himself a new Cutlass Supreme and some clothes. He bought his parents a new color television. Then he lost the rest of the money in a poker game.

In 1971, the Oakland Athletics were owned by Charlie Finley, a maverick who'd moved the team from Kansas City in 1968. He fancied himself a visionary but acted more like a buffoon. He delighted in shaking up the baseball world with such innovations as multicolored uniforms, ball girls, orange baseballs (an idea with a very brief life), and a mechanical jackrabbit that hauled fresh baseballs to the home plate umpire. Anything for more attention. He bought a mule, named it Charley O., and paraded it around the field and even into hotel lobbies.

But while he was hogging the headlines with his eccentricities, he was also building a dynasty. He hired an able manager, Dick Williams, and put together a team that included Reggie Jackson, Joe Rudi, Sal Bando, Bert Campaneris, Rick Monday, Vida Blue, Catfish Hunter, Rollie Fingers, and Tony LaRussa.

The A's of the early 1970s were without a doubt the coolest team in baseball. They wore white cleats—the first and only team to do so—and they had a dazzling array of uniforms, different combinations of green, gold, white, and gray. California cool, with longer hair, facial hair, and an air of nonconformity. For a game that was by then over a hundred years old and demanded that its traditions be worshipped, the A's were outrageous. They had attitude. The country was still hungover from the 1960s. Who needed authority? All rules could be broken, even in such a hidebound place as pro baseball.

In late August 1971, Ron made his third trip to Oakland, this time as an Athletic, a member of the club, one of the boys, a star of the future, though he'd yet to play a game as a professional. He was well received, got the pats on the back and the words of encouragement. He was eighteen years old, but with a round baby face and bangs down to his eyes he looked no more than fifteen. The veterans knew that the odds were stacked against him, as they were for every kid who signed a contract, but they nonetheless made him feel welcome. They'd once been in his shoes.

Less than 10 percent of those who sign pro contracts make it to the big leagues for just one game, but no eighteen-year-old wants to hear it.

Ron loitered around the dugout and the field, hung out with the players, took in pregame batting practice, watched the rather thin crowd file into Oakland Alameda County Coliseum. Long before the first pitch, he was led to a prime seat behind the A's dugout where he watched his new team play. The following day he returned to Ada, determined more than ever to breeze through the minors and crack The Show at the age of twenty. Maybe twenty-one. He'd seen, felt, absorbed the electric atmosphere of a major-league ballpark, and he would never be the same.

His hair got longer, then he tried to grow a mustache, though nature failed to cooperate. His friends thought he was rich, and he certainly worked hard to give that impression. He was different, cooler than most folks around Ada. He'd been to California!

Throughout September he watched with great amusement as the A's won 101 games and clinched the American League West. Soon he'd be up there with them, catching or playing center, wearing the colorful uniforms, long hair and all, part of the hippest crew in the game.

In November, he signed a contract with Topps Chewing Gum, giving the company the exclusive right to exhibit, print, and reproduce his name, face, photo, and signature on a baseball card.

Like every boy in Ada, he'd collected thousands of them; saved them, swapped them, framed them, hauled them around in a shoe box, and saved his coins to buy more. Mickey Mantle, Whitey Ford, Yogi Berra, Roger Maris, Willie Mays, Hank Aaron, all the great players with the valuable cards. Now he would have his own!

The dream was rapidly coming true.

HIS FIRST assignment, though, was Coos Bay, Oregon, Class A in the Northwest League, far from Oakland. His 1972 spring training in Mesa, Arizona, had not been remarkable. He'd turned no heads, caught no one's attention, and Oakland was still trying to figure out where to play him. They put him behind the plate, a position he did not know. They put him on the mound, simply because he could throw so hard.

Bad luck hit late in spring training. His appendix ruptured, and he returned to Ada for surgery. As he waited impatiently for his body to heal, he began drinking heavily to pass the time. Beer was cheap at the local Pizza Hut, and when he grew tired of that place, he drove his new Cutlass over to the Elks Lodge and washed things down with a few bourbon and Cokes. He was bored and anxious to get to a ballpark somewhere, and for some reason, he wasn't sure why, he found refuge in booze. Finally he got the call and left for Oregon.

Playing part-time for the Coos Bay–North Bend Athletics, he had 41 hits in 155 at-bats, an unimpressive average of .265. He caught forty-six games and played a few innings in center field. Late in the season, his contract was assigned to Burlington, Iowa, of the Midwest League, still Class-A ball, but a step up and much closer to home. He played in only seven games for Burlington, then returned to Ada for the off-season.

Every stop in the minor leagues is temporary and unsettling. The players earn very little and live off meager meal money and whatever generosity the host club might offer. At "home," they live in motels offering bargain monthly rates, or cluster in small apartments. On the road, along the bus routes, it's more motels. And bars and nightclubs and strip joints. The players are young, rarely married, far away from their families and whatever structure that gave them, and so they tend to keep late hours. Most are barely out of their teens, immature, pampered for most of their short lives, and all are convinced they'll soon be making the big bucks playing in the big ballparks.

They party hard. Games start at 7:00 p.m. Over by 10:00. A quick shower, and it's time to hit the bars. Staying out all night, sleeping all day, either at home or on the bus. Drinking hard, chasing women, playing poker, smoking grass—it's all part of the seedier side of the minors. And Ron embraced it with enthusiasm.

LIKE any father, Roy Williamson followed his son's season with great curiosity and pride. Ronnie called occasionally and wrote even less, but Roy managed to keep up with his statistics. Twice he and Juanita drove to Oregon to watch their son play. Ronnie was suffering through his rookie year, trying to adjust to hard sliders and sharp curveballs.

Back in Ada, Roy received a phone call from an A's coach. Ron's off-field habits were of some concern—lots of partying, drinking, late nights, hangovers. The kid was being excessive, which was not that unusual for a nineteen-year-old in his first season away from home, but perhaps a strong word from the father might settle him down.

Ron was making calls, too. As the summer wore on and his playing time remained marginal, he became frustrated with the manager and staff and felt he was being underutilized. How could he improve if they left him on the bench?

He chose the risky and seldom-used strategy of going over the heads of his coaches. He began calling the A's front office with a list of complaints. Life was miserable way down in A ball, he simply wasn't playing enough, and he wanted the big shots who'd drafted him to know all about it.

The front office had little sympathy. With hundreds of players in the minors, and most of them miles ahead of Ron Williamson, such calls and complaints quickly wore thin. They knew Ron's numbers and knew he was struggling.

Word came down from the top that the boy needed to shut up and play ball.

WHEN he returned to Ada in the early fall of 1972, he was still the local hero, now with some California edges and affectations. He continued his late-night routines. When the Oakland A's won the World Series for the first time in late October, he led a boisterous celebration in a local honky-tonk. "That's my team!" he yelled repeatedly at the television while his drinking buddies admired him.

Ron's habits changed suddenly, though, when he met and began dating Patty O'Brien, a beautiful young lady and former Miss Ada. The two quickly got serious and saw each other regularly. She was a devout Baptist, drank nothing, and didn't tolerate bad habits from Ron. He was more than happy to clean up and promised to change his ways.

IN 1973 he found himself no closer to the big leagues. After another mediocre spring in Mesa, he was reassigned to the Burlington Bees, where he played in only five games before being transferred to the Key West Conchs of the Florida State League. Class A. In fifty-nine games there, he hit a dismal .137.

For the first time in his life, he was beginning to wonder if he would make it to the big leagues. With two very unimpressive seasons behind him, he had quickly learned that professional pitching, even at the Class-A level, was far more difficult to hit than anything he'd seen at Asher High School. Every pitcher threw hard, every curveball broke sharper. Every player on the field was good, some would make it to the big leagues. His signing bonus had long since been spent and wasted. His smiling face on a baseball card was not nearly as exciting as it had been only two years earlier.

And he felt as though everyone was watching him. All his friends and the fine folks of Ada and Asher were expecting him to fulfill their dreams, to put them on the map. He was the next great one from Oklahoma. Mickey cracked The Show at nineteen. Ron was already behind schedule.

He returned to Ada, and to Patty, who strongly suggested that he find meaningful employment in the off-season. An uncle knew someone in Texas, and Ron drove to Victoria and worked several months with a roofing contractor.

On November 3, 1973, Ron and Patty were married in a large wedding at the First Baptist Church in Ada, her home church. He was twenty years old, still a prospect as far as he was concerned.

Ada saw Ron Williamson as its biggest hero. Now he'd married a beauty queen from a nice family. His life was charmed.

THE NEWLYWEDS drove to Mesa for spring training in February 1974. A new wife added pressure to finally make his move up—maybe not to triple A but at least to double A. His contract for 1974 was with Burlington, but he had no plans to go back there. He was tired of Burlington and Key West, and if the A's sent him back to those places, then the message was clear—they no longer considered him a prospect.

He pushed harder in training, ran more, took extra batting practice, worked as hard as he had back at Asher. Then, during routine infield practice one day, he made a hard throw to second base, and a sharp pain shot through his elbow. He tried to ignore it, telling himself, as all players do, that he could simply play through it. It would go away, just a little spring-training soreness. It was back the next day, and worse after that. By late March, Ron could barely toss a ball around the infield.

On March 31, the A's cut him, and he and Patty made the long drive back to Oklahoma.

Avoiding Ada, they settled in Tulsa, where Ron got a job as a service representative with Bell Telephone. It wasn't a new career, but rather a paycheck while his arm healed and he waited for some baseball person, someone who really knew him, to call. After a few months, though, he was doing the calling, and there was no interest.

Patty got a job in a hospital, and they went about the business of getting themselves established. Annette began sending them $5 and $10 a week, just in case they needed help with the bills. The little supplements stopped when Patty called and explained that Ron was using the money for beer, something she did not approve of.

There was friction. Annette was worried because he was drinking again. She knew little, though, of what was happening in the marriage. Patty was very private and shy by nature, and never really relaxed around the Williamsons. Annette and her husband visited the couple once a year.

When Ron was passed over for a promotion, he quit Bell and began selling life insurance for Equitable. It was 1975, and he still had no baseball contract, still no inquiries from teams looking for neglected talent.

· But with his athletic confidence and outgoing personality, he sold a lot of life insurance. Selling came naturally, and he found himself enjoying the success and the money. He was also enjoying late hours in bars and clubs. Patty hated the drinking and couldn't tolerate the carousing. His pot smoking was now a habit and she detested it. His mood swings were becoming more radical. The nice young man she'd married was changing.

Ron called his parents one night in the spring of 1976, crying and hysterical with the news that he and Patty had fought bitterly and separated. Roy and Juanita, as well as Annette and Renee, were shocked at the news and hopeful that the marriage could be saved. All young couples weather a few storms. Any day now Ronnie would get the phone call, get back in a uniform, and resume his career. Their lives would be on track; the marriage would survive a few dark days.

But it was beyond repair. Whatever their problems, Ron and Patty chose not to talk about them. They quietly filed for divorce on the grounds of irreconcilable differences. The separation was complete. The marriage lasted less than three years.

ROY WILLIAMSON had a childhood friend named Harry Brecheen, or Harry the Cat, as he was known in his baseball days. Both had grown up in Francis, Oklahoma. Harry was scouting for the Yankees. Roy tracked him down and passed along his phone number to his son.

Ron's powers of persuasion paid off in June 1976, when he convinced the Yankees that his arm was fully healed and better than ever. After seeing enough good pitching to realize he couldn't hit it, Ron decided to play to his strength—his right arm. It had always caught the attention of the scouts. Oakland had continually talked of converting him to a pitcher.

He signed a contract with the Oneonta Yankees of the New York–Penn League, Class A, and couldn't wait to get out of Tulsa. The dream was alive again.

He could certainly throw hard, but oftentimes had little idea where the ball was going. His breaking stuff was unpolished; he'd simply not had enough experience. Throwing too hard too quick, the soreness came back, slowly at first, then practically a full-blown limpness. The two-year layoff took its toll, and when the season was over, he was cut again.

Again avoiding Ada, he returned to Tulsa and sold insurance. Annette dropped by to check on him, and when the conversation shifted to baseball and his failures, he began crying hysterically and couldn't stop. He admitted to her that he had long, dark bouts of depression.

Once more accustomed to life in the minors, he fell into his old habits, hanging around bars, chasing women, and drinking a lot of beer. To pass the time, he joined a softball team and enjoyed being the big star on a small stage. During a game, on a cool night, he fired a throw to first base and something snapped in his shoulder. He quit the team and gave up softball, but the damage was done. He saw a doctor and put himself through a strenuous rehab program, but felt little improvement.

And he kept the injury quiet, hoping once again that a good rest would have things healed by spring.

Ron's final sally into professional baseball came the following spring, in 1977. He again talked his way into a Yankee uniform. He survived spring training, still as a pitcher, and was assigned to Fort Lauderdale in the Florida State League. There he endured his final season, all 140 games, half of them on the road, on the buses, as the months dragged by and he was used as sparingly as possible. He pitched in only fourteen games, thirty-three innings. He was twenty-four years old with a damaged shoulder that wouldn't heal. The glory of Asher and the Murl Bowen days were far away.

Most players get a sense of the inevitable, but not Ron. There were too many people back home counting on him. His family had sacrificed too much. He'd bypassed college and an education to become a major leaguer, so quitting was not an option. He had failed at marriage, and he was not accustomed to failure. Plus, he was wearing a Yankee uniform, a vivid symbol that kept the dream alive every day.

He gamely hung on until the end of the season, then his beloved Yankees cut him again.

CHAPTER 3

A few months after the season was over, Bruce Leba was casually walking through the Southroads Mall in Tulsa when he saw a familiar face and stopped cold. Just inside Toppers Menswear was his old pal Ron Williamson, wearing very nice clothes and peddling the same to customers. The two bear-hugged and launched into a lengthy session of catch-up. For two boys who'd practically been brothers, they were surprised at how radically they'd drifted apart.

After graduating from Asher, they went their separate ways and lost touch. Bruce played baseball for two years at a junior college, then quit when his knees finally gave out. Ron's career had not fared much better. Each had notched one divorce; neither knew the other had been married. Neither was surprised to learn that the other had continued a fondness for the nightlife.

They were young, nice-looking, single again, working hard with money in their pockets, and they immediately began hitting the clubs and chasing women together. Ron had always loved the girls, but a few seasons in the minors had brought an even higher intensity to his skirt chasing.

Bruce was living in Ada, and whenever he passed through Tulsa, it was time for an all-nighter with Ron and his friends.

Though the game had broken their hearts, baseball was still their favorite topic: the great days at Asher, Coach Bowen, the dreams they'd once shared, and old teammates who'd tried and failed just like them. Helped mightily by two bad knees, Bruce had managed a clean break from the game, or at least the dreams of major-league glory. Ron had not. He was convinced he could still play, that one day something would change, his arm would miraculously heal, someone would call. Life would be good again. At first Bruce shrugged it off; it was just the residue of fading fame. As he had learned himself, no star fades faster than that of a high school athlete. Some deal with it, accept it, then move on. Others keep dreaming for decades.

Ron was almost delusional in his belief that he could still play the game. And he was greatly troubled, even consumed, by his failures. He constantly asked Bruce what people were saying about him back in Ada. Were they disappointed in him because he had not become the next Mickey Mantle? Were they talking about him in the coffee shops and cafés? No, Bruce assured him, they were not.

But it didn't matter. Ron was convinced that his hometown saw him as a failure, and the only way to change their minds was to get one last contract and claw his way up to the major leagues.

Lighten up, pal, Bruce kept telling him. Let go of the game. The dream is over.

Ron's family began to notice drastic changes in his personality. At times he was nervous, agitated, unable to concentrate or focus on one subject before ricocheting to the next. At family gatherings, he would sit quietly, mute-like for a few minutes, then barge into the conversation with comments only about himself. When he spoke, he insisted on dominating the conversation, and every topic had to relate to his life. He had trouble sitting still, smoked furiously, and developed the odd habit of simply vanishing from the room. For Thanksgiving in 1977, Annette hosted the entire family and covered the table with the traditional feast. As soon as everyone was seated, Ron, without a word, abruptly bolted from the dining room and walked across Ada to his mother's house. No explanation was given.

At other family gatherings he would withdraw to a bedroom, lock the door, and stay by himself, which, though unsettling for the rest of the family, did allow them some time for pleasant conversation. Then he would burst out of the room, ranting about whatever happened to be on his mind, always a subject completely disconnected from what everybody else was chatting about. He would stand in the middle of the den and rattle on like a madman until he got tired, then dash back to the bedroom and relock the door.

Once, his rowdy entrance included a guitar, which he began strumming furiously while singing badly and demanding that the rest of the family sing along. After a few disagreeable songs, he gave up and stomped back to the bedroom. Deep breaths were taken, eyes were rolled, then things returned to normal. Sadly, the family had become accustomed to such behavior.

Ron could be withdrawn and sullen, pouting for days over nothing or everything, then a switch would flip on and the gregarious personality was back. His baseball career depressed him, and he preferred not to talk about it. One phone call would find him dejected and pitiful, but during the next he would be hyper and jovial.

The family knew he was drinking, and there were strong rumors of drug use. Maybe the alcohol and chemicals were causing an imbalance and contributing to the wild mood swings. Annette and Juanita inquired as delicately as possible, and were met with hostility.

Then Roy Williamson was diagnosed with cancer, and Ron's problems became less important. The tumors were in his colon and progressing rapidly. Though Ronnie had always been a mama's boy, he loved and respected his father. And he felt guilty for his behavior. He no longer attended church and was having serious problems with his Christianity, but he clung to the Pentecostal belief that sin gets punished. His father, who'd led a clean life, was now being punished because of the son's long list of iniquities.

Roy's failing health added to Ron's depression. He dwelled on his selfishness—the demands he'd made on his parents for nice clothes, expensive sports gear, baseball camps and trips, the temporary move to Asher, all repaid in glorious fashion with a single color television set extracted from the signing bonus the A's gave him. He remembered Roy quietly buying secondhand clothes so his spoiled son could dress with the best in high school. He recalled his father trudging along the hot sidewalks of Ada with his bulky sample cases, peddling vanillas and spices. And he remembered his father up in the bleachers, never missing a game.

Roy underwent exploratory surgery in Oklahoma City early in 1978. The cancer was advanced and spreading and the surgeons could do nothing. He returned to Ada, rejected chemotherapy, and began a very painful decline. During his final days, Ron drove home from Tulsa and hovered over his father, distraught and tearful. He apologized repeatedly and begged his father to forgive him.

Roy, at one point, had heard enough. It's time to grow up, son, he said. Be a man. Stop all the crying and hysterics. Get on with your life.

Roy died on April 1, 1978.

In 1978, Ron was still in Tulsa and sharing an apartment with Stan Wilkins, an ironworker four years his junior. The two had a fondness for guitars and popular music and spent hours strumming and singing. Ron had a strong, untrained voice and promising talent with his guitar, an expensive Fender model. He could sit and play it for hours.

The disco scene was hot in Tulsa, and the two roommates went out often. After work they'd have a few drinks, then head for the clubs, where Ron was well known. He loved the ladies and was utterly fearless in his pursuit of them. He would survey the crowd, pick out the hottest woman, and ask her to dance. If she agreed to dance, then he usually took her home. His goal was a different woman every night.

Though he loved to drink, he was careful when he was on the prowl. Too much booze might hamper his performance. Certain chemicals, however, did not. Cocaine was roaring through the country and widely available in the clubs in Tulsa. There was little thought given to sexually transmitted diseases. The biggest concern was herpes; AIDS had yet to appear. For those so inclined, the late 1970s were wild and hedonistic. And Ron Williamson was out of control.

On April 30, 1978, the Tulsa police were called to the apartment of Lyza Lentzch. When they arrived, she told them that Ron Williamson had raped her. He was arrested on May 5, posted bail of $10,000, and was released.

Ron hired John Tanner, a veteran criminal defense attorney, and freely admitted to having sex with Lentzch. He swore it was consensual; they'd met in a club, and she'd invited him back to her apartment, where they eventually went to bed. Tanner actually believed his client, a rare occurrence.

To Ron's friends, the idea of rape was ridiculous. Women practically threw themselves at him. He could take his pick in any bar, and he wasn't exactly stalking young maidens at church. The women he met in the clubs and discos were looking for action.

Though he was humiliated by the charges, he was determined to act as though nothing bothered him. He partied as hard as ever and laughed off any suggestion that he was in trouble. He had a good lawyer. Bring on the trial!

Privately, though, he was frightened by the process, and for good reason. To be charged with such a serious crime was sobering enough, but to face a jury that could send him to prison for many years was a terrifying prospect.

He kept most of the details from his family—Ada was two hours away—but they soon noticed an even more subdued personality. And even wilder mood swings.

As his world became gloomier, Ron fought back with the only tools he had. He drank more, kept even later hours, chased even more girls, all in an effort to live the good life and escape his worries. But the alcohol fueled the depression, or maybe the depression required more alcohol—whatever the combination, he became moodier and more dejected. And less predictable.

On September 9, the Tulsa police received a call regarding another alleged rape. An eighteen-year-old woman named Amy Dell Ferneyhough returned to her apartment around 4:00 a.m. after a long night in a club. She was feuding with her boyfriend, who was in the apartment asleep with the doors locked. She couldn't locate her key, and since she really needed to find a restroom, she hustled down the block to an all-night convenience store. There, she bumped into Ron Williamson, who was also enjoying another late night. The two did not know each other but struck up a conversation, then disappeared behind the store and into some tall grass, where they had sex.

According to Ferneyhough, Ron struck her with his fist, ripped off most of her clothes, and raped her.

According to Ron, Ferneyhough was mad at her boyfriend for locking her out of their apartment and agreed to a quick roll in the weeds.

For the second time in five months, Ron posted bail and called John Tanner. With two rapes hanging over his head, he finally throttled back on the nightlife, then went into seclusion. He was living alone and talking to virtually no one. Annette knew a few of the details because she was sending money. Bruce Leba knew very little about what was happening.

In February 1979, the Ferneyhough rape went to trial first. Ron testified and explained to the jury that, yes, indeed they had had sex, but it had been by mutual consent. Oddly enough, the two had agreed to have relations behind a convenience store at four in the morning. The jury deliberated for an hour, believed him, and returned a verdict of not guilty.

In May, another jury was impaneled to hear the accusations of rape by Lyza Lentzch. Again, Ron gave a full explanation to the jury. He had met Lentzch in a nightclub, danced with her, liked her, and she evidently liked him, because she invited him back to her apartment, where they had consensual sex. The victim told the jury that she decided she didn't want to have sex, that she tried to stop it long before it got started, but she was afraid of Ron Williamson and finally gave in to keep from being hurt. Again, the jury believed Ron and found him not guilty.

BEING called a rapist the first time had humiliated him, and he knew the label would stick for many years. But few people got tagged with it twice, and in less than five months. How could he, the great Ron Williamson, be branded as a rapist? Regardless of what the juries said, people would whisper and gossip and keep the stories alive. They would point at him when he walked by.

He was twenty-six years old, and for most of his life he'd been the baseball star, the cocky athlete headed for big-league glory. Later, he was still the confident player with a sore arm that just might heal itself. People in Ada and Asher hadn't forgotten him. He was young; the talent was still there. Everybody knew his name.

It all changed with the rape charges. He knew he would be forgotten as a player and would be known only as an accused rapist. He kept to himself, withdrawing more each day into his own dark and confused world. He began missing work, then quit his job at Toppers Menswear. Bankruptcy followed, and when he'd lost everything, he packed his bags and quietly left Tulsa. He was crashing, spinning downward into a world of depression, booze, and drugs.

Juanita was waiting, and she was deeply concerned. She knew little about the trouble up in Tulsa, but she and Annette knew enough to be worried. Ron was obviously a mess—the drinking, the wild, nasty mood swings, the increasingly bizarre behavior. He looked awful—long hair, unshaven face, dirty clothes. And this was the same Ron Williamson who had enjoyed being so stylish and dapper, who sold fine clothes and had always been quick to point out that a certain tie did not exactly match the jacket.

He parked himself on the sofa in his mother's den and went to sleep. It wasn't long before he was sleeping twenty hours a day, always on the sofa. His bedroom was available, but he refused to even walk into it after dark. Something was in there, something that frightened him. Though he slept soundly, he sometimes jumped up screaming that the floor was covered with snakes and there were spiders on the walls.

He began hearing voices, but wouldn't tell his mother what they said. Then he began answering them.

Everything tired him—eating and bathing were enormous chores, always followed by long naps. He was listless, unmotivated, even during short stretches of sobriety. Juanita had never tolerated alcohol in her house—she hated drinking and smoking. A truce of sorts was reached when Ron moved into a cramped garage apartment next to the kitchen. There, he could smoke and drink and play his guitar and not offend his mother. When he wanted to sleep, he drifted back to the den and crashed on the sofa, and when he was awake, he stayed in his apartment.

Occasionally, the moods would swing, his energy would return, and he needed the nightlife again. Drinking and drugs, chasing the ladies, albeit with a little more caution. He would be gone for days, living with friends, bumming money off any acquaintance he ran into. Then another shift in the wind, and he was back on the sofa, dead to the world.

Juanita waited and worried endlessly. There was no history of mental illness in the family, and she had no idea how to handle it. She prayed a lot. She was very private and worked hard to keep Ronnie's problems away from Annette and Renee. Both were married and happy, and Ronnie was her burden, not theirs.

Ron occasionally talked of finding a job. He felt rotten for not working and supporting himself. A friend knew someone in California who needed employees, so, much to the relief of his family, Ron went west. A few days later he called his mother, crying, saying he was living with some devil worshippers who terrified him and wouldn't allow him to leave. Juanita sent him a plane ticket, and he managed to escape.

He went to Florida and New Mexico and Texas, looking for work, but never lasted more than a month. Each brief trip away exhausted him, and he crashed even harder on the sofa.

Juanita eventually convinced him to see a mental health counselor, who diagnosed him as manic-depressive. Lithium was prescribed, but he wouldn't take it regularly. He worked part-time here and there, never able to keep a job. His only talent had been in sales, but in his current state he was in no condition to meet and charm anyone. He still referred to himself as a professional baseball player, a close friend of Reggie Jackson's, but by then the locals in Ada knew better.

Late in 1979, Annette made an appointment with the district court judge Ronald Jones at the Pontotoc County Courthouse. She explained her brother's condition and asked if the state or the court system could do anything to help. No, Judge Jones said, not until Ron became a danger to himself or to others.

ON ONE particularly good day, Ron applied for training at a vocational rehabilitation center in Ada. The counselor there was alarmed at his condition and referred him to Dr. M. P. Prosser at St. Anthony Hospital in Oklahoma City, where he was admitted on December 3, 1979.

Trouble soon began when Ron demanded privileges that the staff could not provide. He wanted far more than his share of their time and attention and acted as though he was their only patient. When they did not comply with his wishes, he left the hospital, only to return a few hours later and ask to be readmitted.

On January 8, 1980, Dr. Prosser noted: "This boy has demonstrated rather bizarre and sometimes psychopathic behavior whether he is manic as the counselor in Ada thought or a schizoid individual with sociopathic trends, or the reverse, sociopathic individual with schizoid trends may never be determined ... Long term treatment may be required but he does not feel he needs treatment for schizophrenia."

Ron had been living in a dream since early adolescence, since his glory days on the baseball field, and had never accepted the reality that his career was over. He still believed that "they"—the powers that be in baseball—were going to come get him, put him in the lineup, and make him famous. "This is the real schizophrenic part of his disorder," Dr. Prosser wrote. "He just wants to get in the ballgame and preferably as one of the stars."

Long-term treatment for schizophrenia was suggested, but Ron would not consider it. A complete physical exam was never completed, because he was uncooperative, but Dr. Prosser did observe "a healthy young muscular, active, ambulatory man ... in better trim than most persons his age."

When he could function, Ron peddled Rawleigh home products door-to-door, through the same Ada neighborhoods where his father had worked. But it was tedious labor, the commissions were small, he had little patience with the required paperwork, and, besides, he was Ron Williamson, the great baseball star, now going door-to-door hawking kitchen products!

Untreated, unmedicated, and drinking, Ron became a regular at the local watering holes around Ada. He was a sloppy drunk, talking loud, bragging about his baseball career, and bothering women. He frightened many people, and the bartenders and bouncers knew him well. If Ron Williamson showed up to drink, everyone knew it. One of his favorite clubs was the Coachlight, and the bouncers there watched him closely.

It didn't take long for the two rape charges in Tulsa to catch up with him. The police began watching, sometimes following him around Ada. He and Bruce Leba were barhopping one night and stopped to fill their car with gas. A cop followed them for a few blocks, then stopped them and accused them of stealing the gas. They hadn't, but they narrowly avoided being arrested.

The arrests, however, began soon enough. In April 1980, two years after his father died, Ron was jailed on his first drunk-driving charge.

In November, Juanita Williamson convinced her son to seek help for his drinking. At her prodding, Ron walked into the Mental Health Services of Southern Oklahoma office in Ada and was seen by Duane Logue, a substance abuse counselor. He freely admitted his problems, said he'd been drinking for eleven years and doing drugs for at least the past seven, and that the booze increased dramatically after the Yankees cut him. He did not mention the two rape charges in Tulsa.

Logue referred him to a facility called the Bridge House in Ardmore, Oklahoma, sixty miles away. The following day Ron presented himself at the Bridge House and agreed to twenty-eight days of alcohol treatment in a lockdown environment. He was very nervous and kept telling the counselor he'd done "terrible things." Within two days he became a loner, sleeping long hours and missing meals. After a week, he was caught smoking in his bedroom, a clear rule violation, and announced that he was through with the place. He left with Annette, who happened to be in Ardmore to visit him, but the next day he was back, asking to be readmitted. He was told to return to Ada and reapply in two weeks. Fearing the wrath of his mother, he chose not to go home, but instead drifted for a few weeks without telling anyone where he was.

On November 25, Duane Logue sent Ron a letter requesting an appointment on December 4. Logue said, in part, "I am concerned about your well-being and I hope to see you then."

On December 4, Juanita informed Mental Health Services that Ron had a job and was living in Ardmore. He had met some new friends, had become involved with a church, had accepted Christ again, and no longer needed the help of the mental health service. His case was closed.

It was reopened ten days later when he was seen again by Duane Logue. Ron needed long-term treatment, but he would not agree to it. Nor would he consistently take the prescribed medications, primarily lithium. At times he would freely admit to abusive drinking and drug use, then he would adamantly deny it. Just a few beers, he would say if asked how much.

Since he couldn't keep a job, he was always broke. When Juanita refused to "loan" him money, he would roam around Ada, looking for another source. Not surprisingly, his circle of friends was shrinking; most people avoided him. Several times he drove to Asher, where he could always find Murl Bowen at the baseball field. They'd chat, Ron would deliver another hard-luck tale, and his old coach would fork over another twenty bucks. While Ron was promising to pay it back, Murl was delivering a stern lecture about cleaning up his life.

Ron's refuge was Bruce Leba, who had remarried and was living a much quieter life in his home a few miles out of town. About twice a month, Ron would stagger up to the door, drunk and disheveled, and beg Bruce to give him a place to sleep. Bruce always took him in, sobered him up, fed him, and usually loaned him ten bucks.

In February 1981, Ron was again arrested for drunk driving and pleaded guilty. After a few days in jail, he went to Chickasha to see his sister Renee and her husband, Gary. They found him in their backyard one Sunday when they returned from church. He explained that he had been living in a tent behind their rear fence, and he certainly looked the part. Further, he had just escaped from some Army men down the road in Lawton, and these soldiers had stashed weapons and explosives in their homes and were planning to overthrow the base. Luckily, he had escaped in time and now needed a place to live.

Renee and Gary allowed him to stay in their son's bedroom. Gary found him a job on a farm hauling hay, a gig that lasted two days before he quit because he said he'd found a softball team that needed him. The farmer later called and told Gary that Ron was not welcome back and that, in his opinion, he had some serious emotional problems.

Ron's interest in American presidents was suddenly rekindled, and for days he talked of nothing else. Not only could he quickly name them in order and reverse order, but he knew everything about them—

birth dates, birthplaces, terms, vice presidents, wives and children, administration highlights, and so on. Every conversation around the Simmonses' home had to center on an American president. Nothing else could be discussed as long as Ron was present.

He was thoroughly nocturnal. Though he was willing to sleep at night, he was incapable of doing so. Plus, he enjoyed all-night television, at full volume. With the first rays of sunlight, he became drowsy and drifted away. The Simmonses, tired and red-eyed, enjoyed a quiet breakfast before going off to work.

He often complained of headaches. Gary heard noises one night and found Ron sorting through the medicine cabinet, looking for something to deaden the pain.

When the nerves had frayed enough, Gary sat Ron down for the inevitable serious chat. Gary explained that Ron was welcome to stay but he had to adjust to their schedule. Ron showed no signs of understanding that he had problems. He left quietly and returned to his mother's, where he was either comatose on the sofa or holed up in his apartment, twenty-eight years old and unable to admit that he needed help.

ANNETTE and Renee were worried about their brother, but there was little they could do. He was as headstrong as always and seemed content to live the life of a drifter. His behavior was getting even stranger; there was little doubt he was deteriorating mentally. But this subject was off-limits; they had made the mistake of broaching it with him. Juanita could cajole him into seeing a counselor, or seeking treatment for his drinking, but he never followed through with prolonged therapy. Each brief stint of sobriety was followed by weeks of uncertainty about where he was or what he was doing.

For enjoyment, if he had any, he played his guitar, usually on the front porch at his mother's house. He could sit and strum and sing to the birds for hours, and when he grew bored with the porch, he would take his act on the road. Often without a car or without money to buy gas, he would simply roam around Ada and could be seen at various places and at all hours with his guitar.

Rick Carson, his childhood friend, was an Ada policeman. When he pulled the graveyard shift, he often saw Ron strolling down sidewalks, even between houses, strumming chords on the guitar and singing, well past midnight. Rick would ask him where he was going. No place in particular. Rick would offer a ride home. Sometimes Ron said yes; other times he preferred to keep walking.

On July 4, 1981, he was arrested for being drunk in public and pleaded guilty. Juanita was furious and insisted that he seek help. He was admitted to Central State Hospital in Norman, where he was seen by a Dr. Sambajon, a staff psychiatrist. Ron's only complaint was that he wanted to "get help." His self-esteem and energy were very low, and he was burdened with thoughts of worthlessness, hopelessness, even suicide. He said, "I cannot do good to myself and the people around me. I cannot keep my job and I have a negative attitude." He told Dr. Sambajon that his first serious episode with depression had been four years earlier, when his baseball career ended at about the same time his marriage collapsed. He admitted abusing alcohol and drugs, but believed such behavior did not contribute to his problems.

Dr. Sambajon found him to be "unkempt, dirty, untidy . . . careless in his grooming." The patient's judgment was not grossly impaired, and he had insight into his present condition. The diagnosis was dysthymic disorder, a chronic form of low-grade depression. Dr. Sambajon recommended medications, more counseling, more group therapy, and continued family support.

After three days at Central State, Ron demanded his release and was discharged. A week later he was back at the mental health clinic in Ada, where he was seen by Charles Amos, a psychological assistant. Ron described himself as a former professional baseball player who'd been depressed since the end of that career. He also blamed his depression on religion. Amos referred him to Dr. Marie Snow, the only psychiatrist in Ada, and she began seeing him weekly. Asendin, a commonly used antidepressant, was prescribed, and Ron showed slight improvement. Dr. Snow tried to convince her patient that more intensive psychotherapy was needed, but after three months Ron was finished.

On September 30, 1982, Ron was again charged with operating a motor vehicle while under the influence of alcohol. He was arrested, jailed, and later pleaded guilty.

CHAPTER 4

Three months after the murder of Debbie Carter, Detectives Dennis Smith and Mike Kieswetter went to the Williamson home and interviewed Ron for the first time. Juanita was present and took part in the meeting. When asked where he was on the night of December 7, Ron said he did not remember—it had been three months earlier. Yes, he frequented the Coachlight, as well as the other clubs around Ada. Juanita went to her diary, checked the date, and informed the detectives that her son had been at home at ten that night. She showed them the entry for December 7.

Ron was asked if he knew Debbie Carter. He said he wasn't sure. He certainly knew the name because everybody in town had talked of little else since the murder. Smith produced a photograph of the victim, and Ron studied it carefully. Maybe he'd met her before, maybe not. Later, he asked to see the photo again. She was vaguely familiar. He vehemently denied knowing anything about the murder, but did offer the opinion that the killer was probably a psychopath who followed her home, broke in on her, then fled town as soon as the crime was committed.

After about thirty minutes, the police asked Ron if he would provide fingerprint and hair samples. He agreed to do so, and followed them to the station when the interview was over.

Three days later, on March 17, they were back with the same questions. Ron again stated that he had nothing to do with the murder and that he was at home on the night of December 7.

The police also interviewed a man by the name of Dennis Fritz, whose only possible link to the murder investigation was his friendship with Ron Williamson. According to an early police report, Fritz was "a suspect or at least an acquaintance of a suspect in the Carter murder case."

Dennis rarely went to the Coachlight and had not been there for months prior to the murder. No witness placed him there; in fact, by March 1983 no witness had mentioned his name. He was new to the area and not well known around town. He had never driven Ron Williamson to the Coachlight. He did not know Debbie Carter, wasn't sure he'd ever seen her before, and had no idea where she lived. But since the investigators were now on the trail of Ron Williamson, and were apparently operating under the knee-jerk theory that there were two killers, they needed another suspect. Fritz was their man.

DENNIS FRITZ grew up near Kansas City, finished high school there, and earned a degree in biology from Southeastern Oklahoma State University in 1971. In 1973, his wife, Mary, gave birth to their only child, Elizabeth. They were living in Durant, Oklahoma, at the time. Mary was working for a nearby college, and Dennis had a good job with the railroad.

On Christmas Day 1975, while Dennis was working out of town,

Mary was murdered by a seventeen-year-old neighbor, shot in the head as she sat in a rocking chair in her own den.

For two years afterward, Dennis was unable to work. He was emotionally scarred and did nothing but care for Elizabeth. When she started school in 1981, he managed to pull himself together and get a job teaching junior high science in the town of Konawa. After a few months, he moved into a rental home in Ada, not far from the Williamsons, and not far from the apartment Debbie Carter would one day lease. His mother, Wanda, joined him in Ada to help with Elizabeth.

He took another job teaching ninth-grade biology and coaching basketball in the town of Noble, an hour away. The school officials allowed him to live in a small trailer on campus, and he commuted back and forth on weekends to spend time with Elizabeth and his mother. Noble had no nightlife, and occasionally Dennis would drive to Ada on a weeknight to see his daughter, then get a drink or perhaps meet a girl.

One night in November 1981, Dennis was in Ada. He was bored and wanted a beer, so he drove to a convenience store. Parked outside and sitting in the front seat of his mother's old Buick was Ron Williamson, strumming his guitar and watching the world go by. Dennis also played the guitar and just happened to have his in the backseat. The two struck up a conversation about music. Ron said he lived a few blocks away and invited Dennis over for a jam session. Both men were looking for friends.

The apartment was cramped and dirty, a sad little place, Fritz thought. Ron explained that he lived with his mother, who didn't tolerate tobacco or alcohol. He had no job, and when Dennis asked what he did all day, he replied that he usually slept. He was friendly enough, easy with conversation and quick with a laugh, but Fritz noticed a detached air. He would gaze off for long periods of time, then stare at Dennis as if he weren't there. A strange guy, thought Dennis.

But they enjoyed playing their guitars and talking about music. After a few visits, Fritz began to notice Ron's excessive drinking and mood swings. Ron loved beer and vodka, and his routine was to start drinking late in the afternoon, once he was fully awake and away from his mother. He was flat and depressed until the booze kicked in, then his personality came to life. They began to frequent the bars and lounges in town.

Dennis stopped by one afternoon, earlier than usual and before Ron had a drink. He chatted with Juanita, a pleasant but long-suffering soul who said little but seemed to be fed up with her son. She disappeared, and Dennis found Ron in his bedroom, staring at the walls. The room made Ron nervous, and he seldom entered it.

There were large color photos of Patty, his ex-wife, and of himself in various baseball uniforms.

"She was beautiful," Fritz said, looking at Patty.

"I once had it all," Ron said with sadness and bitterness. He was twenty-eight years old and had thoroughly given up.

BARHOPPING was always an adventure. Ron never entered a club quietly, and once inside he expected to be the center of attention. One of his favorite routines was to wear a nice suit and claim to be a rich Dallas lawyer. By 1981, he had already spent enough time in courtrooms to have the lingo and the mannerisms, and his "Tanner Act" was played out in lounges all over Norman and Oklahoma City.

Fritz would stay in the background and enjoy the show. He gave Ron plenty of room. He was also becoming a little tired of the adventures. A night out with Ron usually involved a conflict of some sort and an unexpected ending.

During the summer of 1982, they were returning to Ada after a night in the bars when Ron announced he wanted to go to Galveston. Fritz had made the mistake of telling a story about deep-sea fishing out of Galveston, and Ron claimed that he'd always wanted to do that. They were drunk, and an unplanned eight-hour drive did not seem totally far-fetched. They were in Dennis's pickup truck. As always, Ron had no car, no license, and no money for gas.

School was out, Fritz had some cash in his pocket, so why not go fishing? They bought some more beer and headed south.

Somewhere in Texas, Dennis needed a nap, so Ron took the wheel. When Dennis woke up, there was a strange black man in the back of the pickup. "Picked up a hitchhiker," Ron said proudly. Somewhere in Houston, just before dawn, they stopped at a convenience store to buy beer and food, and when they returned, the truck was gone, stolen by the hitchhiker. Ron said he forgot and left the keys in the ignition, and upon further reflection admitted that he had not only left the keys in the ignition but had probably left the engine running as well. They drank a few beers and pondered their bad luck. Fritz insisted on calling the police, but Ron wasn't so sure. They argued, and Dennis called them anyway. When the cop heard the story, he laughed in their faces.

They were in a very rough part of town, but they found a Pizza Hut. They ate pizza and drained several pitchers of beer, and began roaming around the city, quite lost. At dusk they stumbled upon a black honky-tonk, and Ron was determined to go inside and party. It was a crazy idea, but Fritz soon realized that things were probably safer inside the club than out. At the bar, Dennis sipped a beer and prayed no one would notice them. Ron, typically, began talking loud and attracting attention. He was wearing a suit and was now the hotshot Dallas lawyer. Dennis was worrying about his truck and hoping they didn't get knifed, while his sidekick was telling tall tales about his close, personal friend Reggie Jackson.

The main man of the club was a guy named Cortez, and he and Ron soon became pals. When Ron told the story of the stolen pickup, Cortez roared with laughter. When the honky-tonk closed, Ron and Dennis drove away with Cortez, whose apartment was nearby and did not have enough beds. The two white boys slept on the floor. When he awoke, Fritz was hungover, angry about his truck, and determined to get back to Ada in one piece. He jolted Ron out of his coma, and together they convinced Cortez to drive them, for a small fee, to a bank where Dennis could hopefully withdraw some money. At the bank, Cortez waited in the car while Ron and Dennis went inside. Dennis got the cash, and as they were leaving, a dozen police cars came screaming from all directions and surrounded Cortez. Heavily armed officers yanked him out of his car and threw him into the backseat of one of theirs.

Ron and Dennis ducked back into the bank, quickly assessed the raid in the parking lot, and made a hurried exit on the other side. They bought bus tickets. The ride home was long and painful. Fritz was sick of Ron and angry that he'd let the truck get away from them. He vowed to avoid him for a long time.

A month later, Ron called Dennis and wanted to go out. Since the adventure in Houston, the friendship had cooled considerably. Fritz enjoyed going out for a few beers and some dancing, but he kept things under control. Ron was fine as long as they were having a drink and playing guitars in his apartment, but once he hit the bars, anything could happen.

Dennis picked him up and they went out for a drink. Fritz explained that it would be a short night because he had a rendezvous with a young lady planned for later. He was actively on the prowl for a love interest. His wife had been dead for seven years, and he longed for a stable relationship. Ron did not. Women were for sex and nothing else.

Ron, though, proved difficult to shake that night, and when Dennis went to visit his lady friend, Ron went with him. When he finally realized he wasn't welcome, he got mad and left, but not on foot. He stole Dennis's car and drove to Bruce Leba's house. Fritz stayed with the woman, and when he got up the next morning, he realized his car was gone. He called the police, filed a report, then called Bruce Leba and asked if he'd seen Ron. Bruce agreed to drive Ron and the stolen car back to Ada, and when they arrived, both were stopped by the police. The charges were dropped, but Dennis and Ron did not speak for months.

FRITZ was at home in Ada when he received a phone call from Detective Dennis Smith. The police wanted him to come down to the station and answer some questions. What kinds of questions? Fritz asked. We'll tell you when you get here, Smith replied.

Fritz reluctantly went to the station. He had nothing to hide, but any such encounter with the police was unnerving. Smith and Gary Rogers asked him about his relationship with Ron Williamson, an old friend he hadn't seen in months. The questions were businesslike at first, but slowly became accusatory. "Where were you on the night of December 7?" Dennis wasn't sure at that moment; he'd need some time to think about it. "Did you know Debbie Carter?" No. And so on. After an hour, Fritz left the station, mildly concerned that he was even involved in the investigation.

Dennis Smith called again and asked Fritz if he would take a polygraph. With his science background, Fritz knew that polygraphs are wildly unreliable, and he wanted no part of an exam. At the same time, he'd never met Debbie Carter, and he wanted to prove this to Smith and Rogers. He reluctantly agreed, and a test was scheduled at the OSBI offices in Oklahoma City. As the day approached, Fritz became more and more nervous, and to calm his nerves, he took a Valium right before the exam.

The test was administered by OSBI agent Rusty Featherstone, with Dennis Smith and Gary Rogers lurking nearby. When it was over, the cops huddled over the graphs, grimly shaking their heads at the bad news.

Fritz was informed that he had "severely flunked" the exam.

"Impossible" was his first response.

You're hiding something, they said. Fritz admitted to being nervous and finally confessed that he'd taken a Valium. This upset the cops, and they insisted that he take another polygraph. He felt as though he had no choice.

A week later Featherstone brought his machine to Ada and set it up in the basement of the police department. Fritz was even more nervous than before, but answered the questions truthfully and easily.

He "severely flunked" it again, only this time even worse, according to Featherstone, Smith, and Rogers. The post-polygraph interrogation began with a fury. Rogers, playing the bad cop, began cursing and threatening and saying, "You're hiding something, Fritz," over and over. Smith tried to play the role of Fritz's true friend, but it was a juvenile act and an old one at that.

Rogers was dressed like a cowboy, boots and all, and his style was to strut around the room, fuming, cursing, threatening, talking about death row and lethal injections, then suddenly he would lunge at Fritz, jab him in the chest, and tell him that he was going to confess. The routine was frightening enough, but not very effective. Fritz said over and over, "Get out of my face."

Rogers finally accused him of the rape and murder. He got angry, and his language became even more abusive as he described how Fritz and his sidekick, Williamson, broke in on the girl, raped her and killed her, and now he, Rogers, was demanding a confession.

With no evidence, only a confession could've solved the case, and the cops were desperate to squeeze one out of Fritz. But he didn't budge. He had nothing to confess, but after two hours of verbal abuse he wanted to give them something. He told the story of a road trip he and Ron had made to Norman the previous summer, a rowdy night in bars looking for girls, one of whom hopped in the backseat of Dennis's car and became hysterical when he wouldn't let her out. She finally jumped, ran away, called the cops, and Ron and Dennis slept in the car, in a parking lot, hiding from the police. No charges were filed.

That story seemed to placate the cops, for a few minutes anyway. Their clear focus was Williamson, and now they had more proof that he and Fritz were friends and drinking buddies. The relevance to the Carter murder was unclear to Fritz, but then most of what the cops were saying made little sense. Fritz knew he was innocent, and if Smith and Rogers were after him, then the real killer had little to worry about.

After hammering away for three hours, the cops finally quit. They were convinced Fritz was involved, but the case wouldn't be solved with a confession. Good police work was needed, so they began watching

Fritz, following him around town, stopping him for no reason. Several times Fritz woke up to the sight of a police car parked in front of his house.

Fritz voluntarily submitted hair, blood, and saliva samples. Why not give them everything? He had nothing to fear. The thought of talking to a lawyer crossed his mind briefly, but why bother? He was completely innocent, and the cops would soon realize this.

Detective Smith dug into Fritz's background and discovered a 1973 conviction for growing marijuana in the town of Durant. Armed with the information, an Ada policeman contacted the junior high school in Noble where Dennis was teaching and informed the authorities that Fritz not only was under investigation for murder but also had a drug conviction he'd neglected to disclose when he applied to teach. Fritz was fired immediately.

ON MARCH 17, Susan Land at the OSBI received from Dennis Smith "the known scalp and pubic hairs of Fritz and Williamson."

On March 21, Ron went to the police station and voluntarily submitted to a polygraph test administered by B. G. Jones, another examiner with the OSBI. Jones declared the exam to be inconclusive. Ron also gave a saliva sample. A week later, this was submitted to the OSBI, along with a sample from Dennis Fritz.

On March 28, Jerry Peters with the OSBI completed his fingerprint analysis. In his report he stated, without qualification, disclaimer, or equivocation, that the palm print on the Sheetrock sample did not belong to Debbie Carter, Dennis Fritz, or Ron Williamson. This should have been good news for the police. Find a match to the palm print, and they had their killer.

WITHIN a month of the murder the police had quietly informed the Carter family that Ron Williamson was their prime suspect. Though they did not have enough evidence, they were pursuing all leads and slowly, methodically, building a case against him. He certainly seemed suspicious; he acted strange, kept weird hours, lived with his mother, didn't have a job, was known to pester women, was a regular at the honky-tonks, and, most damning of all, lived close to the murder scene. By cutting through a back alley, he could be at Debbie Carter's apartment in minutes!

Plus, he'd had those two problems up in Tulsa. The man had to be a rapist, regardless of what the juries decided.

Not long after the murder, Debbie's aunt Glenna Lucas received an anonymous phone call in which a male voice said, "Debbie's dead, and you next will die." Glenna recalled, with horror, the words scrawled in nail polish: "Jim Smith next will die." The similarities sent her into a panic, but instead of notifying the police, she called the district attorney.

Bill Peterson, a heavyset young man from a prominent Ada family, had been the prosecutor for three years. His district covered three counties—Pontotoc, Seminole, and Hughes—and his office was in the Pontotoc County Courthouse. He knew the Carter family, and like any small-town prosecutor, he was anxious to find a suspect and solve the crime. Dennis Smith and Gary Rogers were routinely updating Peterson on the investigation.

Glenna described the anonymous call to Bill Peterson, and they agreed that Ron Williamson was probably the caller, and the killer. By walking a few steps from his garage apartment to the back alley, he could actually see Debbie's place, and by walking a few steps down his mother's driveway, he could see Glenna's home. He was right there in the middle, the weird man with no job and strange hours, just watching the neighborhood around him.

Bill Peterson arranged for a recorder to be placed on Glenna's phone, but there were no other calls.

Her daughter, Christy, was eight years old and very aware of the family's ordeal. Glenna kept her close, never allowed her to be alone or use the phone, and made sure she was watched carefully at school.

There were whispers around the house, and around the family, about Williamson. Why would he kill Debbie? What were the police waiting for?

The whispers and gossip continued. Fear quickly spread throughout the neighborhood, then the entire town. The murderer was loose, out there for all to see, and everybody knew his name. Why didn't the police get him off the streets?

A YEAR and a half after his last session with Dr. Snow, Ron certainly needed to be off the streets. He was in desperate need of long-term care in an institution. In June 1983, again at the urging of his mother, he made the familiar trek, on foot, over to the mental health clinic in Ada. He asked for help, again saying he was depressed and unable to function. He was referred to another facility in Cushing, and there he was evaluated by Al Roberts, a rehabilitation counselor. Roberts noted that Ron's IQ was 114, "in the bright-normal range of intellectual functioning," but cautioned that he might be suffering some degree of brain impairment because of the alcohol abuse.

Roberts wrote, "This man may be exhibiting a cry for help." Ron was insecure, tense, worried, nervous, and depressed.

> He is a very nonconforming person and is resentful of authority. His behavior is going to be erratic and unpredictable. He does have problems with impulse control. He is very suspicious and distrustful of others around him. He lacks social skills and is very uncomfortable in social situations. This individual is one who would accept little responsibility for his own behavior and he is likely to strike out in anger or hostility as a defense against being hurt. He sees the world as a very threatening and scary place and defends himself by being hostile or being withdrawn. Ron seems very immature and will present a picture of one who is rather unconcerned.

Ron applied to a vocational training program at East Central University in Ada, stating that he wanted to get a degree in chemistry or, in the alternative, one in physical education so he could coach. He agreed to a more thorough psychological evaluation using a series of tests. The examiner was Melvin Brooking, a psychological assistant with Vocational Rehabilitation.

Brooking knew Ron and the Williamson family well, perhaps too well. His behavorial observations were loaded with anecdotes, and he referred to him as "Ronnie."

On his athletic career, Brooking wrote, "I don't know what kind of student Ronnie was in high school, but I do know that he was an outstanding athlete but was always handicapped by temper tantrums on and off the court and generally rude, immature behavior, and a highly self-centered, arrogant attitude. His prima donna attitude, his inability to get along with people, and his disregard for rules and regulations made him an unfit player about everywhere he went."

On the family, he said, "Ronnie's mother has been a hard working woman all of her life. She has owned and operated a beauty shop downtown for many years. Both Ronnie's mother and father have stood by him through many, many crises, and his mother is evidently still providing support, although she is just about emotionally, physically and financially drained."

On the failed marriage, he wrote, "He married a very beautiful girl, who was a former Miss Ada, but she finally could not tolerate Ronnie's mood swings and inability to make a living and divorced him."

Evidently, Ron was forthcoming about his alcohol and drug abuse. Brooking observed, "Ronnie has had serious alcohol and drug abuse problems in the past . . . He has been a serious pill taker. Most of his drug taking seems to be an attempt to medicate himself out of serious depression. He says that he is no longer drinking or doing drugs."

Brooking began his diagnosis with bipolar disorder and described it as follows:

Bipolar disorder means that this young man suffers from tremendous mood swings, going from manic highs to stupor level depressive lows. I will diagnose depressed type because that is characteristically where he stays most of the time. His manic highs are usually drug induced and short lived. For the last three or four years, Ronnie has been seriously depressed, living in the back room of his mama's house, sleeping most of the time, working very, very little and totally dependent on those around him for his upkeep. He's come out of the house three or four times and made major moves as though he were going to rehabilitate himself, but they've never worked out.

Brooking also diagnosed a paranoid personality disorder because of "a pervasive and unwarranted suspiciousness and mistrust of people, hypersensitivity and restricted affectivity."

And, for good measure, he added alcohol and substance dependence. His prognosis was "guarded," and he concluded by saying, "This young man has never gotten it together since he left home more than ten years ago. His life has been a series of problems and devastating crises. He continues to try and get his feet on solid ground, but so far he has never been able to make it."

Brooking's job was to evaluate Ron, not to treat him. By the late summer of 1983, Ron's mental condition was worsening, and he was not getting the help he needed. Long-term, institutionalized psychotherapy was required, but the family couldn't afford it, the state couldn't provide it, and Ron wouldn't agree to it anyway.

His application to East Central University included a request for financial aid. The request was granted, and he was notified that a check was available at the business office of the school. He arrived to pick it up, in his usual unkempt condition with long hair and a mustache, accompanied by two other shady characters, both of whom seemed very interested in the prospect of Ron getting some money. The check was made payable to Ron, but also to an officer of the school. Ron was in a hurry, but he was told to wait in a long line. He felt the money was right-fully his, and he didn't feel like waiting. His two buddies were anxious to get the cash, so Ron quickly forged the name of the school official.

He left with $300.

The forgery was witnessed by Nancy Carson, the wife of Rick Carson, Ron's childhood friend who was an Ada policeman. Mrs. Carson worked in the business office and had known Ron for many years. She was appalled at what she had just seen, so she called her husband.

An official from the college knew the Williamson family. He drove straight to Juanita's beauty shop and told her about Ron's forgery. If she would reimburse the school the $300, no criminal charges would be pursued. Juanita quickly wrote a check for the money and went to find her son.

The following day Ron was arrested for uttering a forged instrument, a felony that carried a maximum prison sentence of eight years. He was placed in the Pontotoc County jail. He could not post bail, and his family couldn't help him.

THE MURDER investigation was proceeding slowly. There was still no word from the OSBI lab on the initial fingerprint, hair, and saliva submissions. Samples from thirty-one Ada men, including Ron Williamson and Dennis Fritz, were being processed. Glen Gore still had not been asked to provide hair and saliva.

By September 1983, all hair samples were on the backlogged desk of Melvin Hett, an OSBI hair analyst.

On November 9, Ron, while in jail, submitted to another polygraph exam, this one also administered by the OSBI agent Rusty Featherstone. It was a two-hour meeting, with lots of questions before Ron was wired for the polygraph. He continually and adamantly denied any involvement in, or knowledge of, the murder. The test was again deemed inconclusive, and the entire interview was videotaped.

Ron adjusted to life behind bars. He kicked the booze and pills because he had no choice, and he managed to continue his habit of sleeping twenty hours a day. But without medication or treatment of any type, he continued a slow mental decline.

Later in November, another inmate, Vicki Michelle Owens Smith, told Detective Dennis Smith an odd story about Ron. Dennis Smith made the following report:

> At 0300 or 0400 hours Saturday morning, Ron Williamson looked out his window and saw Vicki. Williamson yelled that she was a witch and that Vicki was the one who took him to Debbie Carter's house and now she had brought him Debbie's spirit into his cell and it was haunting the hell out of him. Williamson also screamed for his mother to forgive him.

In December, one year after the murder, Glen Gore was asked to stop by the police station and give a statement. He denied any involvement in the death of Debbie Carter. He said he'd seen her at the Coachlight a few hours before she was killed, and added the new wrinkle that she had asked him to dance with her because Ron Williamson was making her uncomfortable. The fact that no one else at the Coachlight reported seeing Ron there was apparently insignificant.

But as anxious as the cops were to paste together a case against him, the evidence was simply too scant. There was not a single fingerprint lifted from the Carter apartment that matched either Ron or Dennis Fritz, a gaping hole in the theory that the two were there during the prolonged and violent attack. There were no eyewitnesses; no one heard a sound that night. The hair analysis, always shaky at best, was still bottlenecked in Melvin Hett's office at the OSBI.

The case against Ron consisted of two "inconclusive" polygraph exams, a bad reputation, a residence not far from that of the victim's, and the delayed, half-baked eyewitness identification of Glen Gore.

The case against Dennis Fritz was even weaker. One year after the murder, the only tangible result of the investigation had been the firing of a ninth-grade science teacher.

IN JANUARY 1984, Ron pleaded guilty to the forgery charge and was sentenced to three years in prison. He was transported to a correctional center near Tulsa, and it wasn't long before his odd behavior attracted the attention of the staff. He was transferred to an intermediate mental health unit for observation. Dr. Robert Briody interviewed him on the morning of February 13 and noted: "He is usually subdued and appears in control of his actions." But during an interview that afternoon, Dr. Briody saw a different person. Ron was "hypomanic, loud, irritable, easily excited, has loose associations, flight of ideas, irrational thoughts, and some paranoid ideation." Further evaluation was suggested.

Security was not tight at the intermediate unit. Ron found a baseball field nearby and enjoyed sneaking over at night for the solitude. A policeman found him once, napping on the field, and escorted him back to the unit. The staff slapped his wrist and made him write a report. It reads:

> I was feeling down the other nite and needed some time to think
> things out. I've always felt peaceful on a ballfield. I strolled out to the
> ballfield's southeast corner and kind of like an old blue-tick hound I
> curled up under the shade tree. A few minutes later a police officer
> asked me to go back to the CTC Building. I met Brents halfway up the
> field and we walked in the front door together. He said that, after
> seeing I wasn't up to no good, that he'd forget it. However, as this
> letter attests, I've been given a write-up.

WITH the prime suspect behind bars, the investigation into the murder of Debbie Carter came to a virtual halt. Weeks passed with little activity. Dennis Fritz worked for a short time in a nursing home, then a factory.

The Ada police harassed him occasionally but eventually lost interest. Glen Gore was still in town but of little interest to the cops.

The police were frustrated, tensions were high, and the pressure was about to increase dramatically.

In April 1984, another young woman was murdered in Ada, and though her death was unrelated to Debbie Carter's, it would eventually have a profound impact on the lives of Ron Williamson and Dennis Fritz.

DENICE HARAWAY was a twenty-four-year-old student at East Central who worked part-time at McAnally's convenience store on the eastern edge of Ada. She had been married for eight months to Steve Haraway, also a student at East Central and the son of a prominent dentist in town. The newlyweds lived in a small apartment owned by Dr. Haraway and were working their way through college.

On Saturday night, April 28, around 8:30, a customer was approaching the entrance to McAnally's when he was met by an attractive young woman who was leaving the store. She was accompanied by a young man. His arm was around her waist; they appeared to be just another pair of lovers. They walked to a pickup truck, where the woman got in first, on the passenger's side. Then the young man got in and slammed the door, and a few seconds later the engine started. They left going east, away from town. The truck was an old Chevrolet with a spotty, gray-primered paint job.

Inside the store, the customer saw no one. The cash register drawer was open and had been emptied. A cigarette was still burning in the ashtray. Beside it was an open beer can, and behind the counter was a brown purse and an open textbook. The customer tried to find the clerk, but the store was empty. Then he decided that perhaps there had been a robbery, so he called the police.

In the brown purse an officer found a driver's license belonging to Denice Haraway. The customer looked at the photo on the license and made a positive identification. That was the young lady he'd passed on the way into the store less than half an hour earlier. Yes, he was sure it was Denice Haraway because he stopped at McAnally's often and knew her face.

Detective Dennis Smith was already in bed when the call came. "Treat it like a crime scene," he said, then went back to sleep. His orders, though, were not followed. The manager of the store lived nearby and he soon arrived. He checked the safe; it had not been opened. He found $400 in cash under the counter, awaiting transfer to the safe, and he found $150 in another cash drawer. As they waited for a detective, the manager tidied up the place. He emptied the ashtray with a single cigarette butt in it and threw away the beer can. The police didn't stop him. If there were fingerprints, they were gone.

Steve Haraway was studying and waiting for his wife to come home after McAnally's closed at 11:00 p.m. A phone call from the police stunned him, and he was soon at the store, identifying his wife's car, textbooks, and purse. He gave the police a description and tried to remember what she was wearing—blue jeans, tennis shoes, and a blouse he couldn't recall.

Early Sunday morning, every policeman on Ada's thirty-three man force was called in for duty. State troopers arrived from nearby districts. Dozens of local groups, including Steve's fraternity brothers, volunteered to help in the search. OSBI agent Gary Rogers was assigned to lead the investigation from the state level, and once again Dennis Smith was to direct the Ada police. They divided the county into sections and assigned teams to search every street, highway, road, river, ditch, and field.

A clerk at JP's, another convenience store a half a mile from McAnally's, came forward and told the police about two strange young men who'd stopped by and spooked her not long before Denice disappeared. Both were in their early twenties with long hair and weird behavior. They shot a game of pool before leaving in an old pickup truck.

The customer at McAnally's had seen only one man leaving with

Denice, and she did not appear to be frightened by him. His general description sort of matched the general description of the two weird boys at JP's, so the police had the first hint of a trail. They were looking for two white males, between twenty-two and twenty-four years of age, one between five feet eight and five feet ten with blond hair below his ears and a light complexion, the other with shoulder-length light brown hair and a slim build.

The intense manhunt on Sunday produced nothing, not a single clue. Dennis Smith and Gary Rogers called it off after dark and made plans to reassemble early the next morning.

On Monday, they obtained a college photograph of Denice and printed flyers with her pretty face and general description—five feet five inches tall, 110 pounds, brown eyes, dark blond hair, light complexion. The flyer also listed a description of the two young men seen at JP's, along with one of the old pickup truck. These were placed in every store window in and around Ada by cops and volunteers.

A police artist worked with the clerk from JP's and put together two sketches. When the drawings were shown to the customer at McAnally's, he said that one of them was at least "in the ballpark." The two composites were given to the local television station, and when the town got its first look at the possible suspects, calls poured in to the police station.

Ada had four detectives at the time—Dennis Smith, Mike Baskin, D. W. Barrett, and James Fox—and they were soon overwhelmed with the number of calls. More than a hundred, with about twenty-five names given for potential suspects.

Two names stood out. Billy Charley was suggested by about thirty of the callers, so he was invited in for questioning. He arrived at the police station with his parents, who said that he had been at home with them throughout Saturday night.

The other name given by about thirty concerned citizens was that of Tommy Ward, a local boy the police knew well. Tommy had been arrested several times for misdemeanors—public drunkenness, petty theft—

but nothing violent. He had family all over Ada, and the Wards were known as generally decent folks who worked hard and tended to their own business. Tommy was twenty-four years old, the second youngest of eight children, a high school dropout.

He voluntarily came in for questioning. Detectives Smith and Baskin asked him about last Saturday night. He'd been fishing with a friend, Karl Fontenot, then they'd gone to a party, stayed out until 4:00 a.m., then walked home. Tommy didn't own a vehicle. The detectives noticed that Ward's blond hair had been cut very short, a hack job that was uneven and obviously unprofessional. They took a Polaroid of the back of his head and dated it May 1.

The suspects in the composites both had long, light-colored hair.

Detective Baskin found Karl Fontenot, a man he did not know, and asked him to stop by the station for some questions. Fontenot agreed, but never arrived. Baskin didn't pursue it. Fontenot had long, dark hair.

As the search continued with great urgency in and around Pontotoc County, Denice Haraway's name and description were broadcast to law enforcement officials nationwide. Calls came from everywhere, but not one was of any benefit. Denice had simply vanished without leaving a single clue.

When Steve Haraway wasn't handing out flyers or driving the back roads, he was secluded in his apartment with a few friends. The phone rang constantly, and with each call there was a moment of hope.

There was no reason for Denice to run away. They had been married less than a year and were still very much in love. Both were seniors at East Central, looking forward to graduation and leaving Ada for a life somewhere else. She had been taken against her will, he was certain of that.

Each passing day brought a greater likelihood that Denice would not be found alive. If she had been grabbed by a rapist, she would have been released after the assault. If she had been kidnapped, someone would have demanded a ransom. There were rumors of an old lover down in Texas, but they came and went. And there were rumors of drug traffickers and such, but then most bizarre crimes had a few of those.

Ada, again, was shocked by the crime. Debbie Carter had been murdered seventeen months earlier, and the town had just settled down from that nightmare. Now doors were locked and double-locked, curfews were tightened on teenagers, and there was a brisk run of gun sales at the local pawnshops. What was happening to the nice little college town with two churches on every corner?

Weeks passed, and life slowly returned to normal for most of Ada's population. It was soon summertime and the kids were out of school. The rumors died down but didn't stop altogether. A suspect in Texas boasted of killing ten women, and the Ada police raced off to interview him. A woman's body was found in Missouri, with tattoos on her legs. Denice had no tattoos.

And so it went through the summer and into the fall. Not a single break or piece of evidence of any kind that would lead the police to the body of Denice Haraway.

And no progress in the Carter investigation. With two sensational murders remaining unsolved, the atmosphere around the police department was heavy and strained. Long hours were worked, with nothing to show for the time. Old leads were reviewed and chased again, with the same results. The lives of Dennis Smith and Gary Rogers were consumed with the two murders.

For Rogers, the pressure was even worse. One year before the disappearance of Denice Haraway, a similar crime had been committed in Seminole, thirty miles north of Ada. An eighteen-year-old girl named Patty Hamilton was working at an all-night convenience store when she vanished. A customer walked in and found the store empty, the cash register cleaned out, two open soft drink cans on the counter, no sign of a struggle. Her locked car was found outside the store. She was gone without a clue, and for a year the police had assumed she'd been abducted and murdered.

The OSBI agent in charge of the Patty Hamilton case was Gary
Rogers. Debbie Carter, Denice Haraway, Patty Hamilton—Agent Rogers
had the unsolved murders of three young women on his desk.

WHEN Oklahoma was still a territory, Ada had a colorful and richly deserved reputation as an open haven for gunslingers and outlaws. Disputes
were settled with six-shooters, and the quickest on the draw walked away
with no fear of punishment from civil authorities. Bank robbers and cat-
tle thieves drifted to Ada because it was still Indian territory and not a
part of the States. Sheriffs, when they could be found, were no match for
the professional criminals who settled in and around Ada.

The town's reputation for lawlessness changed dramatically in 1909,
when the locals finally got fed up with living in fear. A respected rancher
named Gus Bobbitt was gunned down by a professional killer hired by
a rival landowner. The killer and three conspirators were arrested, and
an epidemic of hanging fever swept through the town. Led by the Ma-
sons, the upstanding members of Ada, a lynch mob formed early on the
morning of April 19, 1909. Forty members marched solemnly out of the
Masonic Hall on Twelfth at Broadway in downtown Ada and arrived at
the jail a few minutes later. They subdued the sheriff, yanked the four
thugs out of their cells, and dragged them across the street to a livery stable that had been chosen for the occasion. Each of the four had his wrists
and ankles bound with baling wire, then each was ceremoniously hanged.

Early the next morning a photographer set up his camera in the
barn and took some pictures. One survived over the years, a faded black
and white that clearly shows all four men suspended by their ropes, motionless, almost peaceful, and quite dead. Years later, the photo was re-
produced on a postcard and handed out at the Chamber of Commerce
office.

For decades, the lynchings were Ada's proudest moment.

CHAPTER 5

With the Carter case, Dennis Smith and Gary Rogers not only had an autopsy, hair samples, and "suspicious" polygraph exams but also were confident they had their killer. Ron Williamson was away for a spell doing time, but he would be back. They'd nail him sooner or later.

With Haraway, though, they had nothing—no body, no witnesses, not a single solid clue. The sketches by the police artist could realistically fit half the young men in Ada. The cops were due for a break.

It came out of nowhere early in October 1984, when a man named Jeff Miller walked into the Ada Police Department and asked to speak to Detective Dennis Smith. He said he had information about the Haraway case.

Miller was a local boy with no criminal record, but the police knew him vaguely as one of the many restless young people in the town who kept late hours and moved from job to job, usually in factories. Miller pulled up a chair and proceeded to tell his story.

The night Denice Haraway disappeared, there had been a party near the Blue River, at a spot some twenty-five miles south of Ada. Jeff Miller had not actually been at the party, but he knew two women who were there. These two women—and he gave Smith their names—later told him that Tommy Ward was there, and that at some point early in the party there was a shortage of alcohol. Ward, who did not own a vehicle, volunteered to go get some beer, and he borrowed a pickup truck from one Janette Roberts. Ward left by himself in the truck, was gone for a few hours, and when he returned without the beer, he was distraught and crying. When asked why he was crying, he said he'd done something terrible. What? everyone at the party wanted to know. Well, for some reason he had driven all the way back to Ada, passing many beer stores along the way, and had found himself at McAnally's out east of town, where he snatched the young female clerk, raped her, killed her, disposed of her body, and now he felt awful about it.

Confessing all this to a random group of hard drinkers and dope smokers seemed like the logical thing to do.

Miller offered no clue as to why the two women would tell him and not the police, nor did he suggest any reason why they had waited five months.

As absurd as the story was, Dennis Smith quickly pursued it. He tried to find the two women, but they had already moved away from Ada. (When he finally tracked them down a month later, they denied being at the party, denied seeing Tommy Ward there or at any other party, denied ever hearing a story about a young female store clerk getting kidnapped and killed, or any other young female for that matter, and denied everything Jeff Miller had included in his tale.)

Dennis Smith located Janette Roberts. She was living in Norman, seventy miles away, with her husband, Mike Roberts. On October 12, Smith and Detective Mike Baskin drove to Norman and dropped in unannounced on Janette. They asked her to follow them down to the police station for a few questions, which she reluctantly did.

During the interview, Janette admitted that she, Mike, Tommy Ward, and Karl Fontenot, among many others, had often partied down by the

Blue River, but she was almost positive they had not done so on the Saturday night the Haraway girl disappeared. She often loaned Tommy Ward her pickup, but he had never left with it from a party at the river (or any other place), nor had she ever seen him crying and upset, nor had she ever heard him blubbering about raping and murdering a young woman. No, sir, that had never happened. She was quite certain.

The detectives were pleasantly surprised to learn that Tommy Ward was living with the Robertses and working with Mike. The two men were employed by a siding contractor and putting in long hours, usually from sunrise to dark. Smith and Baskin decided to stay in Norman until Ward came home from work, then ask him some questions.

Tommy and Mike stopped for a six-pack on the way home, and the beer drinking was one reason not to go chat with the cops. More important, Tommy just didn't like them. He was reluctant to go to the police station in Norman. The Ada cops had quizzed him about the murder months earlier, and he thought the matter was closed. One reason he'd left Ada was because so many people commented on how much he looked like one of the suspects in the police composites, and he was tired of it. He'd looked at the drawing many times and could see no resemblance. It was just another sketch, drawn by a police artist who'd never seen the suspect and never would, then broadcast to a community quite anxious to link the face to someone living in Ada. Everybody wanted to help the police solve the crime. It was a small town. The disappearance was big news. At one time or another, everybody Tommy knew had ventured a guess as to the likely identities of the suspects.

Tommy had been through several run-ins with the Ada police over the years, nothing serious or violent, but they knew him and he knew them, and Tommy preferred to avoid Smith and Rogers if at all possible.

In Janette's opinion, if Tommy had nothing to hide, then it was safe to go to the police station and chat with Dennis Smith and Mike Baskin. Tommy had nothing to do with the Haraway girl, but he didn't trust the police. After wrestling with the issue for an hour, he asked Mike to drive him to the Norman Police Department.

Smith and Baskin took him downstairs to a room with video equipment and explained that they wanted to make a tape of the interview. Tommy was nervous, but agreed. The machine was turned on, and they read him his *Miranda* rights, and he signed the waiver.

The detectives began politely enough; it was just another routine interview, nothing important. They asked Tommy if he remembered the last interview, five months earlier. Of course he did. Had he told them the truth then? Yes. Was he telling the truth now? Yes.

Within minutes Smith and Baskin, going back and forth with the questions, confused Tommy with the days of the week back in April. On the day Denice Haraway disappeared, Tommy had worked on the plumbing in his mother's home, then showered and gone to a party at the Robertses' home in Ada. He'd left at four in the morning and walked home. Five months earlier he'd told the cops this had happened the day before the disappearance. "I just got my days mixed up," he tried to explain, but the cops could not be convinced.

The detectives' replies were, "When did you realize you hadn't told us the truth?" and "Are you telling us the truth now?" and "You're getting yourself into more serious trouble."

The tone became harsh and accusatory. Smith and Baskin lied and claimed to have several witnesses who would testify that Tommy was at a party by the Blue River that Saturday night and had borrowed a pickup truck and left.

Wrong day, Tommy said, sticking to his version. He'd gone fishing on Friday, partied at the Robertses' on Saturday, and gone to a party at the river on Sunday.

Why were the cops lying? Tommy asked himself. He knew the truth.

The lying continued. "Isn't it true you were going to rob McAnally's? We've got people who are going to testify to that."

Tommy shook his head and held firm, but he was deeply troubled. If the police were willing to lie so casually, what else might they do?

Dennis Smith then pulled out a large photograph of Denice Haraway and held it close to Tommy's face. "Do you know that girl?"

"I don't know her. I've seen her."

"Did you kill that girl?"

"No, I didn't. I wouldn't take nobody's life from them."

"Who did kill her?"

"I don't know."

Smith continued to hold the photo while asking if she was a pretty girl. "Her family would like to bury her. They'd like to know where she is so they could bury her."

"I don't know where she's at," Tommy said, staring at the photo and wondering why he was being accused.

"Would you tell me where she's at so her family could bury her?"

"I don't know."

"Use your imagination," Smith said. "Two guys took her, got her in a pickup, took her away. What do you think they did with the body?"

"No telling."

"Use your imagination. What do you think?"

"She could be alive for all I know, for all you know, for all anyone knows."

Smith continued to hold up the photo as he asked questions. Every answer by Tommy was immediately disregarded, treated as if it weren't true or weren't heard by the detectives. They asked him repeatedly if he thought she was a pretty girl. Did he think she screamed during the attack? Don't you think her family should be able to bury her?

"Tommy, have you prayed about this?" Smith asked.

He finally put the photo aside and asked Tommy about his mental health, about the composite sketches, about his educational background. Then he picked up the photo again, thrust it near Tommy's face, and started over with questions about killing the girl, burying the body, and wasn't she a pretty girl?

Mike Baskin attempted a tearjerker when he talked about Denice's family's ordeal: "All it would take to end their suffering would be to tell where she's at."

Tommy agreed, but said he had no idea where the girl was.

The machine was finally turned off. The interview lasted an hour and forty-five minutes, and Tommy Ward never wavered from his original statement—he knew nothing about the disappearance of Denice Haraway. He was quite rattled by the meeting, but agreed to take a lie detector test in a few days.

The Robertses lived only a few blocks from the Norman police station, and Tommy decided to walk to their home. The fresh air felt good, but he was angry at being treated so harshly by the cops. They had accused him of killing the girl. They had lied repeatedly to try to trick him.

Driving back to Ada, Smith and Baskin were convinced they had found their man. Tommy Ward looked like the sketch of one of the strange-acting boys who'd stopped by JP's store that Saturday night. He'd changed his story about where he was on the night Denice vanished. And he seemed nervous during the interview they had just completed.

AT FIRST, Tommy was relieved that he would be taking a polygraph exam. He would tell the truth, the test would prove it, and the cops would finally stop hassling him. Then he began having nightmares about the murder; the accusations by the police; the comments about his resemblance to the man in the sketch; the pretty face of Denice Haraway and her family's anguish. Why was he being accused?

The police believed he was guilty. They wanted him to be guilty! Why should he trust them with a lie detector exam? Should he talk to a lawyer?

He called his mother and told her he was scared of the police and the polygraph. "I'm afraid they'll make me say something I'm not supposed to say," he told her. Tell the truth, she advised him, and everything will be fine.

Thursday morning, October 18, Mike Roberts drove Tommy to the OSBI offices in Oklahoma City, twenty minutes away. The exam was to take about an hour. Mike would wait in the parking lot, then the two would drive to work. Their boss had given them a couple of hours off.

As Mike Roberts watched Tommy enter the building, he could not imagine that the boy was taking his last steps in the free world. The rest of his life would be behind prison walls.

Dennis Smith met Tommy with a big smile and a warm handshake, then put him in an office where he waited, alone, for half an hour—a favorite police trick to make the suspect even more nervous. At 10:30, he was led to another room, and waiting there was Agent Rusty Featherstone and his trusty polygraph.

Smith disappeared. Featherstone explained how the machine worked, or how it was supposed to work, as he strapped Tommy in and hooked up the electrodes. By the time the questions started, Tommy was already sweating. The first questions were easy—family, education, employment—everybody knew the truth and the machine complied. This could be a cakewalk, Tommy started thinking.

At 11:05, Featherstone read Tommy his *Miranda* rights and began probing into the Haraway matter. For two and a half hours of tortuous questioning, Tommy gamely stuck to the truth—he knew nothing about the Denice Haraway matter.

Without a single break, the exam lasted until 1:30, when Featherstone unplugged everything and left the room. Tommy was relieved, even elated because the ordeal was finally over. He had aced the test; finally the cops would leave him alone.

Featherstone was back in five minutes, poring over the graph paper, studying the results. He asked Tommy what he thought. Tommy said he knew he'd passed the exam, the matter was over, and he really needed to get to work.

Not so fast, Featherstone said. You flunked it.

Tommy was incredulous, but Featherstone said it was obvious he was lying and clear that he was involved in the Haraway kidnapping. Would he like to talk about it?

Talk about what!

The polygraph doesn't lie, Featherstone said, pointing to the results right there on the paper. You know something about the murder, he said repeatedly. Things would go much smoother for Tommy if he came clean, talked about what happened, told the truth. Featherstone, the nice cop, was anxious to help Tommy, but if Tommy refused his kindness, then he would be forced to hand him over to Smith and Rogers, the nasty cops, who were waiting, ready to pounce.

Let's talk about it, Featherstone urged him.

There's nothing to talk about, Tommy insisted. He said again and again that the polygraph was rigged or something because he was telling the truth, but Featherstone wasn't buying it.

Tommy admitted to being nervous before the exam, and anxious while it was under way because he was late for work. He also admitted that the interview six days earlier with Smith and Rogers had upset him and caused him to have a dream.

What kind of dream? Featherstone wanted to know.

Tommy described his dream: He was at a keg party, then he was sitting in a pickup truck with two other men and a girl, out by the old power plant near Ada where he grew up. One of the men tried to kiss the girl, she refused, and Tommy told the man to leave her alone. Then he said he wanted to go home. "You're already home," one of the men said. Tommy looked through his window, and he was suddenly at home. Just before he woke up, he was standing at a sink, trying in vain to wash a black liquid off his hands. The girl was not identified; neither were the two men.

That dream doesn't make sense, Featherstone said.

Most dreams don't, Tommy retorted.

Featherstone remained calm but continued to press Tommy to come clean, tell him everything about the crime, and, especially, tell him where the body was. And he threatened again to turn Tommy over to those "two cops" waiting in the next room, as if a lengthy torture session could be in the works.

Tommy was stunned and confused and very frightened. When he refused to confess to Featherstone, the nice cop turned him over to Smith and Rogers, who were already angry and seemed ready to throw punches.

Featherstone stayed in the room, and as soon as the door closed, Smith lunged at Tommy, yelling, "You, Karl Fontenot, and Odell Titsworth grabbed that girl, took her out to the power plant, raped and killed her, didn't you?"

No, Tommy said, trying to think clearly and not panic.

Talk to us, you little lying sonofabitch, Smith growled. You just flunked the polygraph, we know you're lying, and we know you killed that girl!

Tommy was trying to place Odell Titsworth, a name he had heard but a man he'd never met. Odell lived somewhere around Ada, he thought, and he had a bad reputation, but Tommy could not remember meeting him. Maybe he'd seen him once or twice, but at the moment he couldn't remember, because Smith was yelling and pointing and ready to punch him.

Smith repeated his theory about the three men snatching the girl, and Tommy said no. No, I had nothing to do with it. "I don't even know Odell Titsworth."

Yes, you do, Smith corrected him. Stop lying.

Karl Fontenot's involvement in their theory was easier to understand because he and Tommy had been friends off and on for a couple of years. But Tommy was bewildered by the accusations and terrified of the smug certainty of Smith and Rogers. Back and forth they went with their threats and verbal abuse. The language deteriorated and soon included every profanity and obscenity on the list.

Tommy was sweating and dizzy and trying desperately to think rationally. He kept his responses short. No, I didn't do it. No, I wasn't involved. A few times he wanted to lash out with sarcastic comments, but he was scared. Smith and Rogers were erupting, and armed, and Tommy was locked in a room with them and Featherstone. His interrogation showed no signs of ending anytime soon.

After sweating through three hours with Featherstone and suffering an hour of torment from Smith and Rogers, Tommy really needed a break. He needed to find a restroom and smoke a cigarette and clear his head. He needed help, to talk to someone who could tell him what was going on.

Can I take a break? he asked.

Just a few more minutes, they said.

Tommy noticed a video camera on a nearby table, unplugged and neglecting the verbal battering under way. Surely, he thought, this cannot be standard police procedure.

Smith and Rogers repeatedly reminded Tommy that Oklahoma uses lethal injection to kill its killers. He was facing death, certain death, but there might be a way to avoid it. Come clean, tell what happened, lead them to the body, and they would use their influence to get him a deal.

"I didn't do it," Tommy kept saying.

He had a dream, Featherstone informed his two colleagues.

Tommy repeated the dream, and again it was met with disapproval. The three cops agreed that the dream made little sense, to which Tommy replied again, "Most dreams don't."

But the dream gave the cops something to work with, and they began adding to it. The other two men in the truck were Odell Titsworth and Karl Fontenot, right?

No, Tommy insisted. The men in his dream were not identified. No names.

Bullshit. The girl was Denice Haraway, right?

No, the girl was not identified in his dream.

Bullshit.

For another hour, the cops added the necessary details to Tommy's dream, and every new fact was denied by him. It was just a dream, he kept saying over and over and over.

Just a dream.

Bullshit, said the cops.

AFTER two hours of nonstop hammering, Tommy finally cracked. The pressure came from fear—Smith and Rogers were angry and seemed perfectly able and willing to slap him around if not outright shoot him—but also from the horror of wasting away on death row before finally getting executed.

And it was obvious to Tommy that he would not be allowed to leave until he gave the cops something. After five hours in the room, he was exhausted, confused, and almost paralyzed with fear.

He made a mistake, one that would send him to death row and eventually cost him his freedom for life.

Tommy decided to play along. Since he was completely innocent, and he assumed Karl Fontenot and Odell Titsworth were too, then give the cops what they want. Play along with their fiction. The truth would quickly be discovered. Tomorrow, or the next day, the cops would realize that the story did not check out. They would talk to Karl, and he would tell the truth. They would find Odell Titsworth, and he would laugh at them.

Play along. Good police work will find the truth.

If his dream confession was sufficiently ridiculous, how could anyone believe it?

Didn't Odell go in the store first?

Sure, why not, Tommy said. It was only a dream.

Now the cops were getting somewhere. The boy was finally breaking under their clever tactics.

Robbery was the motive, right?

Sure, whatever, it was only a dream.

Throughout the afternoon, Smith and Rogers added more and more fiction to the dream, and Tommy played along.

It was only a dream.

Even as the grotesque "confession" was happening, the police should have realized they had serious problems. Detective Mike Baskin was waiting back in Ada at the police department, sitting by the phone and wishing he was at the OSBI in the thick of things. Around 3:00 p.m.,

Gary Rogers called with great news—Tommy Ward was talking! Get in the car, drive out to the power plant west of town, and look for the body. Baskin raced off, certain the search would soon be over.

He found nothing, and realized he would need several men for a thorough search. He drove back to the police station. The phone rang again. The story had changed. There was an old burned house on the right as you approach the power plant. That's where the body is!

Baskin took off again, found the house, picked through the rubble, found nothing, and drove back to town.

His goose chase continued with the third call from Rogers. The story had changed yet again. Somewhere in the vicinity of the power plant and the burned house there was a concrete bunker. That's where they put the body.

Baskin rounded up two more officers and some floodlights, and took off again. They found the concrete bunker, and were still searching when darkness fell.

They found nothing.

With each call back from Baskin, Smith and Rogers made modifications to Tommy's dream. The hours dragged on, the suspect was beyond fatigue. They tag-teamed, back and forth, good cop, bad cop, voices low and almost sympathetic, then bursts of yelling, cursing, threatening. "You lyin' little sonofabitch!" was their favorite. Tommy had it screamed at him a thousand times.

"You'd better be glad Mike Baskin ain't here," Smith said. "Or he would blow your brains out."

A bullet to the head would not have surprised Tommy.

After dark, when they realized that the body would not be found that day, Smith and Rogers decided to wrap up the confession. With the video camera still unplugged, they walked Tommy through their story, beginning with the three killers riding around in Odell Titsworth's pickup, planning the robbery, realizing Denice would identify them so they grabbed her, then decided to rape and kill her. The details on the location of the body were vague, but the detectives felt sure it was hidden somewhere near the power plant.

Tommy was brain-dead and barely able to mumble. He tried to recite their tale but kept getting the facts mixed up. Smith and Rogers would stop him, repeat their fiction, and make him start over. Finally, after four rehearsals with little improvement and their star fading fast, the cops decided to turn on the camera.

Do it now, they said to Tommy. Do it right, and none of that dream bullshit.

"But the story ain't true," Tommy said.

Just tell it anyway, the cops insisted, then we'll help you prove it's not true.

And none of that dream bullshit.

At 6:58 p.m., Tommy Ward looked at the camera and stated his name. He had been interrogated for eight and a half hours, and he was physically and emotionally wasted.

He was smoking a cigarette, his first of the afternoon, and sitting before him was a soft drink can, as if he and cops were just finishing up a friendly little chat, everything nice and civilized.

He told his tale. He, Karl Fontenot, and Odell Titsworth kidnapped Denice Haraway from the store, drove out to the power plant on the west side of town, raped her, killed her, then tossed her body somewhere near a concrete bunker out by Sandy Creek. The murder weapon was Titsworth's lock-blade knife.

It was all a dream, he said. Or meant to say. Or thought he said.

Several times he used the name "Titsdale." The detectives stopped him and helpfully suggested the name "Titsworth." Tommy corrected himself and plodded on. He kept thinking, Any blind cop could see that I'm lying.

Thirty-one minutes later, the video was turned off. Tommy was handcuffed, then driven back to Ada and thrown in jail. Mike Roberts was still waiting in the parking lot of the OSBI building. He'd been there for almost nine and a half hours.

The next morning, Smith and Rogers called a press conference and announced they had solved the Haraway case. Tommy Ward, age twenty-four, of Ada, had confessed and implicated two other men who were not yet in custody. The cops asked the press to sit on the story for a couple of days, until they could round up the other suspects. The newspaper complied, but a television station did not. The news was soon broadcast over southeastern Oklahoma.

A few hours later, Karl Fontenot was arrested near Tulsa and driven back to Ada. Smith and Rogers, fresh from their success with Tommy Ward, handled the interrogation. Though a video recorder was ready, no tape was made of the questioning.

Karl was twenty years old and had been living on his own since he was sixteen. He grew up in Ada, in wretched poverty—his father had been an alcoholic and Karl had witnessed his mother's death in an auto accident. He was an impressionable kid with few friends and virtually no family.

He insisted he was innocent and knew nothing about the Haraway disappearance.

Karl proved to be considerably easier to break than Tommy, and in less than two hours Smith and Rogers had another taped confession, one suspiciously similar to Ward's.

Karl repudiated his confession immediately after he was placed in jail, and would later state: "I've never been in jail or had a police record in my life and no one in my face telling me I'd killed a pretty woman, that I'm going to get the death penalty so I told them the story hoping they would leave me alone. Which they did after I taped the statement. They said I had a choice to write it or tape it. I didn't even know what the word statement or confessing meant till they told me I confessed to it. So that's the reason I gave them an untrue statement so they would leave me alone."

The police made sure the story got to the press. Ward and Fontenot had made full confessions. The Haraway mystery was solved, most of it anyway. They were working on Titsworth, and expected to charge all three with murder in a matter of days.

The site of the burned house was located, and the police found the remains of what appeared to be a jawbone. This was soon reported in the *Ada Evening News*.

IN SPITE OF the careful coaching, Karl's confession was a mess. There were huge discrepancies between his version of the crime and Tommy's. The two were in direct contradiction on such details as the order in which the three raped Denice, whether or not she was stabbed by her attackers during the rape, the location and number of stab wounds, whether or not she managed to break free and run a few steps before being caught, and when she finally died. The most glaring discrepancy was how they killed her and what they did with her body.

Tommy Ward said she received multiple knife wounds while lying in the back of Odell's pickup during the gang rape. She died there, and they flung her body into a ditch near a concrete bunker. Fontenot didn't recall it that way. In his version, they took her into an abandoned house where Odell Titsworth stabbed her, stuffed her beneath the floor, then poured gasoline over her and burned down the house.

But the two were in almost complete agreement on Odell Titsworth. He had been the organizer, the mastermind who rounded up Ward and Fontenot to go riding in his pickup, to drink some beer, smoke some pot, and at some point rob McAnally's. Once the gang had decided on which store to rob, Odell went in and stole the money, grabbed the girl, and told his buddies they would have to kill her so she couldn't identify them. He drove out to the power plant. He directed the gang rape, going first himself. He produced the weapon, a six-inch lock-blade knife. He stabbed her, killed her, and either he burned her or he did not.

Though they admitted their involvement, the real blame rested on Odell Titsworth, or Titsdale, or whatever his name was.

LATE in the afternoon of Friday, October 19, the police arrested Titsworth and questioned him. He was a four-time convicted felon with a lousy attitude toward cops and far greater experience with their interrogation tactics. He didn't budge an inch. He knew nothing about the Haraway case, didn't give a damn what Ward and Fontenot said, on tape or off. He had never met either of the gentlemen.

No video was made of his interrogation. Titsworth was thrown in jail, where he soon recalled that on April 26 he had broken his arm in a fight with the police. Two days later, when Denice disappeared, he had been at his girlfriend's house, wearing a heavy cast and in great pain.

In both confessions, he had been described as wearing a T-shirt, with tattoos covering his arms. In truth, his left arm had been covered with a cast and he'd been nowhere near McAnally's. When Dennis Smith investigated this, he found hospital and police records that clearly verified Odell's story. Smith spoke with the treating physician, who described the break as a spiral fracture between the elbow and shoulder and very painful. It would have been impossible for Titsworth to carry a body or commit a violent attack only two days after the fracture. His arm was in a cast, and the cast was in a sling. Impossible.

The confessions continued to unravel. As the police sifted through the rubble of the burned house, its owner appeared and asked what they were doing. When he was told that they were looking for the remains of the Haraway girl, and that one of the suspects had confessed to burning her with the house, the owner said that was not possible. He'd burned the old house himself in June 1983, ten months before she disappeared.

The state medical examiner completed an analysis of the jawbone and concluded that it came from a possum. This was given to the press.

However, the press was not told of the burned house or Odell

Titsworth's broken arm, nor of the fact that Ward and Fontenot had immediately repudiated their confessions.

In jail, Ward and Fontenot were adamant about their innocence and told anyone who would listen that the confessions were extracted by threats and promises. The Ward family scraped together enough money to hire a good lawyer, and Tommy described to him in great detail the tricks used by Smith and Rogers during the interrogation. It was just a dream, he said a thousand times.

There was no family for Karl Fontenot.

The search for the remains of Denice Haraway continued in earnest. The obvious question asked by many was, "If those two confessed, then why don't the police know where the body is buried?"

THE FIFTH AMENDMENT to the U.S. Constitution protects against self-incrimination, and since the easiest way to solve a crime is to get a confession, there is a thick and rich body of law that governs police conduct during interrogations. Much of this law was well established before 1984.

A hundred years earlier, in *Hopt v. Utah*, the Supreme Court ruled that a confession is not admissible if it is obtained by operating on the hopes or fears of the accused, and in doing so deprives him of the freedom of will or self-control necessary to make a voluntary statement.

In 1897, the Court, in *Bram v. United States*, said that a statement must be free and voluntary, not extracted by any sorts of threats or violence or promises, however slight. A confession obtained from an accused who has been threatened cannot be admissible.

In 1960, in *Blackburn v. Alabama*, the Court said, "Coercion can be mental as well as physical." In reviewing whether a confession was psychologically coerced by the police, the following factors are crucial: (1) the length of the interrogation, (2) whether it was prolonged in nature, (3) when it took place, day or night, with a strong suspicion around nighttime confessions, and (4) the psychological makeup—intelligence, sophistication, education, and so on—of the suspect.

And in *Miranda v. Arizona*, the most famous of all self-incrimination cases, the Supreme Court imposed procedural safeguards to protect the rights of the accused. A suspect has a constitutional right *not* to be compelled to talk, and any statement made during an interrogation *cannot* be used in court unless the police and the prosecutor can prove that the suspect clearly understood that (1) he had the right to remain silent, (2) anything said could be used against him in court, and (3) he had a right to an attorney, whether or not he could afford one. If, during an interrogation, the accused requests an attorney, then the questioning stops immediately.

Miranda was decided in 1966 and became instantly famous. Many police departments ignored it, at least until guilty criminals were set free because they had not been properly advised of their rights. It was harshly criticized by law-and-order types who accused the Court of coddling the bad guys. It worked its way into our culture, with every cop on TV spitting out the words "You have the right to remain silent" as he made his arrest.

Rogers, Smith, and Featherstone knew its importance because they made sure Tommy's *Miranda* procedure was properly recorded. What was not seen on the video was the five and a half hours of nonstop threats and verbal abuse.

The confessions of Tommy Ward and Karl Fontenot were constitutional disasters, but at the time, in October 1984, the cops still believed they would find the body, and thus some credible evidence. Any trial was months away. They still had plenty of time to build a solid case against Ward and Fontenot, or so they thought.

But Denice was not found. Tommy and Karl had no idea where she was, and they repeatedly told this to the police. Months dragged on with no evidence, not a shred of it. The confessions became more and more important; indeed, they were to become the only evidence the state had at trial.

CHAPTER 6

Ron Williamson was well aware of the Haraway case. He had the best seat in the house—a bed in the Pontotoc County jail. After serving ten months of his three-year sentence, he was paroled back to Ada and placed under house arrest, a rather loose arrangement that severely restricted his movements. Not surprisingly, it didn't work. Ron was unmedicated and unable to keep track of time and dates or anything else.

In November, while living at home, he was charged with "willfully and wrongfully, having been sentenced to confinement with the Department of Corrections for the crime of Uttering a Forged Instrument, and while on house arrest status did escape from such status and confinement by leaving his house during a time not consented to by the D.O.C."

Ron's version was that he walked down the street to buy a pack of cigarettes and returned home thirty minutes later than expected. He was arrested, jailed, and four days later charged with the felony of escape from a penal institution. He made a pauper's oath and requested court-appointed counsel.

The jail was buzzing with the Haraway matter. Tommy Ward and Karl Fontenot were already there. The inmates, with absolutely nothing to do, talked and talked. Ward and Fontenot had center stage because their crime was the most recent and certainly the most sensational. Tommy described the dream confession and the tactics used by Smith, Rogers, and Featherstone. The detectives were well known to his audience.

Tommy insisted over and over that he had nothing to do with Denice Haraway, that the real killers were out there laughing at the two stupid boys who confessed and the cops who tricked them into it.

WITHOUT the body of Denice Haraway, Bill Peterson had an enormous legal challenge. His case consisted of the two taped confessions, with absolutely no physical evidence as a foundation. Indeed, the truth contradicted virtually everything on the tapes, and the confessions clearly contradicted each other. Peterson had the two sketches of the suspects, but even they were problematic. Arguably, one favored Tommy Ward, but no one had suggested that the other drawing even remotely resembled Karl Fontenot.

Thanksgiving came and went with no body. Then Christmas. In January 1985, Bill Peterson convinced a judge that there was sufficient evidence that Denice Haraway was dead. During a preliminary hearing, the confessions were played to a packed courtroom. The reaction was generally one of shock, though many noted the glaring discrepancies between Ward's account and Fontenot's. Nevertheless, it was time for a trial, with or without a dead body.

But the legal wrangling went on and on. Two judges recused themselves. The search lost steam and was finally called off a year after Denice disappeared. Most of Ada was convinced Ward and Fontenot were guilty—why else would they confess?—but there was also speculation about the lack of evidence. Why was it taking so long for a trial?

In April 1985, a year after the disappearance of Denice Haraway, the *Ada Evening News* ran a story by Dorothy Hogue about the town's frustration with the pace of the investigations. "Unsolved, Violent Crimes Haunt Ada" was the headline, and Hogue summarized both. On Haraway, she wrote: "Although authorities have searched many local areas, both before and after the arrests of Ward and Fontenot, no trace of Haraway has ever been found. However, Detective Dennis Smith said he is convinced the case is solved." The alleged confessions were not mentioned.

On the Carter case, Hogue wrote: "Evidence found at the murder scene and evidence concerning the suspect were sent to the Oklahoma State Bureau of Investigation laboratory less than two years ago and the police said they are still waiting for results." The backlog at the OSBI was noted. Dennis Smith said, "The police have narrowed their focus to one suspect in the case but no one has ever been arrested in connection with the crime."

IN FEBRUARY 1985, Ron was in court on the escape charge. His court-appointed lawyer was David Morris, a man who knew the Williamson family well. Ron entered a plea of guilty to the escape charge and received a two-year sentence, most of which would be suspended if Ron (1) completed some mental health counseling, (2) stayed out of trouble, (3) stayed in Pontotoc County, and (4) refrained from using alcohol.

A few months later he was arrested for public drunkenness in Pottawatomie County. Bill Peterson filed a motion to revoke his suspended sentence and to require him to serve the remainder of his sentence. David Morris was again appointed by the court to represent him. A revocation hearing was held on July 26 before the special district judge John David Miller; or at least it was attempted. Ron, unmedicated, wouldn't shut up. He argued with Morris, Judge Miller, and the deputies, and he became so disruptive that the hearing was postponed.

Three days later they tried again. Judge Miller asked the jailers and deputies to warn Ron about his behavior, but he entered the courtroom yelling and cursing. The judge warned him repeatedly, and he repeatedly rebuked the judge. He demanded a new lawyer, but when the judge asked for a reason, he had none.

His conduct was repulsive, but even in the midst of the turmoil it was obvious that he needed help. At times he seemed connected to what was happening, then a moment later his rantings were incoherent. He was angry, bitter, and lashing out at the world.

After several warnings, Judge Miller ordered him back to the jail, and the hearing was postponed again. The next day David Morris filed a motion requesting a hearing into Ron's mental competency. He also filed a motion to withdraw as counsel.

In his twisted world, Ron saw himself as perfectly normal. He was insulted by the fact that his lawyer would question his mental stability, so he stopped speaking to him. Morris was fed up.

The motion for a competency hearing was granted. The motion to withdraw was denied.

Two weeks later the hearing was initiated, and quickly called off. Ron was even crazier than before. Judge Miller ordered a psychiatric evaluation.

EARLY in 1985, Juanita Williamson was diagnosed with ovarian cancer, and it progressed rapidly. For two and a half years she had lived with the constant rumors that her son killed Debbie Carter, and she wanted to settle the issue before she passed away.

Juanita was fastidious about paperwork. She had kept a detailed daily journal for decades. Her business records were perfect; give her a minute, and she could tell any customer the dates of her last five appointments. She threw away nothing—paid bills, canceled checks, receipts, her children's report cards, and other mementos.

She had checked her diary a hundred times and knew that on the night of December 7, 1982, Ron had been at home with her. She had shared this with the police on more than one occasion. Their theory was that he could easily have sneaked out of the house, darted through a back alley, committed the crime, then returned home. Forget motive. Forget Glen Gore's lies about seeing Ron at the Coachlight that night harassing Debbie Carter. Minor points; the cops had their man.

But the cops also knew that Juanita Williamson was highly respected. She was devout in her Christian faith and well known throughout the Pentecostal churches. She had hundreds of customers at her beauty shop and treated them all like close friends. If Juanita took the witness stand and said Ronnie was at home on the night of the murder, the jury would believe her. Maybe her son was having problems, but he'd certainly been raised better.

Now Juanita remembered something else. In 1982, videocassette rentals were becoming popular. A store down the street had discovered the business. On December 7, Juanita rented a VCR unit and five of her favorite movies, which she and Ron watched until early the next morning. He was there at home that night, in the den, on the sofa, having a wonderful time watching old movies with his mother. And Juanita had the rental receipt.

David Morris had always tended to the light legal matters Juanita needed. He admired her greatly, and as a favor he occasionally represented Ron in some of his escapades, though he was far from an ideal client. Morris listened to her story, looked at the receipt, and had no doubt she was telling the truth. He was also relieved, because he, like most folks in town, had heard the constant rumors about Ron's involvement in the Carter murder.

Most of Morris's work was criminal defense, and he had little respect for the Ada police. But he knew them, and he arranged a meeting with Dennis Smith and Juanita. He even drove her down to the police station and sat with her while she explained things to Dennis Smith. The detective listened carefully, studied the rental record, and asked her if she would video a statement. Certainly.

David Morris watched through a window as Juanita was placed in a chair, faced the camera, and answered Smith's questions. Driving home, she was relieved and certain that she had laid the matter to rest.

If the video camera was loaded with a tape, it was never seen. If Detective Smith made a report of the interview, it was never produced in the legal proceedings that followed.

SITTING in jail, killing days and weeks, Ron worried about his mother. By August, she was dying in the hospital, and he was not allowed to see her.

That month, by court order, he was examined again by Dr. Charles Amos, who planned to administer some tests. During the first one, though, he noted that Ron was simply marking "True" for all the answers. When Amos quizzed him, he replied, "What's more important, this test or my mother?" The evaluation was called off, but Amos did note, "It should be pointed out that this examiner's interview with Mr. Williamson shows a marked deterioration of emotional function since our last encounter in 1982."

Ron begged the police to allow him to see his mother before she died. Annette pleaded, too. Over the years, she had become acquainted with the officers at the jail. When she took Ronnie cookies and brownies, she took enough for all the inmates and all the jailers. She even cooked entire meals for them in the jail's kitchen.

The hospital was not far away, she reasoned. It was a small town; everybody knew Ron and his family. He was unlikely to somehow get a weapon and hurt people. Finally a deal was made and Ron was led out of jail after midnight, handcuffed and chained, surrounded by heavily armed deputies, and driven to the hospital, where he was placed in a wheelchair and rolled down the hallway.

Juanita had been clear that she did not want to see her son in handcuffs. Annette had begged the police to comply, and they had reluctantly agreed. But somewhere along the way the agreement was forgotten. The cuffs and leg chains were not removed. Ron pleaded with the cops—just remove the handcuffs for a few minutes while he saw his mother for the last time. It couldn't be done. He was told to remain seated in the wheelchair.

Ron asked for a blanket to hide the handcuffs and shackles. The cops hesitated—could be a security risk—then relented. They wheeled him into Juanita's room and insisted that Annette and Renee leave. They asked to stay so the family could be together one last time. Too risky, the cops said. Go wait in the hall.

Ron told his mother how much he loved her, how sorry he was for the mess he'd made of his life, sorry for all the disappointments. He cried and begged her to forgive him, and of course she did. He quoted some Scripture. Intimacy, though, was somewhat difficult because the cops stayed in the room, hovering over Ron so he couldn't jump out a window or harm someone.

The farewell was brief. The cops cut it off after a few minutes, saying they had to get back to the jail. Annette and Renee could hear their brother crying as they rolled him away.

Juanita died on August 31, 1985. Initially, the police declined the family's request to allow Ron to attend the funeral. They relented only after Annette's husband offered to pay two former deputies, two of his cousins, to help guard Ron throughout the service.

For dramatic effect, the police treated his presence at the funeral as a major security event. They insisted that everyone be seated first, before the criminal could enter. And they refused to unshackle him.

Such precautions were obviously needed for a felon who forged a $300 check.

The sanctuary was packed. The open casket was in place in front of the altar so that everyone could see Juanita's gaunt profile. The rear doors opened, and her son was escorted down the aisle by his guards. His ankles were chained together, as were his wrists, with both chains secured to a belly chain around his waist. As he shuffled along in half steps, the clinking and rattling of the hardware frayed whatever nerves were left in the crowd. When he saw his mother in the open casket, Ron began sobbing and saying, "I'm sorry, Mother. I'm so sorry." The sobbing turned to wailing as he neared the casket.

They settled him into his seat, guards on both sides, chains clattering with every move. He was nervous, upset, manic, and unable to be still and quiet.

Ron sat in the First Pentecostal Holiness Church, in the sanctuary where he had worshipped as a boy, where Annette still played the organ every Sunday morning, where his mother had seldom missed a meeting, and wept as he stared at her withered face.

A lunch was served in the church's fellowship hall after the service. Ron shuffled over to it, guards within striking distance. He'd been living off jail food for almost a year, and the potluck spread before him was a feast. Annette asked the cop in charge to remove his handcuffs so he could eat. The request was refused. She quietly pleaded. No, came the answer.

Family and friends watched with pity as his sisters, Annette and Renee, took turns feeding him.

At the grave site, after some Scripture and a prayer, the mourners filed past Annette, Renee, and Ron and offered their condolences and kind thoughts. There were polite hugs and warm embraces, but not from Ron. Unable to lift his arms, he was forced to respond with awkward pecks on the cheeks for the women and clumsy, chain-rattling handshakes for the men. It was September, still very hot, and sweat rolled down his forehead and dripped onto his cheeks. He was unable to wipe his face, so Annette and Renee did it for him.

DR. CHARLES AMOS submitted to the court a report in which he stated that Ron Williamson was a mentally ill person as defined by Oklahoma law, that he could not appreciate the nature of the charges against him, that he could not assist his attorney in his defense, and that he could attain mental competency only after undergoing treatment. He also stated that if Ron was released without treatment, he would pose a danger to himself and others.

Judge Miller adopted the findings of Dr. Amos and entered an order that declared Ron mentally incompetent. He was transported to Eastern State Hospital in Vinita for further evaluation and treatment. There he was seen by Dr. R. D. Garcia, who prescribed Dalmane and Restoril for insomnia, Mellaril for hallucinations and delusions, and Thorazine for schizophrenia, hyperactivity, combativeness, and the hyper-energy phase of manic depression. The drugs were adjusted over a few days, and Ron settled down and began improving.

After a couple of weeks, Dr. Garcia concluded: "He is a sociopath and has a history of alcohol abuse. He must continue to take Thorazine, 100mg, four times a day. He is not an escape risk."

This was somewhat ironic since the prison sentence being revoked was for an escape.

Answering written questions from the court, Dr. Garcia said: "(1) He is a person able to appreciate the nature of the charges against him, and (2) . . . is able to consult with his lawyer and rationally assist in the preparation of his defense, and (3) . . . is no longer mentally ill, and (4) . . . even if he is released without treatment, therapy, or training he probably would not pose a significant threat to the life or safety of himself or others, not unless he becomes more sociopathic and may be considered potentially dangerous, especially when drinking heavily."

Ron was returned to Ada, where his revocation process was to be resumed. However, instead of holding a post-examination inquiry into his competency, Judge Miller simply accepted Dr. Garcia's findings at face value. Ron, mentally incompetent by court order, was never adjudicated to be competent.

Based on Dr. Garcia's conclusions, the suspended sentence was revoked, and Ron was sent back to prison for the remainder of his two-year term. When he left Eastern State, he was given a two-week supply of Thorazine.

In September, Tommy Ward and Karl Fontenot were put on trial in Ada. Their lawyers had argued strenuously to have their cases separated and, more important, to get them out of Pontotoc County. Denice Haraway was still missing and still talked about, and hundreds of locals had helped look for her. Her father-in-law was a local dentist who was greatly respected. Ward and Fontenot had been in jail for eleven months. Their confessions had been hot topics in the coffee shops and beauty parlors since October, when first reported in the newspaper.

How could the defendants expect to draw an impartial jury? Notorious trials are moved every day to other venues.

The motions to change venue were denied.

The other pretrial war was over the confessions. Attorneys for Ward and Fontenot attacked the statements, and especially the methods used by Detectives Smith and Rogers to obtain them. The tales told by the boys were clearly not true; not a shred of physical evidence backed up anything they said.

Peterson fought back with a vengeance. Without the tapes, he had no case whatsoever. After lengthy and heated arguments, the judge ruled that the confessions could be seen by the jury.

The state called fifty-one witnesses, few of whom said anything substantive. Many were friends of Denice Haraway, put on the stand to help prove she was in fact missing and presumed dead. The trial had only one surprise. A career criminal by the name of Terri Holland was called as a witness. She told the jury that she was in the county jail back in October when Karl Fontenot was brought in. The two talked occasionally, and he admitted to her that he, Tommy Ward, and Odell Titsworth had kidnapped, raped, and killed the girl.

Fontenot denied ever meeting the woman.

Terri Holland wasn't the only jailhouse snitch to testify. A petty criminal named Leonard Martin was also behind bars. The prosecution hauled him over, and at trial, he told the jury that he once overheard Karl in his cell talking to himself and saying, "I knew we'd get caught. I knew we'd get caught."

Such was the quality of the state's evidence—proof offered to persuade a jury of guilt beyond a reasonable doubt.

With no physical evidence, the taped confessions were beyond crucial, but they were filled with discrepancies and obvious lies. The prosecution was forced into the bizarre position of admitting Ward and Fontenot were lying while asking the jurors to believe them anyway.

Please disregard all that stuff about Titsworth, because he wasn't really involved.

Please overlook such trifling matters as the burned house with the dead body, because the house had been torched ten months earlier.

Monitors were rolled in. The lights were dimmed. The tapes were played. The grisly details emerged, and Ward and Fontenot were headed for death row.

In his closing argument, his first in a murder case, Assistant D.A. Chris Ross aimed for high drama. In graphic narrative, he recalled the gory details from the tapes—the stab wounds, the blood and guts, the brutal raping and knifing of such a pretty girl, then the horrible burning of her body.

The jurors were sufficiently angered. After brief deliberations, they returned with guilty verdicts and death penalties.

THE TRUTH, though, was that the body was not stabbed and it was not burned, regardless of what Ward and Fontenot said in their bogus confessions and regardless of what Bill Peterson and Chris Ross told the jury.

Denice Haraway was killed by a single gunshot wound to the head. Her remains were found the following January by a hunter deep in the woods near the settlement of Gerty, in Hughes County, twenty-seven miles from Ada and far from any place that had been searched.

The true cause of death should have convinced everyone involved that Ward and Fontenot had indeed dreamed up their ridiculous tales and had been coerced into confessing. It did not.

The true cause of death should have prompted the authorities to admit they were wrong and begin searching for the real murderer. It did not.

AFTER the trial, but before the body was found, Tommy Ward was waiting to be transferred to death row at McAlester, a prison fifty-five miles east of Ada. Still stunned by the events that had led him to now face death by lethal injection, he was frightened, confused, and depressed. One year earlier he had been a typical Ada twenty-something looking for a good job and a good party and a cute girl.

The real killers are out there, he kept thinking, laughing at us. Laughing at the cops. He wondered if they, the killers, had been brazen enough to watch his trial. Why not? They were safe.

One day he had visitors—two Ada cops. They were his friends now, his buddies, very concerned about what would happen to him once he got to McAlester. They were thoughtful, quiet, and measured with their words—no threats, yelling, or cursing, no promises of death by injection. They really wanted to find the body of Denice Haraway; thus, they offered a deal. If Tommy would tell them where she was buried, they would lobby hard over at Peterson's office and get the death sentence reduced to life. They claimed to have this authority, but did not. The case was far beyond their control.

Tommy didn't know where the body was. He repeated what he had been saying for almost a year—he had nothing to do with the crime. Now facing death, Tommy Ward still could not give the cops what they wanted.

Not long after the arrests of Ward and Fontenot, their story came to the attention of a respected New York journalist, Robert Mayer, then living in the Southwest. He heard the story from the woman he was dating; her brother was married to one of Tommy Ward's sisters.

Mayer was intrigued by the dream confession and the havoc it was creating. Why, he wondered, would anyone confess to a terrible crime, but fill the confession with lies? He went to Ada and began investigating the story. Throughout the prolonged pretrial process, then during the trial itself, Mayer diligently researched the town, its people, the crime, the police, the prosecutors, and especially Ward and Fontenot.

Ada watched him closely. It was rare to have a real writer in their midst, probing, watching, about to write God knows what. Over time, Mayer gained the trust of most of the players. He interviewed Bill Peterson at length. He sat through meetings with the defense attorneys. He spent hours with the cops. During one meeting, Dennis Smith talked about the pressure of having two unsolved murders in such a small town. He pulled out a photo of Debbie Carter and showed it to Mayer. "We know Ron Williamson killed her," Smith said. "We just can't prove it yet."

When Mayer began the project, he believed that there was an even chance the boys were guilty. But he was soon appalled by the actions of Smith and Rogers, and by the legal proceedings against Ward and Fontenot. There was no evidence other than the confessions, and, as shocking as they were, they were so full of contradictions that they could not be believed.

Nonetheless, Mayer strove to present a balanced picture of the crime and the trial. His book, *The Dreams of Ada*, was published by Viking in April 1987 and was greatly anticipated by the town.

The reaction was swift but predictable. Some people discounted the book because of the author's friendliness with the Ward family. Others were convinced the boys were guilty because they confessed, and nothing could ever change their opinions.

There was also a widespread belief that the police and the prosecutors had botched the case, sent the wrong men to prison, and left the real killers out there.

STUNG by the criticism—it's rare for a small-town prosecutor to have a book written about one of his cases, and a very unflattering one at that—Bill Peterson roared into action in the Debbie Carter matter. He had something to prove.

The investigation was stale—the poor girl had been dead for more than four years—but it was time to nail someone.

Peterson and the police had believed for years that the killer was Ron Williamson. Perhaps Dennis Fritz was involved, maybe not, but they knew Williamson was in Carter's apartment that night. They had no evidence, just gut feelings.

Ron was out of prison and back in Ada. When his mother died in August 1985, he was in jail awaiting a competency hearing and staring at two more years in prison. Annette and Renee reluctantly sold the small house where they had grown up. When Ron was paroled from prison in October 1986, he had no place to live. He moved in with Annette and her husband and son, and for a few days tried hard to fit in. But his old habits returned—the late-night meals he prepared with great noise, the all-night television routine, at full volume, the smoking and drinking, and the daylong naps on the sofa. After a month or so, with nerves frayed and her family on edge, Annette had to ask him to leave.

The two years in prison had done nothing to improve his mental health. He had moved in and out of various state hospitals, with different doctors trying different combinations of drugs. Often there were no medications at all. He would survive for a while in the general prison population, then someone would notice his bizarre behavior, and off he'd go to another mental unit.

Upon his release, the Department of Corrections made an appointment for Ron to see a social worker at Mental Health Services in Ada. On October 15, he met Norma Walker, who noted that he was taking lithium, Navane, and Artane. She found him to be pleasant, controlled, and a little strange, "sometimes staring without saying anything for as long as a minute at a time." He planned to go to a Bible college and maybe become a minister. Or he might start his own construction company. Big plans, a bit grandiose, thought Walker.

Two weeks later, still medicated, he kept his appointment and appeared to be doing fine. He skipped the next two, and when he showed up on December 9, he demanded to see Dr. Marie Snow. He had stopped taking his meds because he'd met a girl who didn't believe in them. Dr. Snow tried to convince him to start taking his pills, but he said that God had told him to give up the booze and all drugs.

He missed appointments on December 18 and January 14. On February 16, Annette called Norma Walker and said his behavior could not be controlled. She described him as "psychotic" and said he had mentioned killing himself with a handgun. The next day he came in, very nervous but somewhat reasonable. He demanded a change in medication. Three days later Walker received a call from McCall's Chapel. Ron was making a scene—yelling and demanding a job. She advised them to treat him with caution and call the police if necessary. That afternoon Annette and her husband brought him in to meet with Walker. They were distraught and desperate for help.

Walker observed Ron to be unmedicated, confused, disoriented, delusional, detached from reality, and completely unable to take care of his own food and shelter. She doubted he could survive on his own even with proper medication. The solution was "long-term institutionalization for his diminished mental capacities and unmanageable behavior."

The three left with no plan, and no meds. Ron drifted around Ada and eventually disappeared. Gary Simmons was at his home in Chickasha one night, chatting with two friends, when the doorbell rang. He answered it, and his brother-in-law rushed in and collapsed on the living room floor. "I need help," Ron said over and over. "I'm crazy and I need help." Unshaven, filthy, his hair thick and matted, he was disoriented and not sure where he was. "I can't take it anymore," he said.

Gary's guests did not know Ron and were shocked by his appearance and desperation. One left, and the other hung around. Ron became quiet, then lethargic. Gary promised Ron he would find help in some way, and they eventually got him in a car. The first stop was the nearest hospital, where they were referred to the local mental health center. From there, they were sent to Central State Hospital in Norman. As they were driving, Ron became almost catatonic. He did manage to say that he was starving. Gary knew a ribs place famous for its large servings, but when they stopped in the parking lot, Ron asked, "Where are we?"

"We're getting something to eat," Gary replied. Ron swore he wasn't hungry, so they drove away, headed for Norman.

"Why did we stop back there?" Ron asked.

"Because you said you were hungry."

"I did not." Ron was irritated by Gary's actions.

A few miles closer to Norman, Ron again said he was very hungry. Gary saw a McDonald's and stopped. "What are we doing here?" Ron asked.

"We're getting something to eat," Gary replied.

"Why?"

"Because you said you were hungry."

"I'm not hungry. Could we just please hurry on to the hospital." They left McDonald's and finally arrived in Norman, at which time Ron announced he was hungry. Gary patiently found another McDonald's, and Ron, not surprisingly, asked why they were stopping.

The last stop before the hospital was for gas at a Vickers station on Main Street. Gary returned to the car with two large candy bars, which Ron grabbed and devoured in seconds. Gary and his friend were startled at how quickly he consumed them.

At Central State, Ron was drifting in and out of whatever stupor he was in. The first doctor became frustrated when he wouldn't cooperate, and as soon as he left the room, Gary chastised his brother-in-law.

Ron responded by standing and facing a blank wall, flexing his arms into a goofy bodybuilder pose, and becoming rigid for several long minutes. Gary tried to speak to him, but he was gone. Ten minutes passed, and Ron didn't flinch. He stared at the ceiling without making a sound or moving a muscle. Twenty minutes passed, and Gary was ready to bolt. After thirty very long minutes, Ron snapped out of it but still would not speak to Gary.

Fortunately, the staff soon arrived and took Ron to his room. He told a doctor, "I just wanted to come here because I needed a place to go to at this time." He was given lithium, for depression, and Navane, an antipsychotic drug used to treat schizophrenia. Once he was stabilized, he checked himself out, against the advice of his doctors, and within a few days was back in Ada.

Gary's next road trip with his brother-in-law was to Dallas, to a Christian mission program for ex-cons and addicts. Gary's pastor had met Ron and wanted to help. Quietly, the pastor confided to Gary, "Ron's lights are on, but no one's home."

They checked into the facility in Dallas. When Ron was situated, Gary said good-bye. In doing so, he slipped Ron $50 in cash, a violation of the rules, though neither knew it. Gary returned to Oklahoma, and so did Ron. Within hours of checking in, he had used the cash to purchase a bus ticket back to Ada and arrived not long after Gary.

His next admission to Central State was not voluntary. On March 21, nine days after being discharged, Ron attempted suicide by swallowing twenty Navane pills. His reason, given to a nurse, was that he was depressed because he could not find a job. He was stabilized and placed on proper medication, which he stopped taking after the third day. His doctors concluded that he was a danger to himself and others and recommended a twenty-eight-day treatment at Central State. On March 24, he was discharged.

BACK in Ada, Ron found a room behind a small house on Twelfth Street, on the west side of town. He had no kitchen and no plumbing. To shower, when he bathed, he used a water hose behind the house. Annette took him food and tried to care for him. During one visit she noticed his wrists were bleeding. He'd cut them with a razor, he said, so that he could suffer like all the others who'd suffered so much because of him. He wanted to die and be with his parents, the two people he'd hurt so much. She begged him to go see a doctor, but he refused. He also refused to get help at the mental services office, where he'd been so many times.

He was completely off his medications.

The old man who owned the house was kind to Ron. Rent was cheap, often free. In the garage there was an ancient lawn mower with one wheel missing. Ron pushed it up and down the streets of Ada, mowing lawns for $5 and giving the money to his landlord.

On April 4, the Ada police received a call from a residence on the west block of Tenth Street. The home owner informed the patrolman that he had to leave town and he feared for the safety of his family because Ron Williamson had been roaming through the neighborhood at all hours of the night. Evidently, the home owner knew Ron and was watching carefully. He told the cop that Ron had made four trips to the Circle K convenience store and two or three to Love's convenience store, all in one night.

The policeman was sympathetic—everyone knew Ron was acting weird—but there was no law against walking the streets after midnight. He promised to patrol the area.

On April 10, at three in the morning, the police received a call from a clerk at the Circle K. Ron Williamson had been in several times, acting really strange. While Officer Jeff Smith was making his report, the suspect showed up again. Smith asked "Ronnie" to leave, which he did.

An hour later Ron walked to the jail and rang the buzzer and announced that he wanted to confess several crimes that he had committed in his past. He was given a form for a voluntary statement and began writing. He admitted to stealing a purse four years earlier at the Coachlight, stealing a gun from a home, touching two girls on their private parts, and hitting and almost raping a girl up at Asher. But he abandoned his confession and left the jail. Officer Rick Carson followed and caught up with him a few blocks away. Ron tried to explain what he was doing at that hour, but was very confused. He finally said he was out looking for mowing jobs. Carson suggested that Ron go home, and that perhaps the mowing jobs might be easier to find during daylight hours.

On April 13, Ron went to the mental health clinic and frightened the workers. One of them described him as "drooling." He demanded to see Dr. Snow and started down a hallway to her office. When told she wasn't in, he left without incident.

Three days later, *The Dreams of Ada* was published.

As MUCH AS the police wanted to pin the Carter murder on Ron Williamson, they simply lacked sufficient proof. By the late spring of 1987, they had little more evidence than they'd had in the summer of 1983. The hair analysis from the OSBI had finally been completed, two years after the murder. Some of the samples taken from Ron and Dennis were "microscopically consistent" with some of the hairs found at the murder scene, but hair comparisons were wildly unreliable.

The prosecution had one significant obstacle—the bloody palm print on the small section of Sheetrock cut from the wall in Debbie Carter's bedroom. Early in 1983 Jerry Peters of the OSBI had examined the print carefully and concluded that it was not from Dennis Fritz or Ron Williamson. Nor did it match Debbie Carter. It was a print left by the killer.

But what if Jerry Peters had been wrong, or perhaps in a hurry, or maybe he had just overlooked something? If the print actually belonged to Debbie Carter, then Fritz and Williamson could not be excluded as suspects.

Peterson seized upon the idea of exhuming her body and examining the palm prints again. With luck, her hands were not too badly decomposed, and a new set of prints just might, if examined perhaps from a different angle, reveal information that could greatly assist the prosecution and finally bring the murderers to justice.

Peggy Stillwell received a call from Dennis Smith. He asked her to come to the police station, but refused to give a reason. She thought, as always, that perhaps there had been a break in the case. When she arrived, Bill Peterson was sitting behind the desk with a sheet of paper in front of him. He explained that they wanted to exhume Debbie's body and he needed her signature to approve it. Charlie Carter had already stopped by and signed off.

Peggy was horrified. The idea of disturbing her daughter was shocking. She said no, but Peterson was prepared for it. He pressed on, asking Peggy if she wanted the murder solved. Of course, but wasn't there some other way? No. If she wanted to find Debbie's killer and bring him to justice, she had to agree to the exhumation. After a few minutes, Peggy scribbled her signature, hurried away from the police department, and drove to the home of her sister Glenna Lucas.

She told Glenna about the meeting with Bill Peterson and the plans to dig up the body. She was actually excited by now, anxious to see her daughter again. "I'll get to touch her and hold her again," she kept saying.

Glenna did not share her enthusiasm and wasn't convinced such a reunion was healthy. And she had doubts about the people running the investigation. In the four and a half years since the murder, she had been forced to chat with Bill Peterson several times about the case.

Peggy was not stable. She had never accepted the fact that Debbie was dead. Glenna had repeatedly asked Peterson and the police to filter any news from the investigation through herself or another family member. Peggy could not handle sudden developments and needed her family's protection.

Glenna immediately called Bill Peterson and demanded to know what he was planning. He explained that the exhumation was necessary if the family wanted Ron Williamson and Dennis Fritz brought to trial for the murder. The bloody palm print stood in the way, and if it actually belonged to Debbie, then he and the police could move with urgency against Fritz and Williamson.

Glenna was confused. How did Peterson know the outcome of the reprinting if the body had yet to be exhumed? How could he be so sure that the exhumation would incriminate Fritz and Williamson?

Peggy was obsessed with seeing her daughter again. At one point she said to Glenna, "I've forgotten what her voice sounded like." Glenna was promised by Bill Peterson that the exhumation would be done quickly and be completed before anyone knew it.

Peggy was at her station at Brockway Glass when a co-worker walked by and asked her what was happening over at Rosedale Cemetery, near Debbie's grave site. She left the factory, raced across town, but found only an empty grave. Her daughter had been removed.

THE FIRST set of palm prints had been taken by OSBI agent Jerry Peters on December 9, 1982, during the autopsy. At that time, the hands had been perfect, and Peters had no doubt that he had taken a full and thorough set of prints. When he issued his report three months later, he'd been certain in his findings that the bloody print from the Sheetrock was not left by Fritz, Williamson, or the victim.

Now, though, four and a half years later, with the murder unsolved and the authorities looking for a break, he suddenly had doubts about his earlier work. Three days after the exhumation, he issued a revised report in which he concluded that the bloody print matched Debbie Carter's palm. For the first and only time in his twenty-four-year career, Jerry Peters changed his mind.

The report was exactly what Bill Peterson needed. Armed with the proof that the bloody print did not belong to some unknown killer but had been left by Debbie as she struggled for her life, he was free to go after his prime suspects. And it was important to alert the townsfolk—the potential jurors.

While the authorities claimed that the exhumation and its details were confidential, Peterson chatted with the *Ada Evening News* anyway. "What we found confirmed our suspicions. We were checking some evidence," he was quoted as saying.

What, exactly, was found? Peterson wouldn't confirm the details, but a source was willing to tell all. The quoted source said, "The body was exhumed so the woman's palm prints could be made and compared with a bloody palm print found on her apartment wall."

The source went on: "Elimination of the possibility that the bloody palm print was someone other than the victim was crucial to the investigation."

"I do feel better about the case," Peterson said.

He obtained warrants for the arrests of Ron Williamson and Dennis Fritz.

ON FRIDAY morning, May 8, Rick Carson saw Ron pushing the lawn mower with three wheels along a street on the west side of town. The two talked for a moment. Ron, with long hair, no shirt, ragged jeans, and sneakers, looked as rough as always. He wanted to get a job with the city, and Rick promised to stop by and pick up an application. Ron said he would wait at home that night.

Carson then informed his lieutenant that he knew their suspect would in fact be hanging around his apartment on West Twelfth later in the evening. The arrest was planned, and Rick asked to be involved. If Ron turned violent, Rick wanted to make sure no one got hurt. Instead, four other policemen were sent, including Detective Mike Baskin.

Ron was taken into custody without incident. He was wearing the same jeans and sneakers and was still shirtless. At the jail, Mike Baskin read him his *Miranda* rights and asked if he would like to talk. Sure, why not. Detective James Fox joined the interview.

Ron repeatedly said he had never met Debbie Carter, had never been in her apartment, and to the best of his knowledge had never seen her. He never wavered, in spite of some yelling and bullying from the cops, who said over and over that they knew Ron was guilty.

Ron was placed in the county jail. At least a month had passed since he had taken any medications.

DENNIS FRITZ was living with his mother and an aunt in Kansas City, keeping busy by painting houses. He'd left Ada a few months earlier. His friendship with Ron Williamson was a distant memory. He hadn't talked to a detective in four years and had almost forgotten about the Carter murder.

Late on the evening of May 8, he was watching television by himself. He had worked all day and was still wearing his dirty painters' whites. The night was warm, the windows were open. The phone rang, and an unidentified female voice asked, "Is Dennis Fritz there?"

"I'm Dennis Fritz," he answered, and she hung up. Perhaps it was a wrong number, or perhaps his ex-wife was up to something. He settled back in front of the television. His mother and aunt were already asleep in the rear of the house. It was almost 11:30.

Fifteen minutes later he heard a series of car doors slam nearby. He got up, barefoot, and was walking to the front door when he saw a small army of combat-ready troops, dressed in black and heavily armed, moving across the lawn. What the hell? he thought. For a split second he considered calling the police.

The doorbell rang, and when he opened the door, two plainclothes cops grabbed him, pulled him outside, and demanded to know, "Are you Dennis Fritz?"

"Yes, I am."

"Then you're under arrest for first-degree murder," one growled while the other slapped on the handcuffs.

"What murder are you talking about?" Dennis asked, then had a quick thought: How many Dennis Fritzes are there in Kansas City? Surely they've got the wrong one.

His aunt appeared at the door, saw the SWAT team advancing on Dennis, submachine guns aimed and ready, and became hysterical. His mother ran from her bedroom as the police entered the house to "secure" it, though, when questioned, they were unclear as to whom and what they wished to secure. Dennis did not own a firearm. There were no other known or suspected murderers on the premises, but the SWAT boys had their procedures.

Just as Dennis was convinced he was about to be gunned down at the front door, he glanced up and saw a white Stetson hat moving his way. Two nightmares from his past were approaching on the driveway. Dennis Smith and Gary Rogers happily joined the fracas, with "shit-eating grins" from ear to ear.

Oh, that murder, Dennis thought. In their finest hour, the two small-town cowboys had conned the Kansas City Fugitive Apprehension Unit into conducting the dramatic but senseless raid.

"Can I get my shoes?" Dennis asked, and the cops reluctantly agreed.

Fritz was placed in the backseat of a police car, where he was joined by an ecstatic Dennis Smith. One of the K.C. detectives did the driving. As they left, Fritz looked at the heavily armed SWAT boys and thought, How stupid. Any part-time deputy could've made the arrest at the local grocery store. As stunned as he was by the arrest, he had to chuckle as he noticed how dejected the K.C. police looked.

His last image was of his mother, standing in the front door, with her hands over her mouth.

They took him to a small interrogation room at a police station in Kansas City. Smith and Rogers went through the *Miranda* warnings, then announced that they intended to get a confession. Dennis kept thinking of Ward and Fontenot and was determined to give them nothing. Smith became the nice guy, his pal who really wanted to help. Rogers was instantly abusive—cursing, threatening, poking Dennis in the chest repeatedly.

Four years had passed since their last session. In June 1983, after Fritz had "severely flunked" the second polygraph, Smith, Rogers, and

Featherstone had kept him in the basement of the Ada Police Department for three hours and badgered him. They got nothing then, and they were getting nothing now.

Rogers was furious. The cops had known for years that Fritz and Williamson raped and murdered Debbie Carter, and now the crime had been solved. All they needed was a confession. "I have nothing to confess," Fritz said over and over. What evidence do you have? Show me the evidence.

One of Rogers's favorite lines was, "You're insulting my intelligence." And each time Fritz was tempted to say, "What intelligence?" But he did not want to get slapped.

After two hours of abuse, Fritz finally said, "All right, I'll confess." The cops were relieved; since they had no proof, they were about to crack the case with a confession. Smith hustled out to find a tape recorder. Rogers quickly arranged his notepad and pens. Let's have it.

When they were all set, Fritz looked directly at the tape recorder and said, "Here's the truth. I did not kill Debbie Carter and know nothing about her murder."

Smith and Rogers went ballistic—more threats, more verbal abuse. Fritz was rattled and frightened, but he held firm. He maintained his innocence, and they finally called off the interrogation. He refused extradition to Oklahoma and waited in jail for the process to run its course.

LATER THAT day, Saturday, Ron was led from the jail to the police station for another interview. Smith and Rogers, back from their thrilling arrest of Fritz, were waiting. Their goal was to make him talk.

The interrogation had been planned since the day before the arrest. *The Dreams of Ada* had just been published, and there was criticism of the methods of Smith and Rogers. They decided that Smith, who lived in Ada, should be replaced by Rusty Featherstone, who lived in Oklahoma City. They also decided not to use video.

Dennis Smith was in the building but stayed away from the interview room. After leading the investigation for over four years, and believing for much of that time that Williamson was guilty, he nonetheless avoided the crucial interrogation.

The Ada Police Department was well stocked with audio and video equipment, and it was frequently used. Interrogations, and especially confessions, were almost always recorded on tape. The police were quite aware of the powerful impact of showing a confession to a jury. Ask Ward and Fontenot. Ron's second polygraph four years earlier had been taped by Featherstone at the Ada Police Department.

When confessions were not recorded on video, they were often taken by audio. The police had plenty of tape recorders.

And when neither audio nor video was used, the suspect was usually asked to write, if he could in fact read and write, his own version of what happened. If the suspect happened to be illiterate, then a detective would write the statement, read it back to the defendant, and ask him to sign it.

None of these methods were used on May 9. Williamson, who was quite literate and had a much wider vocabulary than either of his two interrogators, watched as Featherstone took notes. He said he understood his *Miranda* rights and agreed to talk.

The police version reads as follows:

WILLIAMSON said, "Okay, December the 8th, 1982, I was hanging out at the Coachlight frequently and I was there one night looking at a girl, a pretty girl, and thought I should follow her home."

WILLIAMSON paused, then acted as if he wished to say something that started with the letter F, but then paused again. Then he continued, "Thought what if something bad would happen that night, and followed her home."

WILLIAMSON then paused and talked about when he stole a stereo. WILLIAMSON then said, "I was with DENNIS, and we went to the

Holiday Inn, and told a girl that we had a bar in our car, and got her and she jumped."

WILLIAMSON talked in sporadic phrases and Agent ROGERS asked WILLIAMSON to concentrate and get back to talking about the DEBBIE CARTER case.

WILLIAMSON said, "Okay, I had a dream about killing DEBBIE, was on her, had a cord around her neck, stabbed her, frequently, pulled the rope tight around her neck."

WILLIAMSON said, "I am worried about what this will do to my family," and then he said, "My mother is dead now."

Agent ROGERS asked WILLIAMSON if he and DENNIS were there that night and WILLIAMSON answered "yes." Agent FEATHERSTONE asked WILLIAMSON, "Did you go there with the intention to kill her?" WILLIAMSON responded, "Probably."

Agent FEATHERSTONE asked, "Why?"

WILLIAMSON responded, "She made me mad."

Agent FEATHERSTONE asked, "How do you mean? Mean to you? A bitch?"

WILLIAMSON responded, "No."

WILLIAMSON paused briefly then said, "Oh my God you can't expect me to confess, I've got my family, I've got my nephew to protect. My sister, it will tear her up. It can't hurt my mother now since she is dead. It's been on my mind since it happened."

At about 1938 hours, WILLIAMSON said, "If you're going to try me on this, I want TANNER in Tulsa. No, I want DAVID MORRIS."

The mention of a lawyer spooked the detectives, and they stopped the confession. They called David Morris, who instructed them to stop interrogating Ron immediately.

The statement was not signed by Ron. It was never shown to him.

———

ARMED with another dream confession, the case was coming together nicely for the cops and prosecutors. They had learned with Ward and Fontenot that a lack of physical evidence should not get in the way of an urgent prosecution. The fact that Debbie Carter was not stabbed was of little consequence. Juries will convict if they can be adequately shocked.

If one dream confession could nail Williamson, then another could put him away. A few days later, a jailer named John Christian stopped by Ron's cell. He and Ron had grown up in the same neighborhood. The Christian household was full of boys, one the same age as Ron, and he was often included in lunch and dinner. They played baseball together in the streets and the leagues and attended Byng Junior High.

Untreated and unmedicated, Ron was far from a model inmate. The Pontotoc County jail is a windowless concrete bunker, for some reason built on the west side of the courthouse lawn. The ceilings are low, the atmosphere cramped and claustrophobic, and when someone screams, everyone hears it. Ron screamed often. When he wasn't yelling, he was singing, crying, wailing, complaining, or either protesting his innocence or ranting on about Debbie Carter. He was placed in one of the two solitary cells, as far away from the crowded bullpen as possible, but the jail was so small that Ron could disrupt it from anywhere.

Only John Christian could settle him down, and the other inmates came to appreciate the changing of the guard. When Christian arrived, he immediately went to Ron's cell and calmed him. They would talk about the old days, growing up, playing ball, friends they had known back then. They talked about the Carter case and how unfair it was for Ron to be charged. For eight hours Ron was quiet. His solitary cell was a rat hole, but he managed to sleep and read. Before Christian punched out, he checked on Ron, who was usually pacing, smoking, getting himself psyched up to begin the racket as soon as the new guard arrived.

Late in the evening of May 22, Ron was awake and knew Christian was at the front desk. Ron called him back and wanted to talk about the murder. He had a copy of *The Dreams of Ada* and said he might have a dream confession of his own. According to Christian, Ron said, "Now just imagine this, I dreamed this is what took place. Just imagine that I was living in Tulsa, and I'd been drinking and taking quaaludes all day, and I drove to Buzzy's Club (Coachlight Club), and just imagine that I drank some more and got a bit drunker. Just suppose that I ended up at Debbie Carter's door and knocked on the door and she said just a minute I'm on the phone. Just imagine I busted the door in and I raped and killed her."

Williamson then said, "Don't you think if I was the person that killed her, that I would have gotten some money from my friends and left town?"

Christian thought little of the conversation, but did repeat it to a fellow officer. It was repeated again and again, and finally made it to Gary Rogers. The detective saw an opportunity for additional evidence against their killer. Two months later, he asked Christian to repeat what Ron had told him. Rogers typed up a report, added quotation marks where he thought appropriate, and the police and prosecutor then had their second dream confession. Not a single word was included to reflect Ron's many denials of involvement in the crime.

As usual, the facts were not important. Ron was not living in Tulsa at the time of the murder. He possessed neither a vehicle nor a driver's license.

For Annette Hudson and Renee Simmons, the news that their brother had been arrested and charged with murder was overwhelming. Since his release from prison the previous October, they had been deeply concerned about his deteriorating mental health and his physical well-being, but they had no idea murder charges were looming. The rumors had been around for years, but so much time had passed, the family had assumed the police were busy with other suspects and other cases. When Juanita died two years earlier, she was confident she had given Dennis Smith clear evidence that Ron was not involved. Annette and Renee believed this, too.

Both were living frugally—raising their families, working occasionally, paying the bills, and saving money when possible. They did not have the cash to hire a criminal defense lawyer. Annette talked to David Morris, but he had no interest in the case. John Tanner was in Tulsa, too far away and too expensive.

Though Ron had dragged them through the court system many

times, they were still unprepared for his sudden arrest and the allegations of murder. Friends backed away. The stares and whispers began.
An acquaintance said to Annette, "It's not your fault. You can't help
what your brother did."

"My brother is not guilty," Annette shot back. She and Renee repeated this continually, but few people wanted to hear it. Forget the pre-
sumption of innocence. The cops had their man; why would they have
arrested Ron if he wasn't guilty?

Annette's son, Michael, then a fifteen-year-old sophomore, suffered
through a class discussion on current local events, the principal one being the arrest of Ron Williamson and Dennis Fritz for the murder. Since
his last name was Hudson, none of his classmates knew that Michael's
uncle was the accused killer. Sentiments in the class ran strongly against
the two men. Annette was at the school the following morning and got
the matter resolved. The teacher apologized profusely and promised to
redirect class discussions.

Renee and Gary Simmons were living in Chickasha, about ninety
miles away, and the distance gave them some relief. Annette, though, had
never left Ada, and though she now desperately wanted to flee, she had
to stay and support her little brother.

THE SUNDAY, May 10, edition of the *Ada Evening News* ran a front-page
story about the arrests with a photo of Debbie Carter. Bill Peterson provided most of the details. He confirmed that the body had been exhumed and that the mysterious print in fact belonged to the victim. He
claimed that both Fritz and Williamson had been suspects for more than
a year but did not explain why. As to the investigation itself, he said, "We
came to the end of our rope in this investigation about six months ago
and began to decide how to approach these things."

Of special interest was the news that the FBI had been involved in
the case. Two years earlier the Ada police requested its assistance. The
FBI studied the evidence and provided the police with a psychological

profile of the killers, though Peterson did not share this with the news-paper.

The following day there was another front-page story, this time with mug shots of Ron and Dennis. Even by mug shot standards, their photos were menacing enough to get convictions.

The story repeated the details from the day before, specifically that both men had been arrested and charged with first-degree rape, rape by instrumentation, and first-degree murder. Oddly enough, "officials" re-fused to comment on whether the two men had made statements about the crime. Evidently, the reporters in Ada had become so accustomed to confessions that they assumed such statements were generic to all crim-inal investigations.

Though they withheld news about their first dream confession from Ron, the authorities did release the affidavit used for the arrest war-rants. The story quoted the affidavit as saying "that both pubic and scalp hair were recovered from Miss Carter's body and bedding that were con-sistent microscopically with that of Ronald Keith Williamson and Den-nis Fritz."

And both men had long criminal records. Ron's tally was fifteen misdemeanors—drunk driving and such—plus one felony for the forgery that sent him to prison. Fritz had two DUIs, some driving charges, plus the old marijuana conviction.

Bill Peterson confirmed again that the body had been exhumed to reexamine a palm print, which was found to be the victim's. He added that the two men "had been suspects in the case for more than a year."

The story concluded by reminding everyone that "Carter died from asphyxiation when a washcloth was stuffed down her throat during the rape."

THAT same Monday, Ron was led from the jail, across the lawn to the courthouse, about fifty steps, and made his first appearance before Judge John David Miller, the magistrate who handled preliminary matters. He said he did not have a lawyer and wasn't sure if he could afford one. He was taken back to jail.

A few hours later an inmate by the name of Mickey Wayne Harrell allegedly overheard Ron crying, saying, "I'm sorry, Debbie." This was immediately reported to the jailer. Ron then allegedly asked Harrell if he would draw a tattoo on his arm, one that said, "Ron Loves Debbie."

With a hot new crime on the docket, the gossip festered in the jail. The snitching games, always a part of jail life because the police were so willing to play along, began in earnest. The quickest way to freedom, or at least to a reduced sentence, was to hear or claim to hear a prized suspect confess in whole or in part to his crime, and then trade this off in an attractive plea bargain with the prosecutor. In most jails, snitching was rare because the informants feared retribution from other inmates. In Ada, snitching was widely practiced because it worked so well.

Two DAYS later Ron was taken back to court to discuss the matter of his legal representation. He appeared before Judge John David Miller, and things did not go well. Still unmedicated, he was loud and belligerent and began by yelling, "I didn't do this killing! I'm getting damned tired of being on this rap, now. I feel sorry for the family, but—"

Judge Miller tried to stop him, but Ron wanted to talk. "I didn't kill her. I don't know who killed her. My mother was alive at the time and she knew where I was."

Judge Miller attempted to explain to Ron that the hearing was not designed to allow defendants to plead their case, but Ron kept on. "I want these charges dropped," he said over and over. "This is ridiculous."

Judge Miller asked him if he understood the charges against him, to which Ron replied, "I'm innocent, never been in her company, never been in a car with her."

As his rights were being read into the record, Ron continued ranting. "I've been in jail three times and each time they have tried to say I had something to do with this murder."

When the name of Dennis Fritz was read aloud, Ron interrupted: "This guy didn't have anything to do with it. I knew him at the time. He didn't go to the Coachlight."

The judge finally entered a plea of not guilty. Ron was led away, cursing bitterly as he went. Annette watched and wept quietly.

She went to the jail every day, sometimes twice if the jailers allowed. She knew most of them and they all knew Ronnie, and the rules were often bent slightly to allow more visitation.

He was disturbed, still unmedicated, and in need of professional help. He was irate and bitter for being arrested for a crime he had nothing to do with. He was also humiliated. For four and a half years he had lived with the suspicion that he had committed an unspeakable murder. The suspicion was bad enough. Ada was his hometown, his people, his current and former friends, the folks who watched him grow up in church, the fans who remembered him as a great athlete. The whispers and stares were painful, but he had endured them for years. He was innocent, and the truth, if the cops could ever find it, would clear his name.

But to be suddenly arrested and thrown in jail and have his mug shot on the front page was devastating.

He wasn't sure if he had ever met Debbie Carter.

WHILE Dennis Fritz sat in a jail cell in Kansas City and waited for the extradition process to send him back to Ada, he was struck by the irony of his arrest. Murder? For years he had dealt with the aftermath of his wife's, and many times he'd almost felt like a victim himself.

Murder? He had never physically harmed anyone. He was small, slightly built, averse to fighting and violence. Sure, he'd been in plenty of bars and some rough places, but he'd always managed to slip away when the brawling began. If Ron Williamson didn't start the fight, then he would certainly stay and finish it, but not Dennis. He was a suspect only because of his friendship with Ron.

Fritz wrote a long letter to the *Ada Evening News* to explain why he was fighting extradition. He said he refused to return with Smith and Rogers because he couldn't believe he had been charged with the murder. He was innocent, had nothing to do with the crime, and needed some time to get his thoughts together. He was trying to find a good defense lawyer, and his family was scrambling for money.

He summarized his involvement in the investigation. Because he had nothing to hide and wanted to cooperate, he did everything the police asked: gave samples of saliva, fingerprints, handwriting, and hair (even one from his mustache); took two polygraph exams, which, according to Dennis Smith, he "severely flunked." Fritz said that he found out later that he had not flunked the polygraph tests.

About the investigation, Fritz wrote: "For three-and-a-half years they have had access to my fingerprints, handwriting, and hair samples to match up with the evidence found at the scene of the crime and any other evidence, if any, to have me arrested long ago. But, according to your paper, six months ago they were at the end of their rope and had to decide how to handle 'these things.' I'm not that dumb to know it doesn't take no crime lab three-and-a-half years to match up my volunteered evidence."

Dennis, the former science teacher, had studied hair evidence years earlier after he had submitted samples. His letter included this paragraph: "How can I be charged with rape and murder on just flimsy evidence such as hair which can only distinguish ethnic groups of people and not individual characteristics within the same group of people in the same ethnic group? Any expert witness in their field knows there could be over half a million people that have the same consistencies of hair."

He concluded with a desperate claim of innocence and asked the question "Am I guilty until proven innocent, or innocent until proven guilty?"

PONTOTOC COUNTY did not have a full-time public defender. Those accused of crimes who could not afford a lawyer were required to sign a pauper's oath, then the judge would appoint a local lawyer as indigent counsel.

Since few people of means get themselves charged with felonies, most of the serious crimes involved indigent defendants. Robberies, drugs, and assaults were the crimes of the lower classes, and since most of the defendants were guilty, their court-appointed lawyers could investigate, interview, plea-bargain, do the paperwork, close the file, and pick up a very modest fee.

In fact, the fees were so modest most lawyers preferred to avoid the cases. The haphazard indigent defense system was fraught with problems. Judges often assigned cases to lawyers with little or no criminal law experience. There was no money for expert witnesses and other expenses.

Nothing makes a small-town bar scatter more quickly than a capital murder case. The visibility ensures that the lawyer will be watched carefully as he fights to protect the rights of a low-class defendant accused of some heinous crime. The hours required are burdensome and can virtually shut down a small law office. The fee is nothing compared to the work. And the appeals drag on forever.

The great fear is that no one will agree to represent the accused and that the judge will simply assign the case. Most courtrooms are usually teeming with lawyers when court is in session, but they become empty tombs when a capital murder defendant is hauled in with his pauper's oath. The lawyers flee to their offices, lock the doors, and unplug the phones.

PERHAPS the most colorful courthouse regular in Ada was Barney Ward, a blind lawyer known for his snappy dressing, hard living, tall stories, and penchant for being "involved" in most of the legal gossip in Ada. He seemed to know everything that went on in the courthouse.

Barney lost his eyesight as a teenager when a high school chemistry experiment went awry. He treated the tragedy as a temporary setback and finished high school. He enrolled at East Central in Ada, where his mother served as his reader. After graduation, he went to Norman and studied law at the University of Oklahoma, again with his mother at his side. He graduated, passed the bar exam, returned to Ada, and ran for county attorney. He won and for several years served as the county's chief prosecutor. In the mid-1950s, he established a private practice specializing in criminal defense, and soon had the reputation as a strong advocate for his clients. Quick on his feet, Barney could sniff a weakness in the prosecution's case and would pounce on opposing witnesses. He was a brutal cross-examiner and loved a good scrap.

In one legendary encounter, Barney actually threw a punch at another lawyer. He and David Morris were in court arguing evidentiary matters. Both were frustrated, things were tense, and Morris made the mistake of saying, "Look, Judge, even a blind man can see this." Barney lunged at him, or in his general direction, threw a roundhouse right, and barely missed. Order was restored. Morris apologized but kept his distance.

Everybody knew Barney, and he was often seen around the courthouse with his faithful assistant, Linda, who read everything for him and took his notes. From time to time he used a Seeing Eye dog to help him around, though he preferred a young lady. He was friendly with everyone and never forgot a voice. The other lawyers elected him president of the bar association, and not out of sympathy. Barney was so well liked that he was asked to join a poker club. He produced a set of Braille cards, claimed that only he could deal, and was soon raking in all the chips. The other players decided that perhaps it was best if Barney played but never dealt. His winnings were somewhat reduced.

Each year, the other lawyers invited Barney to deer camp, a weeklong, boys-only getaway with lots of bourbon and poker and dirty jokes and thick stews, and, time permitting, some hunting. Barney's dream was to kill a deer. In the woods his friends found a nice buck and quietly maneuvered Barney into position, handed him the rifle, adjusted it carefully,

138   **John Grisham**

aimed it, then whispered, "Fire." Barney pulled the trigger, and though he missed badly, his friends claimed the deer had narrowly escaped death. Barney told the story for decades.

Like many hard drinkers, he finally had to quit. At the time he was using a dog for guidance, and the dog had to be replaced when he couldn't break the habit of leading Barney to the liquor store. Evidently he went there often, because one lingering bit of lore is that the whiskey store went out of business when Barney went off the booze.

He loved to make money and had little patience with clients who couldn't pay. His motto was "Innocent until proven broke." By the mid-1980s, though, Barney was a bit past his prime. He was known to occasionally miss things in trial because he was asleep. He wore thick dark glasses that covered much of his face, and the judges and lawyers couldn't tell if he was listening or napping. His opponents caught on, and the strategy, whispered because Barney heard everything, was to drag a case or a hearing past lunch and into the afternoon when he always took his nap. If you could make it to 3:00 p.m., your chances of beating Barney rose dramatically.

Two years earlier, he had been approached by the family of Tommy Ward, no relation, but had passed on the case. He was convinced Ward and Fontenot were innocent, but he preferred not to handle capital cases. The paperwork was overwhelming, and not one of his strengths.

Now he was approached again. Judge John David Miller asked Barney to represent Ron Williamson. Barney was the most experienced criminal defense attorney in the county, and his expertise was needed. After a brief hesitation, he said yes. A pure lawyer, he knew the Constitution inside and out, and he believed strongly that every defendant, regardless of how unpopular, was entitled to a vigorous defense.

On June 1, 1987, Barney Ward was appointed by the court to represent Ron, his first death penalty client. Annette and Renee were pleased. They knew him, and they knew of his reputation as one of the best criminal defense lawyers in town.

The lawyer and the client got off to a rocky start. Ron was tired of the jail and the jail was quite tired of him. Conferences took place in a small visitors' room near the front door, a place Barney found too cozy with his unruly client. He made a call and arranged a mental checkup for Ron. A new supply of Thorazine was prescribed, and much to the relief of Barney and the entire jail the drug worked beautifully. In fact, it worked so well the guards overused it to keep peace. Ron was sleeping like an infant again.

During one conference, though, he could barely speak. Barney met with the jailers, the dosage was readjusted, and Ron sprang back to life.

He was generally uncooperative with his lawyer. He offered little but a steady stream of rambling denials. He was being railroaded into a conviction, just like Ward and Fontenot. Barney was frustrated from the day he was appointed, but he plowed ahead.

GLEN GORE was in jail on kidnapping and assault charges. His court-appointed counsel was Greg Saunders, a young lawyer who was building a civil practice in Ada. During a client conference at the jail, he and Gore almost came to blows. Saunders walked next door to the courthouse and asked Judge Miller to remove him from the case. Judge Miller refused, so Saunders said he would take the next capital murder appointment if he could get rid of Gore. A deal, said Judge Miller, you're now representing Dennis Fritz in the Carter murder.

Though Greg Saunders was apprehensive about his death penalty case, he was also excited about working closely with Barney Ward. As an undergraduate at East Central, he had dreamed of being a trial lawyer and had often cut classes when he knew Barney was in action. He had watched Barney rip shaky witnesses and intimidate prosecutors. Barney respected judges but did not fear them, and he could chat with a jury. He never used his disability as a crutch, but at crucial moments he could use it to arouse sympathy. To Greg Saunders, Barney was a brilliant courtroom lawyer.

Working independently, but also quietly working together, they filed a truckload of motions and soon had the district attorney's office scrambling. On June 11, Judge Miller called a hearing on issues raised by both the state and the defense. Barney was demanding a list of the names of all the witnesses the prosecution expected to use in the case. Oklahoma law required such disclosure, but Bill Peterson was having trouble with the statute. Barney explained it to him. The prosecutor wanted to disclose only those witnesses he planned to use at the preliminary hearing. Not so, said Judge Miller, and Peterson was ordered to timely notify the defense of any new witness.

Barney was in a feisty mood and prevailed on most of the motions. He was also showing signs of frustration. In one aside, he commented on being court appointed and not wanting to spend too much time on the case. He vowed to do a proper job, but was worried about getting consumed with his first capital murder trial.

The following day he filed a motion requesting additional counsel for Ron. The state did not object, and on June 16 Frank Baber was appointed by Judge Miller to help Barney. The legal wrangling and paperwork battles continued as both sides prepared for the preliminary hearing.

DENNIS FRITZ was placed in a cell not far from Ron Williamson. He couldn't see Ron, but he could certainly hear him. When he wasn't overmedicated, Ron yelled constantly. For hours, he would stand at the bars in his cell door and bellow over and over, "I am innocent. I am innocent." His deep and husky voice echoed through the cramped building. He was a wounded animal, in a cage, in dire need of help. The prisoners were stressed anyway, but Ron's screeching voice added another thick layer of anxiety.

Other inmates would yell back at him and taunt him about killing Debbie Carter. The bickering and cursing back and forth were occasionally amusing but generally nerve-racking. The jailers moved Ron from his isolation cell into a bullpen with a dozen others, an arrangement that proved disastrous. The men had little privacy and practically lived shoulder to shoulder. Ron respected no one's space. A petition quickly appeared. It was signed by the other prisoners and begged the jailers to take Ron back to isolation. To prevent a riot or a killing, the guards agreed.

Then there were long periods of silence, and everyone, inmates and guards, would breathe easier. Soon the entire jail knew that either John Christian was on duty or the guards had given Ron another toxic dose of Thorazine.

The Thorazine quieted him, though at times there were other side effects. It often made his legs itch, and the "Thorazine shuffle" became part of the jail's routine as Ron stood at the bars of his cell and ducked and weaved from side to side for hours.

Fritz would talk to him and try to calm him, but it was hopeless. Ron's cries of innocence were painful to hear, especially for Dennis, who knew him best. It was obvious that Ron needed much more than a bottle of pills.

NEUROLEPTIC drugs are synonymous with tranquilizers and antipsychotics, and are used primarily on schizophrenics. Thorazine is a neuroleptic, and it has a tortured history. In the 1950s it began flooding state mental hospitals. It's a potent drug that strongly reduces awareness and interest. Psychiatrists who support the drug claim it actually cures the patient by altering or repairing bad brain chemistry.

But critics, who greatly outnumber supporters, cite numerous studies that show the drug to produce a long, frightening list of side effects. Sedation, drowsiness, lethargy, poor concentration, nightmares, emotional difficulties, depression, despair, lack of spontaneous interest in the surroundings, a blunting or dulling of the patient's awareness and motor control. Thorazine is toxic to most brain functions and disrupts nearly all of them.

Its harshest critics have called it "nothing more than a chemical lobotomy." They claim that the only real purpose of Thorazine is to save money for mental institutions and prisons and to make patients and inmates more manageable.

Ron's Thorazine was doled out by his jailers, sometimes with instructions from his lawyer. Often, though, there was no supervision. He got a pill when he got too loud.

EVEN though Dennis Fritz had remained in Ada for four years after the murder, he was considered an escape risk. Like Ron's, his bail was exorbitant and out of the question. Like all defendants, they were presumed to be innocent, but nonetheless kept in jail so they wouldn't flee or be loose on the streets killing others.

Presumed innocent, but they would wait almost a year until they went to trial.

A FEW days after Dennis arrived at the jail, a man by the name of Mike Tenney suddenly appeared outside his cell. Fat and balding and not well spoken, Tenney nonetheless had a big smile and a friendly manner, and he treated Dennis like an old friend. And he desperately wanted to talk about the Carter murder.

Dennis had been around Ada long enough to know the jail was a cesspool of snitches, liars, and cutthroats, and he knew that any conversation with anyone could very well be repeated in a courtroom in a version slanted sharply against the person on trial. Every inmate, guard, cop, trustee, janitor, cook, everyone was a potential snitch, anxious to pick up details and then retail the information to cops.

Tenney said he was new to the place and claimed to be a jailer, but in fact he was not yet on the county's payroll. Though unsolicited, and certainly not based on knowledge or experience, Tenney had plenty of advice for Dennis. In his opinion, Dennis was in deep trouble, staring at an execution, and the best way to save his skin was to come clean, confess, cut a deal with Peterson over at the D.A.'s office, and give up the dirt on Ron Williamson.

Peterson would be fair.

Dennis just listened.

Tenney wouldn't go away. He returned every day, shaking his head gravely at Dennis's predicament, babbling on about the system and how he thought it operated, giving sage advice that was absolutely free.

Dennis just listened.

A PRELIMINARY hearing was scheduled for July 20, before Judge John David Miller. Like in most jurisdictions, preliminaries were crucial in Oklahoma because the state was required to play its hand, to show the court and everyone else who its witnesses would be and what they would say.

The challenge for a prosecutor at a preliminary was to show just enough evidence to convince the judge that there were reasonable grounds that the defendant was guilty while not yet revealing everything to the defense. It was gamesmanship, with a bit of risk.

Normally, though, a prosecutor had little to worry about. Local judges find it hard to get reelected if they dismiss criminal charges.

But with such flimsy evidence against both Fritz and Williamson, Bill Peterson had to push hard at the preliminary. He had so little to offer that he could certainly hold nothing back. And the local newspaper would be there, anxious to report every word. Three months after its publication, *The Dreams of Ada* was still being hotly debated around town. The preliminary hearing would be Peterson's first performance in a major trial since the book came out.

A nice crowd gathered in the courtroom. Dennis Fritz's mother was there, as were Annette Hudson and Renee Simmons. Peggy Stillwell, Charlie Carter, and their two daughters arrived early. The regulars—bored lawyers, local gossips, idle clerks, retirees with nothing to do—waited for their first good look at the two murderers. The trial was months away, but the live testimony was about to be heard.

Before the hearing, and just for the sheer fun of it, the Ada police informed Ron that Dennis Fritz had finally made a full confession that implicated both of them in the rape and murder. The shocking news sent Ron off the deep end.

Dennis was sitting quietly with Greg Saunders at the defense table, looking over some documents, waiting for the hearing to begin. Ron was sitting nearby, still handcuffed and shackled and glaring at Fritz as if he wanted to choke him. Suddenly and without warning, Ron bolted out of his chair and began screaming at Fritz, who was just a few feet away. A table went flying through the air and landed on Barney's assistant, Linda. Dennis jumped up quickly and moved near the witness stand as the guards tackled Ron.

"Dennis! You no good lousy son of a bitch!" he screamed. "We're gonna settle this right now!" His deep, husky voice boomed around the courtroom. Barney got hit and fell out of his chair. The guards grabbed Ron, tackled him, and tried to subdue him. He was kicking and thrashing about like a madman, and the guards had their hands full. Dennis, Greg Saunders, and the court personnel quickly backed away and gawked in disbelief at the sight of the pileup in the middle of the courtroom.

It took several minutes to subdue Ron, who was bigger than any of his guards. As they dragged him away, Ron spewed a vile stream of vulgarities and threats at Fritz.

When the dust settled, the tables and chairs were rearranged and everyone took a deep breath. Barney didn't see the brawl, but he knew he'd been in the middle of it. He rose and said:

> I want the record to show that I am now making an application to withdraw. That boy won't cooperate with me at all. If he was paying me I wouldn't be here. I can't represent him, Judge, I just can't do it. I don't know who's going to, but I can't. And I'm—if I can't get relief

here—I'm going to see if I can't get it from the Court of Criminal Appeals. I'm not going to put up with this. I'm too damned old for it, Judge. I don't want anything to do with him, under any circumstances. I have no idea about his guilt—that has nothing to do with it—but I'm not going to put up with this. The next thing you know, he'll be thumping on me; and when he does, he's in bad trouble, and I'll probably be in worse trouble.

To which Judge Miller quickly replied, "Counsel's motion will be overruled."

IT WAS heartbreaking for Annette and Renee to watch their brother act like a madman and to see him dragged around in chains. He was sick and needed help, a long stint in an institution with good doctors who could get him well. How could the state of Oklahoma put him on trial when he was so obviously sick?

Across the aisle, Peggy Stillwell watched the madman and shuddered at the image of the violence he had inflicted on her daughter.

AFTER a few minutes of order, Judge Miller ordered Williamson brought in again. In the holding room, the guards had explained to Ron that his behavior was inappropriate for a judicial setting and that further outbursts would be dealt with sternly. But as they led him in, he began cursing Dennis Fritz as soon as he saw him. The judge sent him back to jail, cleared the courtroom of all spectators, and waited an hour.

Back in the jail, the guards ramped up their warnings, but Ron didn't care. Bogus confessions were all too common in Pontotoc County, and he couldn't believe the cops had squeezed one out of Dennis Fritz. Ron was an innocent man and determined not to be persecuted like Ward and Fontenot. If he could get his hands around Dennis's neck, he would shake out the truth.

His third entry was identical to the first two. As he stepped into the courtroom, he yelled, "Fritz, we're going to settle this now—you and me is going to settle it."

Judge Miller interrupted him, but Ron didn't slow down. "Me and you is going to settle it," he yelled at Dennis. "I ain't never killed nobody."

"Hold him there," Judge Miller said to the guards. "Mr. Williamson, any further outbursts of anger, this hearing will be conducted without your presence."

"That'll be fine with me," Ron shot back.

"Okay, you understand—"

"I'd rather not be here. If you don't mind, I'd rather go back to my cell."

"You wish to waive your right to be present in the preliminary hearing?"

"Yes, I do."

"Nobody's threatening or forcing you to do this, this is your own personal—"

"I'm threatening," Ron snapped, glaring at Dennis.

"Has anybody threatened you—this is your own personal decision to waive your—"

"I said I'm threatening."

"Okay. You do not wish to appear at this hearing; is that correct?"

"That's correct."

"Okay. You may take him back to the county jail. Court record will reflect that the Defendant Ronald K. Williamson does waive his right to appearance in this courtroom due to his outbursts of anger and total disruption. And the Court finds that this hearing cannot be conducted with his presence based on—to his current statements to this Court and outbursts."

Ron went to his cell, and the preliminary hearing proceeded.

In 1956, the U.S. Supreme Court, in a case known as *Bishop v. United States*, ruled that the conviction of a mentally incompetent person was a denial of due process. Where doubt exists as to a person's mental competency, the failure to conduct a proper inquiry is a deprivation of his constitutional rights.

After Ron Williamson had spent two months in jail, no one involved in his prosecution or defense had questioned his mental competency. The evidence was blatantly obvious. His medical history was extensive and readily available to the court. His rantings in jail, though somewhat regulated by the arbitrary dispensing of medications by his lawyer and his jailers, were clear warnings. His reputation in Ada was well known, especially to the police.

And his behavior in court had been seen before. Two years earlier, when the state attempted to revoke Ron's suspended sentence on the escape charge, he so completely disrupted the hearing that he was sent to a mental hospital for evaluation. Presiding then was John David Miller, the same Judge Miller who was now holding the preliminary hearing. It was Judge Miller who had adjudicated him to be mentally incompetent at that time.

Now, two years later and with the death penalty at issue, Judge Miller evidently saw no need to inquire into Ron's state of mind.

Oklahoma had a statute that allowed a judge, including one presiding over a preliminary hearing, to suspend the proceedings if the competency of a defendant became an issue. No motion from the defense was required. Most trial lawyers would argue strenuously that their client had a history of mental problems and should be evaluated, but absent such a plea it remained the judge's duty to protect the constitutional rights of the defendant.

THE SILENCE of Judge Miller should have been shattered by Barney Ward. As defense counsel, he could have requested a complete psychological evaluation of his client. The next step would have been to seek a competency hearing, the same routine procedure David Morris had pursued two years earlier. A final step would have been an insanity defense.

With Ron out of the courtroom, the preliminary hearing proceeded quietly and in order. It ran for several days, and Ron never left his cell. Whether he was competent enough to assist in his own defense made little difference.

DR. FRED JORDAN testified first and went through the autopsy and the cause of death—asphyxiation by either the belt around the neck or the washcloth stuffed in the mouth, or probably both.

The lying began with the second witness, Glen Gore, who testified that on the night of December 7 he was at the Coachlight with some friends, one of whom was Debbie Carter, a girl he'd gone to school with and had known most of his life. At some point during the night she asked Gore to "save" her or to "rescue" her because Ron Williamson was there, too, and he was pestering her.

He did not see Dennis Fritz at the Coachlight on December 7.

Under cross-examination, Gore said he told the police about this on December 8, but their report of his interview does not mention Ron Williamson. Nor was their report submitted to the defense, as required by the rules of procedure.

Thus, Glen Gore became the only witness with direct evidence against Ron Williamson. By placing him in contact and in conflict with Debbie Carter just hours before her murder, he, technically, established the link between the murderer and his victim. All other evidence was circumstantial.

Only a prosecutor as determined as Bill Peterson would be brazen enough to allow a criminal like Glen Gore anywhere near his case. Gore had been brought to the preliminary hearing in cuffs and chains. He was serving a forty-year prison sentence for breaking and entering, kidnapping, and attempting to kill a police officer. Five months earlier, Gore had broken into the home of his former wife, Gwen, and taken her hostage, along with his young daughter. He was drunk and for five hours held them at gunpoint. When a policeman, Rick Carson, glanced through a window, Gore aimed, fired, and hit Carson in the face. Fortunately, the injuries were not serious. Before sobering up and surrendering, Gore also shot at another police officer.

It was not his first violent altercation with Gwen. In 1986, during the unraveling of their rocky marriage, Gore was charged with breaking into Gwen's house and stabbing her repeatedly with a butcher knife. She survived and pressed charges, and Gore faced two counts of first-degree burglary and one count of assault and battery with a dangerous weapon.

Two months earlier, he'd been charged for assaulting Gwen by choking her.

In 1981, he'd been charged for forcibly entering the home of another woman. Gore also had an assault-and-battery charge from his Army days and a long list of convictions for petty crimes.

One week after his name was listed as an additional witness against Ron Williamson, a plea-bargain agreement was filed. At the same time, one charge of kidnapping and one of assault with a dangerous weapon were dismissed. When Gore was sentenced, his ex-wife's parents filed a letter with the court in which they begged for a long prison sentence. It read, in part:

> We want you to be aware of how dangerous we feel this man is. He intends to kill our daughter, granddaughter, and ourselves. This he has told us. We have gone to great lengths to make our daughter's home burglar proof, but all failed. To go into detail all the times he has attacked her would make too lengthy a letter. Please give our daughter enough time to get the child raised before he is out of prison and the terror starts, so the little one never has to live through that again.

FOR YEARS, Barney Ward had suspected that Glen Gore was involved in the Carter murder. He was a career criminal with a history of violence against women, and he was the last person seen with the victim. It was incomprehensible that the police showed so little interest in Gore.

Gore's fingerprints were never submitted to the OSBI for analysis. Prints from a total of forty-four people were submitted, but not Gore's. At one point, he agreed to take a polygraph exam, but one was never administered. The Ada police lost the first set of hair samples Gore gave them, some two years after the murder. He then submitted another set, and perhaps another. No one could remember exactly.

Barney, with his uncanny ability to hear and remember the courthouse gossip, firmly believed that Gore should have been investigated by the police.

And he knew that his boy, Ronnie Williamson, was not guilty.

THE GORE mystery was partially explained fourteen years after the preliminary hearing. Glen Gore, still in prison, signed an affidavit in which he stated that during the early 1980s he was selling drugs in Ada. He mentioned methamphetamine. Some of his transactions involved Ada policemen, specifically one Dennis Corvin, whom Gore described as a "primary supplier" and who frequented Harold's Club, where Gore worked.

When Gore owed them money, they would arrest him under false pretenses, but for the most part the cops left him alone. Under oath, he said in his affidavit, "However, most of the time during the early 1980's I was aware that I was receiving favorable treatment from Ada law enforcement."

And, "This favorable treatment ended when I was no longer involved in the drug business with Ada police."

He blamed his forty-year prison sentence on the fact that he "was no longer selling drugs to the Ada police."

Regarding Williamson, the police seemed to believe he and Fritz were guilty. Gore said he did not know if Ron was at the Coachlight the night of the murder. The police showed him a lineup of photos, pointed to Ron, and explained that he was the man they were interested in. "Then they directly suggested that I identify Mr. Williamson."

And, "To this day I do not know if Ron Williamson was at the bar on the night that Debbie Carter disappeared. I made the identification because I knew the police expected me to do that."

Gore's affidavit was prepared by an attorney, and it was reviewed by his own lawyer before he signed it.

THE STATE'S next witness was Tommy Glover, a regular at the Coachlight and one of the last to see Debbie Carter. His initial recollection was that she was talking with Glen Gore in the parking lot and that she pushed him away before driving off.

But four years and seven months later, he remembered things a bit differently. Glover testified at the preliminary hearing that he saw Gore speak to Debbie and that she got in her car and drove away. Nothing more or less.

Charlie Carter testified next and told the story of finding his daughter on the morning of December 8, 1982.

OSBI agent Jerry Peters, a "Crime Scene Specialist," was called to the stand. It wasn't long before he was in trouble. Barney smelled a rat and grilled Peters on his conflicting opinions about the palm print on the Sheetrock. A firm opinion in March 1983, then, surprise, an about-face in May 1987. What prompted Peters to rethink his original opinion that the palm print did not belong to Debbie Carter, Ron Williamson, or Dennis Fritz? Could it have been that this opinion didn't really help the prosecution?

Peters did admit that nothing happened for four years, then a phone call early in 1987 from Bill Peterson prompted him to ponder his earlier judgment. After the exhumation and reprinting, he suddenly changed his mind and issued a report that was exactly what the prosecution wanted.

Greg Saunders joined the assault on behalf of Dennis Fritz, and it was obvious the evidence had been reconstructed. But it was only a pre-liminary hearing, not a trial that required proof beyond a reasonable doubt.

Peters also testified that of the twenty-one fingerprints found in the apartment and on the car, nineteen belonged to Debbie Carter herself, one to Mike Carpenter, one to Dennis Smith, and none to either Fritz or Williamson.

THE PROSECUTION'S star was the amazing Terri Holland. From October 1984 to January 1985, Holland had been locked up in the Pontotoc County jail for writing bad checks. As far as unsolved murders went in Oklahoma, it was a productive and remarkable four-month stay.

First she claimed she heard Karl Fontenot admit everything about the Denice Haraway kidnapping and murder. She testified in the first Ward/Fontenot trial in September 1985 and gave the jury all the lurid details that Detectives Smith and Rogers had furnished Tommy Ward during his dream confession. After she testified, she was given a light sentence on the check charges, in spite of having two prior felonies. Ward and Fontenot went to death row; Terri Holland fled the county.

She left behind some unpaid court fines and such, nothing the authorities would take seriously under normal circumstances. But they found her and brought her back anyway. Facing more charges, she suddenly had some astounding news for the investigators. When she was in jail hearing Fontenot's story, she also heard Ron Williamson make a full confession.

What an amazing stroke of luck for the cops! Not only had they generated a dream confession—their favorite investigatory tool—but now they had another snitch, their second-favorite weapon.

Holland was vague on exactly why she had not told anyone about Ron's confession until sometime in the spring of 1987. Over two years had passed without a word. She was never asked why she rushed to tell Smith and Rogers about Fontenot's admissions.

On the stand during the preliminary, she had a grand time with her fiction. With Ron absent from the proceedings, she was free to create all sorts of tales. She told of one episode in which he yelled into the phone at his mother and said, "I'll kill you just like I killed Debbie Carter."

The only telephone in the jail was on a wall in the front office. On the rare occasions when inmates were allowed to make calls, they were forced to lean over a counter, stretch to get the receiver, and talk in the presence of whoever happened to be working the front desk. Eavesdropping by another inmate was unlikely, if not impossible.

Terri Holland testified that Ron once made a phone call to a church, asked someone there for cigarettes, and threatened to burn down the place if they didn't bring him some.

Again, no one could verify this statement. And she was not quizzed on the layout of the jail, and how, exactly, did a female prisoner get so close to the men?

Peterson led her along: "Did he ever say anything that you overheard him say about what he had done to Debbie Carter?"

"Yeah, he was talking in the bullpens," she answered. "It was right after they brought in Tommy Ward and Karl Fontenot."

"What did he say in the bullpens in relationship to what he said he had done to Debbie Carter?"

"He just said that—I don't know how to say it. He said she thought she was better than he was, and that he showed the bitch she wasn't."

"Anything else?"

"He said he made her make love to him, only that's not how he said it. I don't even remember how he said it. He said that he shoved a Coke—catsup bottle up her ass and her panties down her throat, and he taught her a lesson."

Bill Peterson plowed ahead with his leading questions. "Did he say anything in relationship about Debbie should have come off of it or anything like that?" Peterson asked.

"Yeah, he'd tried to go with her, and she didn't want nothing to do with him, and he said she'd been better off if she would just come off of it and give it to him."

"And that he would not have had to do what?" Peterson asked, desperate to prompt his shaky witness.

"Wouldn't have had to kill her."

It was remarkable that Bill Peterson, as an officer of the court and charged with the duty to seek the truth, could elicit such garbage.

A crucial part of snitching is getting paid. Terri Holland was allowed to plea-bargain herself out of trouble and out of jail. She agreed to a monthly payment plan for restitution, but soon abandoned her obligations.

AT THE time, few people knew that Terri Holland had a history with Ron Williamson. Years earlier, when he was peddling Rawleigh products around Ada, he stumbled upon a little unexpected sex. He knocked on a door, and a female voice asked him to step inside. When he did, a woman named Marlene Keutel presented herself completely in the nude. There appeared to be no one else at home, and one thing quickly led to another.

Marlene Keutel was mentally unstable, and a week after the episode she committed suicide. Ron returned several times to sell her more products, but never found her at home. He did not know she was dead.

Her sister was Terri Holland. Shortly after the sexual encounter, Marlene told Terri about it and claimed Ron had raped her. No charges were brought; none were contemplated. Though Terri knew her sister was crazy, she still believed that Ron was responsible for Marlene's death. Ron had long since forgotten about the quickie, and had no idea who Terri Holland was.

THE FIRST day of the preliminary hearing dragged on with the laborious testimony of Dennis Smith, who described in detail the crime scene and the investigation. The only surprise came when Smith discussed the various writings left behind by the killers—the message on the wall scrawled in red fingernail polish, the "don't look fore us or ealse" in catsup on the kitchen table, and the scarcely readable words on Debbie's stomach and back. Detectives Smith and Rogers thought such handwriting might be traceable, so, four years earlier, they asked Dennis Fritz and Ron Williamson to write something on a white index card.

The detectives had virtually no experience with handwriting analysis, but, not surprisingly, they felt strongly that they had a match. The samples given by Fritz and Williamson, words written in pen on an index card, looked suspiciously similar to the red fingernail polish message left on a wall and the smeared catsup in the kitchen.

They took their suspicions to some unidentified agent at the OSBI, and, according to Smith, this agent agreed and gave them a "verbal" confirmation.

Under cross-examination from Greg Saunders, Smith testified, "Well, the handwriting, according to the person we talked to, was similar to the handwriting we found on the wall of the apartment."

"What about the table?"

"Both of them were similar."

A few minutes later, Barney grilled Smith on the handwriting analysis. He asked Smith if he had a report from the OSBI on Ron's handwriting.

"We did not submit it," Smith admitted.

Barney was incredulous. Why wasn't it submitted to the OSBI? They have the experts. Maybe they could have eliminated Ron and Dennis as suspects.

Smith was on the defensive. "There were similarities in the handwriting; but, you know, it was based on our observations, and nothing really scientific. I mean, we were, you know, we saw the similarities in it; but, you know, to compare two different types of writing like this is nearly an impossibility. You have writing with a brush, you have writing with a pencil, and that's two different types of writing."

Barney replied, "Well now, you're not trying to tell this court that there's a possibility that these two boys, Dennis Fritz and Ronnie Williamson, took turns with that fingernail brush, or fingernail polish brush, and wrote a statement about Jim Smith and the other, you know, one of them wrote one letter and just alternated or anything of that nature which would give you the same conclusions, are you?"

"No, but I think it was our opinion that both of them had a hand at the writing, not necessarily on the same writing, but, you know, there was several different writings in the apartment."

Though the handwriting testimony was offered at the preliminary to help prod the case along, it would prove too flimsy even for Bill Peterson to use at trial.

AT THE end of the first day, Judge Miller was concerned about Ron's absence. At a bench conference, he expressed his worries to the lawyers. "I've done some reading about the absence of the defendant. I'm going to have Mr. Williamson brought back over about a quarter till nine and inquire one more time whether or not he still wishes not to be present. If he does, then he's going back again."

To which Dr. Barney added helpfully, "Do you want me to load him down with about a hundred milligrams of—"

"I'm not telling you what to do," Judge Miller interrupted.

At 8:45 the following morning, Ron was escorted into the courtroom. Judge Miller addressed him by saying, "Mr. Williamson, yesterday you had expressed your desire not to be present during the preliminary hearing."

"I don't want to even be up here," Ron said. "I didn't have anything to do with this killing. I never—I don't know who killed her. I don't know anything about it."

"Okay. Your conduct and your disruptive behavior—you can reclaim your right to be present if you so desire, but you'll have to promise and be willing not to be disruptive and disorderly. And you'll have to do that in order to reclaim that right. Do you wish to be present?"

"No, I don't want to be here."

"And you understand that you have the right to be here and listen to all the witnesses' testimony?"

"I don't want to be here. Whatever you all do I can't help it. I'm tired of being crazy about this. It's suffered me so much; I just don't want to be here."

"Okay, and that's your decision. You do not wish to be present?"

"That's correct."

"And you're waiving your right to confront witnesses by doing that under the Constitution?"

"Yes I am. You all can charge me on something I didn't do. You all can do anything you want to do." Ron then looked at Gary Rogers and said, "You scare me, Gary. You can charge me after four and a half years of harassing me, sir, you all can go at it because you all is the ones in control, not me."

Ron was taken back to jail, and the hearing resumed with the testimony of Dennis Smith. Gary Rogers followed with a tedious narrative of the investigation, then OSBI agents Melvin Hett and Mary Long testified about the forensics involved in the case—fingerprints, hair analysis, and the components in blood and saliva.

After the state rested its case, Barney called ten witnesses—all jailers or former trustees. Not a one recalled hearing anything vaguely similar to what Terri Holland claimed she heard.

When the testimony was over, Barney and Greg Saunders asked the court to dismiss the rape charges because they had not been brought within three years of the crime, as required by Oklahoma law. Murder has no statute of limitations, but all other crimes do. Judge Miller said he would rule on the motion at a later date.

Almost lost in the shuffle was Dennis Fritz. The focus of Peterson's prosecution was obviously Ron Williamson, and his star witnesses—

Gore, Terri Holland, Gary Rogers (with the dream confession)—all testified against Ron. The only proof that remotely tied Fritz to the murder was the hair analysis testimony of Melvin Hett.

Greg Saunders argued long and hard that the state had not met its burden of proving probable cause that Dennis Fritz was connected to the killing. Judge Miller took the matter under advisement.

Barney joined in the fray with a noisy motion to dismiss all charges because of such light evidence, and Greg followed suit. When Judge Miller didn't issue a ruling immediately, when it became apparent he was actually considering the merits of the defense motions, the police and prosecutors realized they needed more evidence.

SCIENTIFIC experts carry great weight with juries, especially in small towns, and when the experts are employees of the state and called by the prosecution to testify against criminal defendants, their opinions are deemed infallible.

Barney and Greg Saunders knew the hair and fingerprint testimony from the OSBI crowd was suspect, but they needed some help to dispute it. They would be allowed to cross-examine the state's experts and attempt to discredit them, but they also knew that lawyers rarely win such arguments. Experts are hard to pin down, and jurors are quickly confused. What the defense needed was an expert or two at its table.

They filed a motion requesting such assistance. Such motions were commonly made but rarely granted. Experts cost money, and many local officials, including judges, cringed at the idea of forcing the taxpayers to cover the bill for an indigent defense that ran too high.

The motion was argued. Left unsaid was the fact that Barney was blind. If anyone needed help in analyzing hair fibers and fingerprints, it was Barney Ward.

CHAPTER 8

The paperwork flew back and forth. The D.A.'s office amended the charges and dropped the rapes. The defense lawyers attacked the new indictment. Another hearing was needed.

The district court judge was Ronald Jones from Pontotoc County, which, along with Seminole and Hughes, comprised the Twenty-second Judicial District. Judge Jones was elected in 1982 and, not surprisingly, was known to be pro-prosecution and tough on defendants. He believed strongly in the death penalty. He was a devout Christian, a Baptist deacon whose nicknames included Ron the Baptist and By-the-Book Jones. He did, though, have a weakness for jailhouse conversions, and some defense lawyers quietly advised their clients that a sudden interest in finding the Lord might prove beneficial when facing Judge Jones.

On August 20, Ron, unrepentant, was brought before him for an arraignment, the first time the two met in court. Judge Jones spoke to Ron and asked him how he was doing. He got an earful.

"I have one thing to say, sir," Ron began loudly. "This—I feel strongly for the Carter family, as much as their kinfolks."

Judge Jones asked for silence.

Ron continued, "Sir, I know that you don't want—I, I didn't do this, sir."

The guards squeezed him and he shut up. The arraignment was postponed so Judge Jones could review the transcript from the preliminary hearing.

Two weeks later Ron was back with more motions by his lawyers. The jailers had fine-tuned the Thorazine. When Ron was in his cell and they wanted peace, they pumped him full and everybody was happy. But when he was scheduled to be in court, they reduced the dosage so he would appear louder, more intense, more belligerent. Norma Walker at Mental Health Services suspected the jailers were juicing Ron and made a note in her file.

The second appearance before Judge Jones did not go well. Ron was outspoken. He professed his innocence, claimed people were telling lies about him, and at one point said, "Mother knew I was at home that night."

He was eventually returned to the jail, and the hearing continued. Barney Ward and Greg Saunders had requested separate trials, and they pressed hard on this issue. Saunders especially wanted his own jury without the baggage of a co-defendant like Ron Williamson.

Judge Jones agreed and ordered separate trials. He also broached the issue of Ron's mental competency, telling Barney in court that the matter needed to be dealt with before the trial. Ron was finally arraigned, entered a formal plea of not guilty, and went back to jail.

The Fritz case was now on a different track. Judge Jones had ordered a new preliminary hearing because the state had presented so little evidence against Dennis at the first one.

The authorities didn't have enough witnesses.

NORMALLY, a prosecution with no hard evidence would worry the police, but not in Ada. No one panicked. The Pontotoc County jail was full of potential snitches. The first one they found for Dennis Fritz was a career petty criminal named Cindy McIntosh.

Dennis had been strategically moved to a cell closer to Ron so the two could talk. Their feud was over; Dennis had convinced him that he had not confessed.

Cindy McIntosh claimed she got close enough to hear the two talk, then notified the police that she had the goods. According to McIntosh, Fritz and Williamson discussed some photographs submitted during the first preliminary hearing. Ron wasn't there, of course, and he was curious about what Dennis had seen. The photos were of the crime scene, and Ron asked Dennis, "Was she [Debbie Carter] on the bed or on the floor?"

The floor, Dennis replied.

This, to the police, was clear proof that both men were in the apartment and committed the rape and murder.

Bill Peterson was quickly convinced. On September 22, he filed a motion to add Cindy McIntosh as a witness for the state.

The next snitch was James Riggins, though his career as such was short-lived. Hauled back from prison to face charges in Pontotoc County, Riggins was being returned to his cell one night when he passed another cell. Inside, he heard someone, perhaps Ron, admitting that he killed Debbie Carter, that he had two rape charges up in Tulsa, and that he would beat the murder rap just like he'd walked on the rapes. Riggins wasn't clear who Ron was doing all this confessing to, but in the snitching world such details were not important.

About a month later, Riggins changed his mind. In an interview with the police, he said he was incorrect about Ron Williamson, that in fact the man he heard doing the confessing was Glen Gore.

CONFESSIONS were contagious in Ada. On September 23, a young drug addict named Ricky Joe Simmons walked into the police department and announced he'd killed Debbie Carter and wanted to talk about it. Dennis Smith and Gary Rogers had no trouble locating a video recorder, and Simmons began his story. He admitted that he had abused drugs for years, his favorite being a home brew called crank, which included, among many ingredients, battery acid. He said he had finally kicked drugs, had found God, and had been reading his Bible one December night in 1982—he thought it was 1982 but wasn't sure—and for some strange reason began wandering around Ada on foot. He ran into a girl, presumably Debbie Carter but he wasn't sure, and gave several conflicting versions of how he and the girl got together. He might have raped her, then maybe he didn't, and he thought he choked her to death with his hands, after which he prayed and vomited all over the apartment.

Strange voices were telling him what to do. The details were a blur, and at one point Simmons said, "It seemed like a dream."

Oddly, at this point Smith and Rogers did not get excited over the prospect of yet another dream confession.

When pressed on why he had waited almost five years to come forward, he was finally able to explain that all the recent gossip around town had led him to remember that fateful night back in 1982, or maybe it was 1981. But he couldn't recall how he entered Debbie's apartment, or how many rooms it had, or in which room he killed her. Then, suddenly, he remembered the catsup bottle and scrawling words on the wall. Later, he said a friend at work had been talking about the details.

Simmons claimed to be clean and sober during the confession, but it was obvious to Smith and Rogers that the crank had taken its toll. They dismissed his story immediately. Though it had as many inaccuracies as Tommy Ward's, the detectives were not impressed. Smith finally heard enough and announced, "In my opinion, you didn't kill Debbie Carter." Then he offered to get counseling for Simmons.

Simmons, confused even further, insisted that he had killed her. The two detectives insisted he had not.

They thanked him for his time and sent him away.

GOOD news was rare at the Pontotoc County jail, but early in November, Ron received an unexpected letter. An administrative law judge awarded him disability benefits under the Social Security Act.

A year earlier Annette applied for the benefits on Ron's behalf, claiming that he had been unable to work since 1979. The judge, Howard O'Bryan, reviewed the extensive medical history and ordered a full hearing on October 26, 1987. Ron was driven over from the jail.

In his decision, Judge O'Bryan noted: "Clearly the claimant has adequate medical documentation to show a history of alcoholism, depression that was stabilized with lithium, and has been classified as having an atypical bipolar disorder complicated by an atypical personality disorder, probably borderline, paranoid and antisocial. Clearly, without medications he is belligerent, abusive, physically violent, has religious delusions, and a thought disorder."

And, "There are repeated episodes of disorientation to time, impaired attention span, as well as impaired abstract thinking and level consciousness."

Judge O'Bryan had little trouble reaching his conclusion that Ron had "severe bipolar disorder, personality disorder, and substance abuse disorder." Further, his condition was serious enough to prevent him from obtaining meaningful employment.

Ron's period of disability began on March 31, 1985, and was continuing.

The administrative law judge's primary job was to determine if claimants were disabled, either physically or mentally, and thus entitled to monthly benefits. These were important cases, but not life and death. Judges Miller and Jones, on the other hand, had a duty to ensure that every defendant, especially one facing death, received a fair trial. It was sadly ironic that Judge O'Bryan could see Ron's obvious problems, while Judges Miller and Jones could not.

————

BARNEY was concerned enough to have Ron evaluated. He arranged for testing at the Pontotoc County Health Department. The clinic director, Claudette Ray, administered a series of psychological tests and issued a report to Barney. It ended with: "Ron is consciously anxious due to situational stress. He feels helpless to alter his situation or better himself. He may behave inappropriately, such as not attending preliminary hearings which would benefit him, because of his panic and confused thinking. Most individuals would be demanding to hear information and opinions that would influence their future life or death."

The report was tucked away in Barney's file and left there. A request for a competency hearing was a routine matter, one Barney had handled before. His client was sitting in jail, about a hundred feet from the courthouse, a place Barney visited almost every day.

The case was begging for someone to raise the issue of competency.

THE PROSECUTION of Dennis Fritz got a huge boost from the testimony of a semiliterate Indian by the name of James C. Harjo. At twenty-two, Harjo was already in jail for burglary—he got caught after he broke into the same home twice. In September and October, while he was awaiting transfer to a state prison, his cell mate was Dennis Fritz.

The two became somewhat friendly. Dennis felt sorry for Harjo and wrote letters for the boy, most of them going to his wife. He also knew exactly what the cops had planned. Every other day they would pull Harjo out of the cell for no apparent reason—his court appearances were over—and as soon as he returned, he began quizzing Dennis about the Carter murder. In a jail full of accomplished snitches, Harjo had to be the worst.

The scheme was so obvious that Dennis prepared a one-paragraph statement that he made Harjo sign every time the cops took him out. It read, in part: "Dennis Fritz always says he is innocent."

And Dennis flatly refused to discuss the case with him.

That didn't stop Harjo. On November 19, Peterson listed James C. Harjo as a witness for the state. On that same date, the preliminary hearing for Dennis resumed before Judge John David Miller.

When Peterson announced that his next witness would be Harjo, Dennis flinched. What could this stupid boy dream up?

Harjo, under oath and lying badly, explained to an earnest Bill Peterson that he had been cell mates with Fritz, and while at first things had been friendly, on Halloween night a conversation had turned ugly. Harjo was quizzing Dennis about the details of the murder. Dennis was having trouble with the details, and Harjo deftly managed to poke holes in his story. He became convinced that Dennis was guilty, so he confronted him. This made Dennis very nervous. He began pacing around the bullpen, obviously struggling with his guilt, and when he returned to their cell, he looked at Harjo, with tears in his eyes, and said, "We didn't mean to hurt her."

In court, Dennis couldn't sit through this crap. He yelled at the witness, "You are lying! You are lying!"

Judge Miller settled things down. Harjo and Peterson plowed ahead with their tales. In Harjo's account, Dennis expressed concern for his young daughter. "What would she think if her daddy was a murderer?" he asked. Then, some truly incredible testimony. Dennis confessed to Harjo that he and Ron had taken some beer to Debbie's apartment, and when they finished with the raping and killing, they picked up the empty cans, wiped down the apartment to remove their fingerprints, and left.

On cross-examination, Greg Saunders asked Harjo if Dennis explained how he and Ron wiped off their invisible fingerprints while leaving dozens of others. Harjo had no clue. He admitted that there had been at least six other prisoners nearby when Dennis had made his confession Halloween night, but no one else heard it. Greg produced copies of the statements prepared by Dennis and signed by Harjo.

Harjo was discredited when he took the oath, but after Saunders's cross-examination he looked downright foolish. It didn't matter. Judge Miller had no choice but to bind Dennis over for trial. Under Oklahoma law, a judge at a preliminary hearing was not permitted to determine the credibility of a witness.

TRIAL dates were set, then postponed. The winter of 1987–88 dragged on with Ron and Dennis enduring life in jail and hoping their day in court would soon arrive. After months behind bars, they still believed in the possibility of justice and that the truth would be revealed.

In the pretrial skirmishing the only significant victory for the defense had been the ruling by Judge Jones that they would be tried separately. Even though Bill Peterson had fought the motions for separate trials, there was a huge advantage in trying one before the other. Put Fritz on first, and let the newspaper report the details to an anxious and very curious town.

Since the day of the murder, the police had insisted there were two killers, and the first (and only) pair they'd suspected had been Fritz and Williamson. At every step—suspicion, investigation, accusation, arrest, indictment, preliminary hearing—the two had been linked. Their mug shots were published side by side in the local paper. The headlines repeatedly read, "Williamson and Fritz . . ."

If Bill Peterson could get a conviction for Fritz in the first trial, the Williamson jurors would take their seats and start looking for a noose.

In Ada, the notion of fairness was to try Fritz first, then follow immediately with Ron Williamson—same courtroom, same judge, same witnesses, and the same newspaper reporting it all.

ON APRIL 1, three weeks before Ron's trial was to start, his court-appointed co-counsel, Frank Baber, filed a motion to withdraw from the case. Baber had found a job as a prosecutor in another district.

Judge Jones granted the motion. Baber walked away. Barney was left with no assistance—no legal eyes to help sift through the documents, exhibits, photographs, and diagrams that would be introduced against his client.

On April 6, 1988, five and a half years after the murder of Debbie Carter, Dennis Fritz was escorted into the crowded courtroom on the second floor of the Pontotoc County Courthouse. He was clean-shaven with a fresh haircut, and he wore his only suit, one his mother had purchased for his trial. Wanda Fritz was sitting in the front row, as close to her son as possible. Seated next to her was her sister, Wilma Foss. They would not miss a single word of the trial.

When the handcuffs were removed, Dennis glanced at the crowd and wondered which of the hundred or so potential jurors would eventually make it to the final twelve. Which of those registered voters sitting out there would judge him?

His long wait was over. After enduring eleven months in the suffocating jail, he was now in court. He had a good lawyer; he assumed the judge would guarantee a fair trial; twelve of his peers would carefully weigh the evidence and quickly realize that Peterson had no proof.

The beginning of the trial was a relief, but it was also terrifying. It was, after all, Pontotoc County, and Dennis knew perfectly well that innocent people could be framed. He had briefly shared a cell with Karl Fontenot, a simple and confused soul who was now sitting on death row for a murder he had nothing to do with.

Judge Jones entered and greeted the pool of jurors. Preliminary matters came first, then the jury selection began. It was a slow and tedious process. The hours dragged by as the aged, deaf, and sick were weeded out. Then the questions began, some by the lawyers but most by Judge Jones. Greg Saunders and Bill Peterson haggled over which jurors to keep and which to strike.

At one point in the lengthy process, Judge Jones asked the following question to a prospective juror by the name of Cecil Smith: "What was your past employment?"

Cecil Smith: "The Oklahoma Corporation Commission."

No follow-up questions were asked by the judge or the lawyers. What Cecil Smith failed to include in his abbreviated response was the fact that he'd had a long career in law enforcement.

Moments later, Judge Jones asked Cecil Smith if he knew Detective Dennis Smith, or if he was related to him.

Cecil Smith: "No kin."

Judge Jones: "And how do you know him?"

Cecil Smith: "Oh, I just know of him, and talked to him several times, had a few little deals with him, maybe."

Hours later, a jury was sworn in. Of particular concern to Fritz was the presence of Cecil Smith. When he took his seat in the jury box, Smith gave Dennis a hard look, the first of many.

The real trial began the following day. Nancy Shew, an assistant district attorney, outlined for the jury what the proof would be. Greg Saunders rebutted by saying, in his opening statement, that there was indeed very little proof.

The first witness was Glen Gore, who'd been brought back from prison. Gore, under direct examination from Peterson, presented the rather strange testimony that he did *not* see Dennis Fritz with Debbie Carter on the night of the murder.

Most prosecutors prefer to start with a strong first witness who can put the killer in the same vicinity as the victim, at about the same time of the murder. Peterson chose otherwise. Gore said he may have seen Dennis at the Coachlight at some undetermined point in the past, or perhaps he hadn't seen him there at all.

The state's strategy became apparent with the first witness. Gore talked more about Ron Williamson than about Dennis Fritz, and Peterson asked more questions about Ron. The guilt-by-association scheme was put into play.

Before Greg Saunders got the chance to impeach Gore on his lengthy criminal record, Peterson decided to discredit his own witness. He asked Gore about his criminal career. There were many convictions, for crimes such as kidnapping, aggravated assault, and shooting a police officer.

Not only did the state's prime witness fail to implicate Dennis; he was revealed to be a hardened felon serving a forty-year sentence.

Off to a shaky start, Peterson continued with another witness who knew nothing. Tommy Glover described to the jury how he saw Debbie Carter talking to Glen Gore before she went home from the Coachlight. After a quick appearance on the witness stand, Glover was dismissed without mentioning the name of Dennis Fritz.

Gina Vietta told her story about the strange phone calls from Debbie in the early hours of December 8. She also testified that she had seen Fritz at the Coachlight on several occasions, but not the night of the murder.

Next, Charlie Carter told the heartbreaking story of finding his dead daughter, then Detective Dennis Smith was called to the stand. Smith was led through the lengthy process of describing the murder scene and placing into evidence numerous photographs. He talked about the investigation he led, the collection of saliva and hair samples, and so on. Nancy Shew's first question about possible suspects was, not surprisingly, not about Dennis Fritz.

"Did you interview a man then named Ronald Keith Williamson sometime during your investigation?" she asked.

"Yes, we did." Smith, without interruption or objection, then rambled on about the police investigation into Ron Williamson and explained how and why he became a suspect. Finally Nancy Shew remembered who was on trial and asked about a saliva sample from Dennis Fritz.

Smith described how he collected the saliva and gave it to the OSBI lab in Oklahoma City. Shew finished the direct exam at that point and yielded the witness for cross. When she sat down, the state had provided no clue as to why and how Dennis Fritz became a suspect. He had no history with the victim. No one placed him remotely near her at the time of her murder, though Smith did testify that Fritz lived "close" to Debbie's apartment. There was no mention of motive.

Fritz was finally linked to the murder through the testimony of Gary Rogers, the next witness, who said, "Through our investigation of Ron Williamson, that is when the Defendant, Dennis Fritz' name came into play, as an associate of Ron Williamson."

Rogers explained to the jury how he and Dennis Smith shrewdly concluded that such a crime had required two killers. The crime seemed too violent for just one man, plus the killer(s) had left behind a clue when they wrote, in catsup, "Don't look fore us or ealse." The word "us" implied more than one killer, and Smith and Rogers were quick to pick up on this.

Through good police work they were able to learn that Williamson and Fritz had actually been friends. This, in their theory, linked the two killers.

GREG SAUNDERS had instructed Dennis to ignore the jury, but he found it impossible to do so. Those twelve people held his fate, maybe his life in their hands, and he couldn't help but glance over occasionally. Cecil Smith sat in the front row, and whenever Dennis looked at the jury, Smith was always glaring back.

What is his problem? Dennis thought. He soon found out.

During a recess, Greg Saunders was entering the courthouse when an old lawyer, one of Ada's veterans, asked him, "Who's the smart sonofabitch that left Cecil Smith on the jury?"

Greg said, "Well, I guess that would be me. Who's Cecil Smith?"

"Used to be the chief of police here in Ada, that's all."

Saunders was stunned. He marched into Judge Jones's office and demanded a mistrial on the grounds that the juror had not been forth-

Ronnie as a Police Eagle, age ten.

The Williamson family around 1970: Annette, Ron, and Renee, with their parents, Juanita and Roy.

High school portrait, age eighteen.

Two Asher Players Honored---
On All-State Baseball Teams

Ron Williamson of the state Class B champion Asher Indians was picked as an outfielder on the Daily Oklahoman's South team and was on the Oklahoma Journal's first team. Another Asher star, third baseman Bruce Leba was named to the Daily Oklahoman's South squad.

Bruce Leba   Ron Williamson

Murl Bowen (*right*). His Asher teams won 2,115 games, still a record.

Ron, on the far right, at the beginning of his last season (*below*).

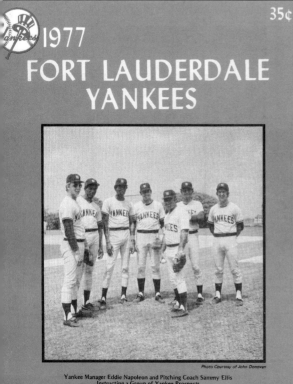

35¢

1977
FORT LAUDERDALE
YANKEES

Photo Courtesy of John Donovan
Yankee Manager Eddie Napoleon and Pitching Coach Sammy Ellis
Instructing a Group of Yankee Prospects

As a minor league Yankee, 1976 (*above*).

Debbie Carter, two days before she was murdered.

The crime scene— Debbie had the upstairs apartment.

Denice Haraway, abducted April 28, 1984.

Tommy Ward and Karl Fontenot being escorted to trial.

Ron Williamson's mug shot.

Dennis Fritz's mug shot.

District Attorney Bill Peterson.

Ron being led away from the Pontotoc County Courthouse after he was found guilty of murder and received the death penalty.

Greg Wilhoit spent four years at F Cellhouse for a murder he did not commit. He and Ron Williamson became close friends on death row.

U.S. District Court Judge Frank H. Seay. As an epilogue to his decision granting a new trial he said, "God help us, if ever in this great country we turn our heads while those who have not had fair trials are executed. That almost happened in this case."

After eleven years in prison, Ron returns to Ada.

The client with his legal team. Front row: Kim Marks and Penny Stewart; second row: Bill Luker, Janet Chesley, Ron, Jenny Landrith, Mark Barrett, and Sara Bonnell. (April 15, 1999.)

Dennis Fritz and Ron Williamson in court as they hear Judge Tom Landrith dismiss the charges. (April 15, 1999.)

Barry Scheck and Mark Barrett celebrate at a press conference after the release of Ron and Dennis. (April 15, 1999.)

Ron at Yankee Stadium two weeks after his release.

Annette and Renee with their brother shortly before his death.

coming during the selection process and that the juror was obviously biased toward the police and prosecution.

The motion was overruled.

DR. FRED JORDAN testified about his autopsy, and the jury heard the gruesome details. Photos of the body were introduced and passed through the jury box, provoking the shock and outrage inherent in any murder trial. Several of the jurors glared in disgust at Fritz.

With the solid, unimpeachable testimony of Dr. Jordan still hanging in the air, the prosecution decided to slip in a few of its off-the-wall witnesses. A man named Gary Allen was sworn in and took the stand. Allen's involvement was quite tenuous. He told the jury that he lived near Dennis Fritz, and that one night in early December 1982, at about 3:30 a.m., he heard two men outside his apartment making noise. He wasn't sure of the exact date, but for some reason was certain that it was before December 10. The two men, neither of whom he saw clearly enough to identify, were in the yard laughing, cursing, and squirting each other with a garden hose. The temperature was cold, and the men had their shirts off. He had known Dennis Fritz for some time and thought he recognized his voice. But he wasn't sure. He listened to the noise for about ten minutes, then went back to bed.

When Allen was excused as a witness, there were a few puzzled looks in the courtroom. What, exactly, was the purpose of his testimony? Things would get even more confusing with the next witness, Tony Vick.

Vick lived in the small apartment under Gary Allen, and he knew Dennis Fritz. He also knew Ron Williamson. He testified that he'd seen Ron on the porch at Dennis's place, and that he knew for a fact that the two had taken a trip together to Texas in the summer of 1982.

What more could the jury ask for?

The damning evidence continued to pile up with Donna Walker, a convenience store clerk who identified Dennis in court and said that she had once known him pretty well. Way back in 1982 Dennis was a frequent customer at her store, a regular coffee drinker who liked to chat her up early in the mornings. Ron was a customer, too, and she knew for a fact that he and Dennis were pals. Then, suddenly, after the murder, the two stopped drinking coffee at her store. They vanished, as far as she was concerned. Then, after staying away for a few weeks, they reappeared as if nothing had happened. But they had changed! How?

"Their character, their dress. They always dressed nice and were clean-shaven before, and they just went completely down, filthy clothing, unshaven, hair was a mess; their character had changed. They seemed kind of nervous and paranoid, I guess."

When pressed by Greg Saunders, Walker couldn't explain why she waited five years before sharing this crucial evidence with the police. She did admit that the cops approached her the previous August, after Dennis and Ron were arrested.

The parade continued with Letha Caldwell, a divorcée who had attended junior high school with Ron at Byng. She told the jury that Dennis Fritz and Ron Williamson were frequent visitors to her home late at night, at irregular hours, and that they were always drinking. At some point, she became frightened of them and asked them to stay away. When they refused, she bought a gun and showed it to them, at which time they decided she was serious.

Her testimony had nothing to do with the murder of Debbie Carter, and in many courtrooms would have been objected to as totally irrelevant to the issues.

The objection finally came when OSBI agent Rusty Featherstone testified. Peterson, in a clumsy attempt to prove that Ron and Dennis were carousing in Norman four months before the murder, put Featherstone on the stand. Featherstone had given Dennis two polygraph exams in 1983, but, for many excellent reasons, the results were inadmissible. During the interviews, Dennis had recounted a night in Norman that involved bars and drinking. When Peterson attempted to elicit this story from Featherstone, Greg Saunders objected loudly. Judge Jones sustained it on the grounds of being irrelevant.

During the skirmish, Peterson, at a bench conference, said, "He (Featherstone) places both Ron Williamson and Dennis Fritz as associating with each other in August of 1982."

"Tell me the relevance of that statement," Judge Jones demanded.

Peterson could not, and Featherstone quickly left the courtroom. It was another appearance by another witness who knew nothing about the murder of Debbie Carter.

The next witness was just as unproductive, though his testimony was somewhat interesting. William Martin was the principal of the junior high in Noble where Dennis taught in 1982. He testified that on the morning of December 8, a Wednesday, Dennis called in sick and a substitute teacher taught his classes. According to the attendance records Martin brought to court, Dennis missed a total of seven days during the nine-month school year.

AFTER twelve witnesses, the state had not laid a glove on Dennis Fritz. The prosecution had proven beyond any doubt whatsoever that he drank alcohol, ran with unsavory people (Ron Williamson), shared an apartment with his mother and daughter in the same neighborhood as Debbie Carter's apartment, and missed school the day after the murder.

Peterson's style was methodical. He believed it was necessary to slowly build a case, block by block, witness by witness, nothing fancy or slick. Gradually pile on the evidence and remove all doubt from the minds of the jurors. But Fritz was quite a challenge because there was no hard evidence.

Snitches were needed.

The first one to testify was James Harjo, brought in, like Gore, from prison. Dull and dim-witted, Harjo had not only burglarized the same house twice but used the identical means of entry—same bedroom, same window. When he was caught, he was interrogated by the police. Using a pen and sheet of paper, articles foreign to Harjo, the cops had walked the boy through his story with diagrams and solved the crime. Evidently, this had impressed Harjo greatly. When he was in jail with Dennis, he, at the urging of the police, decided to crack the Carter murder by doodling on a sheet of paper.

He explained this shrewd strategy to the jury. In the crowded bullpen of the jail, he had quizzed Dennis about the murder. At some point, when his Xs and Os reached their climax, he said to Dennis, "Well, it looks like you're guilty."

Dennis, overcome by the weight of Harjo's deft logic, withered under the burden and tearfully said, "We didn't mean to hurt her."

When Harjo first spun this yarn during the preliminary hearing, Dennis erupted and yelled, "You are lying! You are lying!" But with a jury watching closely, he had to suffer through it again without showing any emotion. While it was difficult, he was encouraged to see several of the jurors suppressing a chuckle at Harjo's silly story.

On cross-examination, Greg Saunders established that Dennis and Harjo were housed in one of the jail's two bullpens—small, open areas accessible to four cells with two bunks each. Each bullpen was designed for eight men but was often more crowded than that. Even in the bullpen the men were practically breathing on each other. Surprisingly, in the Pontotoc County jail, no one else heard Dennis's dramatic confession.

Harjo testified that he enjoyed telling lies to Ron about Dennis, and vice versa. Greg Saunders asked him, "Why were you lying on Dennis and Ron Williamson? Why were you going back and forth and telling them lies about each other?"

"Just to watch and see what they say. They'll cut each other's throats if you watch them."

"And you were lying to Ron about Dennis, or lying to Dennis about Ron; is that right, kind of to get them at each other's throats?"

"Yeah, just see what—see what they'd say."

Harjo later admitted he did not understand the meaning of the word "perjury."

THE NEXT informant was Mike Tenney, the jailer-trainee who'd been used by the police to gather some dirt on Dennis. With little experience or training in law enforcement, Tenney began his career at the jail, and his first assignment had been Dennis Fritz. Eager to impress those who might hire him permanently, he spent a lot of time outside Dennis's cell, chatting about everything but especially about the Carter murder. He had plenty of advice. In his learned opinion, Dennis's situation looked grave, so the best thing to do would be to cut a deal, negotiate a plea bargain, save his own skin, and testify against Ron Williamson. Peterson would be fair.

Dennis had played along, careful to say nothing because anything might be repeated in court.

Being a rookie, Tenney had not testified much and had not fully rehearsed his lines. He began by trying to recall a story about Dennis and Ron hopping bars in Oklahoma City, a story not even remotely connected to the Carter murder. Saunders objected. Judge Jones sustained.

Then Tenney stepped into hot water when he testified that he and Dennis discussed the issue of a plea bargain. Twice he mentioned a plea bargain, a highly prejudicial issue because it strongly implied that Dennis had contemplated pleading guilty.

Greg Saunders objected loudly and moved for a mistrial. Judge Jones overruled.

Tenney finally managed to testify without the lawyers jumping to their feet. He explained to the jury that he had spoken often with Dennis, and after every conversation he had hustled back to the front desk at the jail and written down everything that was said. According to his handler, Gary Rogers, this was the way things were done. Good police work. And during one of their little chats Dennis allegedly said, "Let's say it might have happened this way. Maybe Ron went to the door and broke into Carter's apartment. And then, let's say, he went ahead and got a little. Ron got a little bit carried away and was going to teach her a lesson. She died. Let's say it happened this way. But I didn't see Ron kill her, so how can I tell the D.A. something I really didn't see."

After Tenney, the trial was recessed for the day, and Dennis was taken back to the jail. He carefully removed his new suit and put it on a hanger. A guard took it up front. He stretched out on his bunk, closed his eyes, and wondered how the nightmare would end. He knew the witnesses were lying, but did the jury?

THE NEXT morning Bill Peterson called to the stand Cindy McIntosh, who admitted being in jail on bad-check charges when she met both Dennis Fritz and Ron Williamson. She testified that she overheard the two talking, with Ron asking Dennis about the crime scene photos of Debbie Carter.

"Was she on the bed or on the floor?" Ron asked Dennis.

On the floor, Dennis said.

McIntosh admitted that she was not convicted on the check charges. "I paid off the checks, and they let me out," she said.

With the snitches out of the way, Peterson returned to more credible proof. Slightly more credible. He called to the stand four consecutive witnesses who worked for the state crime lab. Their impact on the jury was profound, as it always is. They were educated, trained, certified, experienced, and they worked for the state of Oklahoma. They were experts! And they were there to testify against the defendant, to help prove his guilt.

The first was the fingerprint expert, Jerry Peters. He explained to the jury that he examined twenty-one prints lifted from Debbie's apartment and car, nineteen of which were Debbie's. One matched Detective Dennis Smith, one matched Mike Carpenter, and not a single fingerprint belonged to either Dennis Fritz or Ron Williamson.

Odd that the fingerprint expert would testify that none of the fingerprints were left behind by the accused.

Larry Mullins described how he reprinted Debbie's palms the previous May when her body was exhumed. He gave the new prints to Jerry Peters, who suddenly saw things he hadn't seen four and a half years earlier.

The prosecution's theory, the same one to be used against Ron Williamson, was that during the prolonged and violent assault Debbie was wounded, her blood somehow ended up on her left palm, and this palm touched a tiny portion of Sheetrock just above the floor of her bedroom. Since the palm print did not belong to Ron or Dennis, and it certainly could not belong to the real killer, it had to be Debbie's.

MARY LONG was a criminalist who worked primarily with body fluids. She explained to the jury that about 20 percent of all people do not show their blood type in body fluids such as saliva, semen, and sweat. This segment is known in the trade as "non-secretors." Based on her examination of the blood and saliva samples from Ron and Dennis, she was certain that they were non-secretors.

The person who left the semen at the crime scene was probably a non-secretor too, though Long was not certain because the evidence was insufficient.

Thus, 80 percent of the population was eliminated from suspicion. Or "around" 80 percent, give or take a few points. Nonetheless, Fritz and Williamson now bore the ominous tag of "non-secretors."

Long's math was blown away on cross-examination when Greg Saunders forced her to admit that most of the blood and saliva samples she analyzed in the Carter case came from non-secretors. Of the twenty samples she examined, twelve were from non-secretors, including Fritz and Williamson.

Sixty percent of those in her pool of suspects were non-secretors, as opposed to the national average of only 20 percent.

It didn't matter. Her testimony excluded many and helped raise the suspicion hanging over the head of Dennis Fritz.

The state's last witness was by far its most effective. Peterson saved his knockout punch for the last round, and when Melvin Hett finished testifying the jury was convinced.

Hett was the OSBI hair man, a veteran testifier who'd helped send many people to prison.

FORENSIC examination of human hair got off to a rocky start as far back as 1882. In a Wisconsin case that year an "expert" for the state compared a "known" hair sample with one found at the crime scene and testified that the two came from the same source. The source was convicted, but on appeal the Wisconsin Supreme Court reversed and said, strongly, "Such evidence is of the most dangerous character."

Thousands of innocent defendants could have been spared if that decision had been heeded. Instead, police, investigators, crime labs, and prosecutors plowed ahead with the analysis of hair, which was often the only real clue left at a crime scene. Hair analysis became so common and so controversial that it was studied many times throughout the twentieth century.

Many of the studies indicated a high rate of error, and in response to the controversy the Law Enforcement Assistance Administration sponsored a crime lab proficiency program in 1978. Two hundred and forty of the best crime labs from throughout the country participated in the program, which compared their analytical findings on different types of evidence, including hair.

Their evaluation of hair was dreadful. A majority of the labs were incorrect four out of five times.

Other studies fueled the debate over hair testimony. In one, the accuracy increased when the examiner compared a crime scene hair with those of five different men, with no indication as to who was the cops' favored suspect. The chance of unintentional bias was removed. During the same study, though, the accuracy fell dramatically when the examiner was told who was the real "suspect." A preconceived conclusion can exist and slant the findings toward that suspect.

Hair experts tread on thin legal ice, and their opinions are weighted heavily with caveats such as: "The known hair and the questioned hair are microscopically consistent and could have come from the same source."

There is an excellent chance that they could *not* have come from the same source, but such testimony was rarely volunteered, at least on direct examination.

THE HUNDREDS of hairs collected at the crime scene by Dennis Smith took a delayed and tortuous route to the courtroom. At least three different OSBI analysts handled them, along with dozens of known hairs collected during the round-up-the-usual-suspects sweep made by Detectives Smith and Rogers shortly after the murder.

First Mary Long collected and organized all the hairs at the crime lab, but soon packed them up and handed them to Susan Land. By the time Susan Land received the hairs in March 1983, Dennis Smith and Gary Rogers were convinced the killers were Fritz and Williamson. To the dismay of the investigators, however, her report concluded that the hairs were microscopically consistent only with those of Debbie Carter.

For a brief period, Fritz and Williamson were off the hook, though they had no earthly means of knowing it. And, years later, their attorneys would not be informed of Susan Land's findings.

The state needed a second opinion.

In September 1983, citing the stress and strain of Land's workload, her boss ordered her to "transfer" the case to Melvin Hett. Such a transfer was highly unusual, and made more so by the fact that Land and Hett worked in different crime labs in different regions of the state. Land worked in the central crime lab in Oklahoma City. Hett worked in a branch in the town of Enid. His region covered eighteen counties, none of which happened to be Pontotoc.

Hett proved to be rather methodical. It took him twenty-seven months to analyze the hair, a lengthy period made even more remarkable by the fact that he was looking only at the samples from Fritz, Williamson, and Debbie Carter. The other twenty-one were not as important and could wait.

Since the police knew who killed Debbie Carter, they helpfully informed Melvin Hett. When he received the samples from Susan Land, the word "suspect" was written by the names of Fritz and Williamson.

Glen Gore had yet to provide samples to the Ada police.

On December 13, 1985, three years after the murder, Melvin Hett finished his first report, finding that seventeen of the questioned hairs were microscopically consistent with known samples of Fritz and Williamson.

After spending more than two years and over two hundred hours analyzing the first samples, Hett picked up steam considerably and knocked out the other twenty-one in less than a month. On January 9, 1986, he finished his second report, finding that all the other samples taken from the young men of Ada were consistent with nothing found in the Carter apartment.

Still Glen Gore had not been asked to provide samples.

It was tedious work, and not without its uncertainties. Hett flip-flopped several times as he labored with his microscope. Once he was certain a hair belonged to Debbie Carter, but later changed his mind and decided it came from Fritz.

Such is the nature of hair analysis. Hett flatly contradicted some of Susan Land's findings, and even managed to impugn his own work. He initially found that a total of thirteen pubic hairs came from Fritz and only two from Williamson. Later, though, he changed his numbers—twelve for Fritz and two for Williamson. Then eleven for Fritz, plus two scalp hairs.

For some reason, Gore's hair finally entered the picture in July 1986.

Someone down at the Ada Police Department woke up and realized Gore had been neglected. Dennis Smith collected scalp and pubic hair from Gore and from the confessed killer Ricky Joe Simmons and mailed them to Melvin Hett, who, evidently, was quite busy because nothing happened for a year. In July 1987, Gore was asked again to provide samples. Why? he asked. Because the police couldn't find his earlier samples.

Months passed with no report from Hett. In the spring of 1988, the trials were approaching, and there was still no report from Hett on the Gore and Simmons samples.

On April 7, 1988, after the Fritz trial was under way, Melvin Hett finally issued his third and last report. The Gore hairs were not consistent with the questioned hairs. It took Hett almost two years to reach this conclusion, and his timing was beyond suspicious. It was another clear indication that the prosecution so firmly believed in the guilt of Fritz and Williamson that it found it unnecessary to wait until all the hair analysis was completed.

IN SPITE of its perils and uncertainties, Melvin Hett was a staunch believer in hair analysis. He and Peterson became friendly, and before the Fritz trial Hett passed along scientific articles touting the reliability of evidence that was famously unreliable. He did not, however, provide the prosecutor with any of the numerous articles condemning hair analysis and testimony.

Two months before the Fritz trial, Hett drove to Chicago and delivered his findings to a private lab called McCrone. There, one Richard Bisbing, an acquaintance of Hett's, reviewed his work. Bisbing had been hired by Wanda Fritz to review the hair evidence and testify at trial. To pay him, Wanda was forced to sell Dennis's car.

Bisbing proved to be far more efficient with his time, but the results were just as conflicting.

In less than six hours, Bisbing refuted almost all of Hett's findings. Looking at only the eleven pubic hairs that Hett was certain were microscopically consistent with Fritz, Bisbing found that only three were accurate. Only three "could" have come from Dennis Fritz. Hett was wrong about the other eight.

Undaunted by such a low estimation of his work by another expert, Hett drove back to Oklahoma, ready to testify without changing his opinion.

HE TOOK the stand on Friday afternoon, April 8, and immediately launched into a windy lecture loaded with scientific terms and words, designed more to impress the jurors than to inform them. Dennis, with a college degree and experience teaching science, could not follow Hett, and he was certain the jurors couldn't, either. He glanced at them several times. They were hopelessly lost, but they were obviously impressed with this expert. He knew so much!

Hett tossed out words like "morphology," "cortex," "scale protrusion," "shallow gapping," "cortical fusi," and "ovoid bodies" as if everyone in the courtroom knew exactly what he meant. He seldom slowed long enough to explain himself.

Hett was the star expert, with an aura of reliability that was bolstered by his experience, vocabulary, confidence, and strong conclusions that some of the known hairs of Dennis Fritz were consistent with some of those found at the crime scene. Six times during his direct testimony he said that Dennis's hair and the suspicious hairs were microscopically consistent and could have come from the same source. Not once did he share with the jury the truth that the hairs could have just as easily *not* come from the same source.

Throughout his testimony, Bill Peterson continually referred to "the Defendant Ron Williamson and the Defendant Dennis Fritz." At the time, Ron was locked away in solitary confinement, strumming his guitar, completely unaware that he was being tried in absentia and that things were not going too well.

Hett wrapped up his testimony by summarizing for the jury his findings. Eleven pubic hairs and two scalp hairs could have come from Dennis. It was the same eleven pubic hairs he'd driven to the McCrone laboratories in Chicago and shown to Richard Bisbing for a second opinion.

The cross-examination by Greg Saunders yielded little. Hett was forced to admit that hair analysis is too speculative to be used for positive identifications. Like most experts, he was able to talk his way out of tough questions by using his endless supply of vague scientific terms.

When he was excused, the state rested.

THE FIRST witness called by the defense was Dennis Fritz. He testified about his past, his friendship with Ron, and so on. He admitted that he had been convicted of cultivating marijuana in 1973 and had lied about this on his application to teach school at Noble seven years later. His reason for doing so was simple; he needed a job. He denied repeatedly that he had ever met Debbie Carter and certainly knew nothing about her murder.

He was then handed over to Bill Peterson for cross-examination.

There's an old adage in bad trial lawyering that when you don't have the facts, do a lot of yelling. Peterson stomped to the podium, glared at the murderer with the suspicious hair, and began yelling.

Within seconds, Judge Jones called him to the bench for a little chastising. "You may not like this defendant," the judge whispered sternly, "but you're not to be angry in this courtroom."

"I'm not angry," Peterson angrily shot back.

"Yes you are. This is the first time you've raised your voice to this bench."

"All right."

Peterson was incensed that Fritz had lied on a job application. Thus, Dennis simply could not be believed. And Peterson dramatically produced another lie, a form Dennis had filled out when he hocked a pistol at a pawnshop in Durant, Oklahoma. Again, Dennis had tried to hide his felony for cultivating pot.

Two clear incidences of outright deception; neither, of course, had anything to do with the Carter murder. Peterson harangued him for as much mileage as he could possibly beat out of his self-confessed lying.

It was ironic, and would have been comical had things not been so tense, that Peterson worked himself into such an indignant lather over a witness who couldn't tell the truth. This, from a prosecutor whose case was built on the testimony of convicts and snitches.

When Peterson finally decided to move on, he had no place to go. He hopscotched from the allegations of one prosecution witness to another, but Dennis did a credible job of holding his ground. After a contentious one-hour cross, Peterson sat down.

The only other witness called by Greg Saunders was Richard Bisbing, who explained to the jury that he disagreed with most of the conclusions reached by Melvin Hett.

It was late on Friday afternoon, and Judge Jones adjourned court for the weekend. Dennis made the short walk back to the jail, changed clothes, and tried to relax in his stuffy rat hole of a cell. He was convinced the state had failed to prove him guilty, but he was far from confident. He had seen the nasty looks from the jurors when they were shown the gruesome crime scene photos. He had watched them as they listened to Melvin Hett and believed his conclusions.

For Dennis, it was a very long weekend.

CLOSING arguments began Monday morning. Nancy Shew went first for the state and plodded through a recitation of each of the prosecution's witnesses and what had been said.

Greg Saunders countered with an argument that not much at all had been proven by the state; that its burden of proving Dennis guilty beyond a reasonable doubt had clearly not been met; that this was nothing more than a case of guilt by association; and that the jury should find his client not guilty.

Bill Peterson had the last shot. For almost an hour, he rambled on and on, regurgitating the high points from each of his witnesses, trying desperately to convince the jurors that his crooks and snitches were worth believing.

The jury retired to deliberate at noon, and six hours later came back to announce it was split eleven to one. Judge Jones sent them back with the promise of dinner. Around 8:00 p.m., they returned with a verdict of guilty.

Dennis listened to the verdict in a frozen silence, stunned because he was innocent, shocked because he'd been convicted with such paltry proof. He wanted to lash out at the jurors, the judge, the cops, the system, but the trial was not over.

Yet he was not totally surprised. He had watched the jurors and seen their distrust. They represented the town of Ada, and the town needed a conviction. If the cops and Peterson were so convinced Dennis was the killer, then he must be.

He closed his eyes and thought of his daughter, Elizabeth, now fourteen and certainly old enough to understand guilt and innocence. Now that he'd been convicted, how would he ever convince her he was innocent?

As the crowd filed out of the courthouse, Peggy Stillwell fainted on the courthouse lawn. She was exhausted and overcome by emotion and grief. She was rushed to the nearest hospital but was soon released.

With the issue of guilt now settled, the trial moved quickly into the penalty phase. In theory, the jury would determine the sentence based on aggravating circumstances presented by the state and designed to get the death penalty, and mitigating circumstances presented by the defendant that would, hopefully, save his life.

The Fritz penalty phase was very brief. Peterson called to the stand Rusty Featherstone, who finally got to tell the jury that Dennis had admitted to him that he and Ron had been barhopping in Norman some four months before the murder. That was the extent of his testimony. The two murder suspects had actually driven seventy miles to Norman and spent a long night in the clubs and lounges.

The next and last witness expanded on this profound story. Her name was Lavita Brewer, and while having a drink in the bar at a Holiday Inn in Norman, she bumped into Fritz and Williamson. After several drinks, the three left together. Brewer got in the backseat. Dennis was behind the wheel. Ron was next to him, and away they went. It was raining. Dennis was driving fast, running red lights and such, and at some point early in the adventure Brewer became hysterical. Though the two never touched or threatened her, she decided that she really wanted to get out. But Dennis wouldn't stop. This went on for fifteen or twenty minutes, then the car slowed enough for her to open the door and jump. She ran to a pay phone and called the police.

No one was injured. No charges were filed. No one was ever convicted.

But to Bill Peterson, the incident was clear proof that Dennis Fritz was an ongoing threat to society and should be put to death to protect other young ladies. Lavita Brewer was the best, and only, witness he could produce.

During his impassioned plea for death to the jury, Peterson looked at Dennis, pointed his finger, and said, "Dennis Fritz, you deserve to die for what you and Ron Williamson did to Debra Sue Carter."

To which Dennis interrupted and said to the jury, "I did not kill Debbie Carter."

Two hours later, the jury returned with a sentence of life in prison. When the verdict was read, Dennis stood, faced the jury, and said, "Ladies and gentlemen of the jury, I would just like to say . . ."

"Excuse me," said Judge Jones.

"Dennis, you can't do that," Greg Saunders said.

But Dennis was not to be denied. He continued: "My Lord, Jesus in heaven knows I didn't do this. I just want you to know that I forgive you. I'll be praying for you."

Back in his cell, in the muggy darkness of his little corner of hell, he found no relief whatsoever in the fact that he had avoided a death sentence. He was thirty-eight years old, an innocent man without a violent tendency in his being, and the prospect of spending the rest of his life in prison was utterly overwhelming.

CHAPTER 9

Annette Hudson had closely followed the Fritz trial by reading the daily reports in the *Ada Evening News*. On Tuesday, April 12, the front-page headline read, "Fritz Found Guilty in Carter Murder."

As usual, the story mentioned her brother. "Ron Williamson, who is also charged with first degree murder in Carter's murder, is scheduled to be tried here on April 21." In fact, all six articles covering the Fritz trial mentioned Ron's involvement and upcoming trial.

How do they expect to find an impartial jury? Annette asked herself repeatedly. If one co-defendant is found guilty, how could the other one get a fair trial in the same town?

She bought Ron a new gray suit, an extra pair of navy slacks, two white shirts, two ties, and new shoes.

ON APRIL 20, the day before his trial began, Ron was taken to court for a chat with Judge Jones. The judge was worried that the defendant might be disruptive, a valid concern given his history. As Ron stood before the bench, the judge said, "I want to see where we stand on your attendance tomorrow and make sure that when you're here that there won't be any disturbances. Do you understand my concern?"

Ron: "As long as they don't start telling me that I've killed somebody."

Judge Jones: "Well, you understand that they're going to do that?"

Ron: "Well, I understand that, but it's not right."

Judge Jones knew that Ron had been a great athlete, so he used the analogy of a sports contest. "It's kind of like a sporting event as far as the adversary process. Each side has an opportunity to be on offense, and they have the opportunity to be on defense, but you can't take issue with the fact that each side gets these opportunities. That's just part of the process."

Ron: "Yeah, but I'm the football being kicked."

FOR THE prosecution, the Fritz trial was a nice warm-up for the main event. Virtually the same witnesses would be used, and in much the same order. But in the next trial, the state had two additional advantages. First, the defendant was mentally incompetent and prone to knock over tables and blurt out obscenities, behavior that most people, including jurors, frowned on. He could be eerily frightening; he scared people. Second, his lawyer was blind, and alone. Since the court-appointed co-counsel, Baber, had withdrawn from the case April 1, there had been no replacement. Barney was quick on his feet and a great cross-examiner, but not effective arguing over fingerprints, photographs, and hair analysis.

For the defense, the trial couldn't start soon enough. Barney was sick of Ron Williamson and frustrated with the sheer number of hours the case was draining away from his other, paying clients. And he was afraid of Ron, physically afraid. He arranged to have his son, not a lawyer, sit closely behind Ron at the defense table. Barney planned to sit as far away as possible, which wasn't far at all, and if Ron made a sudden aggressive move on Barney, then his son was to jump Ron from the rear and take him down.

Such was the level of trust between lawyer and client.

But few people in the packed courtroom on April 21 realized that the son was protecting the father from the client. Most of those present were potential jurors, strangers to such settings and uncertain as to who was who. There were also reporters, curious lawyers, and the usual assortment of gossips that trials in small towns attract. Especially murder trials.

Annette Hudson and Renee Simmons sat in the front row, as close to Ronnie as possible. Several of Annette's close friends had volunteered to sit with her throughout the trial and offer support. She declined. Her brother was sick and unpredictable, and she didn't want her friends to see him in cuffs and shackles. Nor did she want them subjected to explicit and gruesome testimony. She and Renee had suffered through the preliminary hearing and gotten a strong taste of what was coming at trial.

There were no friends there for Ron.

Across the aisle the Carter family held down the front row, the same place they'd been during the Fritz trial. The opposing sides tried not to make eye contact.

It was a Thursday, almost a full year after the exhumation of the victim's body and the arrests of Ron and Dennis. Ron's last significant treatment had been at Central State some thirteen months earlier. At Barney's request, he'd been seen once by Norma Walker in Ada, a brief visit that began and ended like most of his visits to the local clinic. For a year his medications, when he received any at all, had been erratically dispensed by the jailers. The time spent in his solitary hole in the jail had done nothing to improve his mental health.

Yet his mental health concerned no one but his family. Neither the prosecution, the defense, nor the court itself had raised the issue.

It was time for a trial.

THE EXCITEMENT of opening day quickly wore off as the tedium of jury selection hit hard. Hours passed as the lawyers questioned the pool and Judge Jones methodically dismissed one after the other.

Ron, for his part, behaved himself. He looked nice—a haircut, a shave, new clothes. He took pages of notes, all under the eyes of Barney's son, who, though as bored as the others, managed to keep an eye on the client. Ron had no idea why he was being watched so closely.

Late in the afternoon, the final twelve were chosen—seven men, five women, all white. Judge Jones gave them their instructions and sent them home. They would not be sequestered.

Annette and Renee were hopeful. One juror was the son-in-law of a neighbor who lived across the street from Annette. Another was related to a Pentecostal preacher who, surely, knew of Juanita Williamson and her devotion to her church. Another was a distant cousin of a Williamson relative by marriage.

Most of the jurors looked familiar. Annette and Renee had seen them at one time or another around Ada. It was indeed a small town.

THE JURORS were back by nine the following morning. Nancy Shew gave the opening statement for the state, almost a carbon copy of the one she had used for Fritz. Barney deferred his initial remarks until after the state's case-in-chief was finished.

The first witness called by the prosecution was again Glen Gore, but things did not go as planned. After stating his name, Gore went silent and refused to testify. He invited Judge Jones to hold him in contempt; what did it matter? He was serving forty years anyway. His reasons were not clear, but perhaps had something to do with the fact that he was doing time at the state prison, where snitches were held in low regard by their peers, as opposed to the Pontotoc County jail, where snitching was rampant.

After a few moments of confusion, it was decided by Judge Jones that Gore's testimony from the preliminary hearing the previous July would be read to the jury. This was done, and though the impact was somewhat lessened, the jury still heard Gore's fictitious account of seeing Ron at the Coachlight the night of the murder.

Barney was robbed of the opportunity to grill Gore on his numerous felonies and their violent nature. Nor did the defense get the chance to question the witness on his whereabouts and movements on the night of the murder.

With Gore out of the way, the state's case quickly got back on track. Tommy Glover, Gina Vietta, and Charlie Carter gave the same testimony for the third time.

Gary Allen told the same strange story of hearing two men squirt themselves with a water hose at 3:30 a.m. early in December 1982, but emphatically could not identify Ron Williamson. The other man might have been Fritz, but maybe not.

THE TRUTH was that Gary Allen couldn't identify anyone and had no idea when the incident occurred. He was a drug addict, well known to the police. He knew Dennis Smith because they had attended classes at the local college.

Smith approached him shortly after the murder and asked if he'd seen or heard anything suspicious in the early hours of December 8. Allen said he had seen two men squirting themselves with a water hose at the house next door, but could not remember the date. Dennis Smith and Gary Rogers jumped to the conclusion that it was Fritz and Williamson washing off the blood of Debbie Carter. They pressed Allen for details, even showed him a photo of the murder scene. They suggested that the two men were Fritz and Williamson, but Allen could not, and would not, identify the two.

Shortly before the trial, Gary Rogers stopped by Allen's apartment and again suggested details. Wasn't it really Fritz and Williamson, and didn't he see them outside, early in the morning, sometime around December 8?

No, Allen could not be certain. Rogers brushed his coat away from his hip so Allen could see his service revolver. He said that Allen might get lead poisoning if his memory didn't improve. It did, but just barely enough to testify.

DENNIS SMITH then walked the jury through the crime scene, the photographing, fingerprinting, evidence gathering. Photos were passed to the jurors, with the same predictable reactions when they saw the victim. Using a fire-truck ladder, the police photographer had shot some aerials of Debbie's apartment. Peterson used one of them and asked Smith to tell the jury where the Williamson house was located. Only a few blocks away.

Barney said, "Let me see those photos," and they were handed over. As was the unwritten rule in Ada, Barney took the photos and stepped outside with his assistant, Linda. She described each one to him in detail.

The direct examination was matter-of-fact, but Barney had some fireworks on cross. He'd always thought it was odd that the two alleged killers could pull off such a heinous rape and murder without leaving a single fingerprint. He asked Smith to explain the best surfaces for an investigator to dust for prints. Smooth, hard surfaces—glass, mirrors, hard plastic, painted wood, and so on. Then he walked Smith through the small apartment and forced him to admit that he had neglected many obvious locations—kitchen appliances, the glass in the bedroom window that was left open, bathroom fixtures, door facings, mirrors. The list grew and grew, and the impression was clear that Smith had done a poor job of checking for prints.

With the witness on his heels, Barney hammered away. When he became too aggressive, either Bill Peterson or Nancy Shew would object to his tactics, and their objections usually brought an acerbic retort from Barney.

Gary Rogers took the stand next and continued a detailed summary of the investigation. But his most important contribution to the state's case was recounting for the jury the dream confession Ron made the day after he was arrested. It sounded just fine on direct exam, but Barney had a few problems with it.

He was quite curious as to why the statement was not recorded. Rogers admitted that the police owned and often used a video camera, and when pressed by Barney, he admitted that sometimes it wasn't used when the investigators weren't sure what the witness might say. Why run the risk of recording something harmful to the prosecution but helpful to the defendant?

Rogers admitted that the police department owned a tape recorder and that he knew how to operate it. It wasn't used in the interview with Ron, because that would not have been within their normal procedures. Barney didn't buy that, either.

Rogers also admitted that the police department had a ready supply of pencils and paper, but stumbled badly when he tried to explain why he and Rusty Featherstone did not allow Ron to write his own statement. They refused to let him see it, either, after they were through with it, and Barney piled on the suspicion. As he drilled Rogers about his unusual procedures, Rogers made a huge mistake. He mentioned Ron's 1983 interrogation, on video, in which Ron had steadfastly denied any involvement.

Barney was incredulous. Why had he not been told of this tape? Pretrial discovery required the prosecution to hand over all exculpatory evidence. Barney had timely filed the proper motions, months earlier. The prior September the court had ordered the prosecution to provide defense counsel with all statements made by Ron relative to the murder investigation.

How could the police and prosecutor sit on the tape for four and a half years and hide it from the defense?

Barney had very few witnesses at his disposal, since the case against Ron was basically an "admission" case, one in which the state was using a variety of witnesses, albeit a rather sketchy collection, to testify that Ron, at various times and in various ways, admitted to the murder. The only real way to fight such testimony was to deny it, and the only person who could deny making the admissions was Ron himself. Barney planned to put Ron on the stand in his own defense, but he was terrified of the prospect.

The 1983 tape would have been a powerful tool to show the jury. Four and a half years earlier, long before the prosecution had put together its roster of shady witnesses, and long before Ron had such a lengthy criminal record to answer to, he had sat before a camera and repeatedly denied any involvement.

In a famous 1963 decision, *Brady v. Maryland*, the U.S. Supreme Court held that "the suppression by the prosecution of evidence favorable to an accused upon request violates due process where the evidence is material either to guilt or to punishment, irrespective of the good faith or bad faith of the prosecution."

Investigators have all the resources. Frequently, they uncover witnesses or other evidence favorable to a suspect or defendant. For decades they could simply ignore this exculpatory evidence and proceed with a prosecution. *Brady* leveled the field and instantly became ingrained in criminal procedure. A *Brady* request is one of many routine motions a criminal defense lawyer files early in the case. A *Brady* motion. A *Brady* hearing. *Brady* material. "I nailed him on *Brady*." The case worked its way into the vernacular of criminal law practice.

Now Barney stood before Judge Jones, with Rogers still in the witness chair and Peterson studying his shoes, with a clear *Brady* violation. He moved for a mistrial and was overruled. Judge Jones promised to hold a hearing on the matter—after the trial was over!

It was late on Friday, and everyone was tired. Judge Jones recessed until 8:30 Monday morning. Ron was handcuffed, surrounded by deputies, and hustled out of the courtroom. He had behaved himself so far, and it had not gone unnoticed.

The front page of Sunday's *Ada Evening News* ran the headline "Williamson Controlled During Trial's First Day."

THE FIRST witness Monday was Dr. Fred Jordan, who, for the third time in the same seat, testified in detail about the autopsy and cause of death. It was also the third time that Peggy Stillwell had suffered through it, and the ordeal was certainly not getting any easier. Fortunately, she could not see the photos they were passing around to the jurors. She could see their reactions, and that was enough.

Dr. Jordan was followed by Tony Vick, Fritz's neighbor; Donna Walker, the convenience store clerk; and Letha Caldwell, the late-night acquaintance—all three as useless as they'd been in the Fritz trial.

The fireworks started when Terri Holland was called next. During the preliminary hearing she'd been able to spin her yarns with no fear of getting caught. Now, though, with Ron glaring at her and knowing the truth, things would be different.

The tales started immediately—Holland was describing statements Ron allegedly made in jail about Debbie Carter—and it was obvious Ron was about to explode. He shook his head, clenched his jaws, stared at Holland as if he'd like to kill her. Finally she said, "He said if she'd went ahead and went with him, he'd never had to kill her."

Ron said, "Oh," loudly.

Nancy Shew asked, "Did you ever hear a phone conversation that he made that related to Debbie Carter in any way?"

Holland: "I was working in the laundry; I was a trustee. Ron was on the phone to his mom, and he told his mother—he was trying to get her to bring him cigarettes or something, I'm not sure what, but they—

he was hollering at her. And he told her that if she didn't that he'd have to kill her like he did Debbie Carter."

To which Ron yelled, "She is lying!"

Nancy Shew continued: "Ms. Holland, did you ever hear him describe or talk about any of the details of Debbie Carter's death?"

Holland: "He was telling—I guess in the bullpen, the guys back there—that he—he said he shoved a Coke bottle up her ass and her panties down her throat."

Ron jumped up, pointed at her, and yelled, "You are lying! I ain't never said nothing like that in my life! I did not kill this girl, and I call you a liar."

Barney: "Be still, Ron."

Ron: "I don't even know what you're—I mean, you're going to pay for that."

There was a pause as everyone caught their breath, and Barney slowly rose to his feet. He knew exactly what was coming—repair work. The prosecution's star witness had botched a couple of crucial facts—the panties and the Coke bottle—a common problem with fabricated testimony.

With the courtroom tense, a lying witness exposed, and Barney already waiting to pounce, Nancy Shew tried to fix the damage.

Shew: "Ms. Holland, let me ask you about the details you were just relating. As far as your memory goes, are you sure about the objects that he stated he used? You said Coke bottle."

Barney: "If the court please, if the court please—I heard what she said, and I don't want this district attorney changing her testimony any either, and I object to that."

Holland: "He said Coke bottle or catsup bottle or bottle—"

Barney: "See what I mean. If the court please."

Holland: "It's been four years."

Ron: "Yeah, and you're a—"

Barney: "Hush."

Shew: "Ms. Holland, can you—I know you overheard different things—"

Barney: "If the court please—"

Shew: "Can you think of—"

Barney: "I'm going to object to this leading and suggestive questioning that the District Attorney is doing."

The Court: "State a question without posturing anything in front of it."

Shew: "Did he ever tell why—you said that he said that he killed—"

Holland: "He wanted to sleep with Debbie Carter."

Ron: "You're a liar!"

Barney: "Shut up."

Ron (*standing*): "She's a liar. I ain't going to sit for it. I didn't kill Debbie Carter, and you are lying."

Barney: "Ronnie, come on, sit down."

Peterson: "Judge, can we have a recess, please. Barney—I object to counsel's sidebar comments, Your Honor."

Barney: "These aren't sidebar comments, if the court please."

The Court: "Wait a minute."

Barney: "I'm talking to this defendant."

The Court: "Wait a minute. Ask your next question. Mr. Williamson, I must admonish you that you are not allowed to speak from the chair you are now in."

Shew: "Ms. Holland, can you recall if he ever said why he did what he did?"

Holland: "Because she wouldn't sleep with him."

Ron: "You're lying, damn it, tell the truth. I never killed nobody in my life."

Barney: "Judge, I'd like to ask if we could have a recess for a few minutes here."

The Court: "All right. Remember your instructions. The jury may step down."

Ron: "Could I speak to her, please. Let me talk to her. What is she talking about?"

A SHORT break cooled things down. With the jury absent, Judge Jones had a nice chat with Ron, who assured His Honor that he could behave himself. When the jury returned, the judge explained that the case was to be decided on the evidence only, and nothing else. Not comments from the attorneys, and certainly not comments and actions by the defendant.

But Ron's chilling threat of "You're going to pay for that" was clearly heard by the jurors. They, too, were afraid of him.

During the melee, Nancy Shew was unable to completely resuscitate her witness. With leading and suggestive questions she was able to transform the Coke bottle to a catsup bottle, but the little detail of the panties in the mouth went uncorrected. The bloody washcloth was never mentioned by Terri Holland.

THE NEXT hot-check artist called by the state to help find the truth was Cindy McIntosh, but the poor girl was so confused she couldn't remember which story she was expected to tell. She drew a blank, and was finally dismissed without completing her duties.

Mike Tenney and John Christian told of their late-night chats with Ron in his cell and some of the strange things he said. Neither bothered to mention that Ron repeatedly denied any involvement in the murder and would often scream for hours that he was innocent.

After a quick lunch, Peterson lined up the OSBI agents in the same order as in the Fritz trial. Jerry Peters went first and told his story of reprinting Debbie's hands after the exhumation because he was uncertain about a tiny portion of her left palm. Barney tried to pin him down on exactly how and why this became an issue four and a half years after the autopsy, but Peters proved elusive. Did he worry about his initial findings for such a long period of time? Or did Bill Peterson call at random one day early in 1987 and make some suggestions? Peters was vague.

Larry Mullins offered the same opinion as Peters—the bloody print on the Sheetrock belonged to Debbie Carter, not some mysterious killer.

Mary Long testified that Ron Williamson was a non-secretor, thus placed squarely in the minority of about 20 percent of the population. Debbie's rapist was probably in this group. With some effort, Barney pinned her down on the exact number of people she had tested and arrived at a total of twenty, including the victim. And of that number, twelve were non-secretors, or 60 percent of her pool. He then had some fun with the math.

Susan Land testified briefly. She had begun the hair analysis in the Carter case but then transferred it to Melvin Hett. When pressed by Barney as to why, she said: "At that particular time I was working on numerous homicides and all the stress and strain, I just didn't feel that I could be objective, and I didn't want to make a mistake on something."

Melvin Hett was then sworn in and was soon delivering the same scholarly lecture he'd given a few days earlier in the Fritz trial. He described the laborious process of microscopically comparing known hair with questioned hair. He did a fine job of giving the impression that hair analysis was thoroughly reliable. It had to be; it was used all the time in criminal trials. Hett told the jury he'd worked on "thousands" of hair cases. He produced some stock diagrams of different types of hair and explained that hair has between twenty-five and thirty distinguishable characteristics.

When he finally got around to Ron Williamson, he testified that two pubic hairs found on the bed were microscopically consistent and could have come from the same source—Ron Williamson. And, two scalp hairs found on the bloody washcloth were microscopically consistent and could have come from the same source—Ron Williamson.

The four hairs could just as easily *not* have come from Ron, but Hett didn't mention this.

With a slip of the tongue, Hett stepped out of bounds. As he was testifying about the two scalp hairs, he said, "These were the only scalp hairs that matched or were consistent with Ron Williamson."

The word "match" is off-limits in hair analysis because it is extremely misleading. Laypeople on the jury may struggle with the concept of hairs being microscopically consistent, but they have no trouble understanding a match. It's quicker, cleaner, easier to grasp. Like a fingerprint, a match eliminates all doubt.

After Hett used the word "match" for the second time, Barney objected. Judge Jones overruled him, saying he could deal with it on cross-examination.

Hett's most egregious act, though, was the manner in which he testified. Instead of educating the jurors, Hett simply blessed them with his opinions.

To help the jury evaluate the evidence, most hair analysts bring into court enlarged photos of the hair in dispute. A photo of a known hair is mounted next to a questioned hair, and the expert goes into great detail explaining similarities and dissimilarities. As Hett said, there are about twenty-five different characteristics in hair, and a good examiner will show the jury exactly what he or she is talking about.

Hett did nothing of the sort. After working on the Carter murder for nearly five years, hundreds of hours, three different reports, he did not show the jury one single enlarged photo of his work. Not a single hair taken from Ron Williamson was compared with a single hair taken from Debbie's apartment.

Hett was, in effect, telling the jury to simply trust him. Don't ask for proof, just believe his opinions.

THE CLEAR implication of Hett's testimony was that four of the hairs found in the Carter apartment came from Ron Williamson. Indeed, this was the sole purpose of putting Hett on the witness stand.

His presence and testimony highlighted the unfairness of expecting an indigent defendant to get a fair trial without giving him access to forensic experts. Barney had requested such assistance months earlier, and Judge Jones had declined.

Judge Jones should have known better. Three years earlier, a major case from Oklahoma landed at the U.S. Supreme Court, and its outcome rattled the criminal courts of the country. In *Ake v. Oklahoma*, the Court said: "When a State brings its judicial power to bear on an indigent defendant in a criminal proceeding, it must take steps to assure that the defendant has a fair opportunity to present his defense . . . Justice cannot be equal where, simply as a result of his poverty, a defendant is denied the opportunity to participate meaningfully in a judicial proceeding in which his liberty is at stake."

The *Ake* decision required that the basic tools of an adequate defense be provided by the state to an indigent defendant. It was ignored by Judge Jones in both the Fritz and the Williamson trials.

Forensic evidence was a crucial part of the prosecution. Jerry Peters, Larry Mullins, Mary Long, Susan Land, and Melvin Hett were all experts. Ron was left with only Barney, a competent courtroom advocate, but, sadly, one unable to see the evidence.

THE STATE rested after Melvin Hett. At the beginning of the trial, Barney waived his opening statement, reserving it for the start of his defense. It was a risky maneuver. Most defense lawyers can't wait to address the jurors early on to begin sowing doubt about the state's evidence. The opening statement and the closing argument are the only stages in a trial when a lawyer can directly address the jury, and they are opportunities too ripe to pass up.

Barney, after the state rested, surprised everyone by again waiving his right to an opening statement. No reason was given, none was required, but it was a very unusual tactic.

Barney called to the stand seven straight jailers. All denied they had ever heard Ron Williamson in any way implicate himself in the Carter murder.

Wayne Joplin was the Pontotoc County court clerk. Barney called him as a witness to review the records of Terri Holland. She had been arrested in New Mexico in October 1984 and hauled back to Ada and placed in jail, where she promptly helped solve two sensational murder cases, though she waited two years to inform the police about Ron's dramatic confession to her. She pleaded guilty to the bad-check charges, received a five-year sentence with three suspended, and was ordered to pay court costs of $70, restitution of $527.09, $225 for attorneys' fees at the rate of $50 per month, $10 a month to the Department of Corrections, and $50 a month to the Crime Victims Compensation Fund.

She made one payment of $50 in May 1986, then all was apparently forgiven.

Barney was down to his last witness, the defendant himself. Allowing Ron to testify was risky. He was volatile—earlier in the day he had lashed out at Terri Holland—and the jury was already afraid of him. He had a criminal record, which Peterson would hammer him with, attacking his credibility. No one was certain how much, if any, of his meds he was receiving. He was angry and unpredictable, and, worst of all, he had not been prepped by his lawyer.

Barney asked for a conference at the bench and said to Judge Jones: "Now then, the fun starts. I'd like to have a recess to do whatever I can as far as having any kind of calming influence on him. He seems—well, he hasn't been jumping up and down. I'm ready to have a recess anyway."

"You're down to one possible witness?" Judge Jones asked.

"I'm down to one, yeah, and I think you're using the right term too, Judge."

When they adjourned for the noon recess, Ron was led downstairs on his way to the jail. He saw the victim's father and yelled, "Charlie Carter, I did not kill your daughter!" The deputies hustled him away even faster.

At 1:00 p.m., he was sworn in. After a few preliminary questions, he denied having any conversation with Terri Holland and denied ever meeting Debbie Carter.

When did he first learn of Carter's death? Barney asked. "On December the 8th, my sister, Annette Hudson, called over to the house, and mother answered the telephone. And I heard mother say, 'Well, I know Ronnie didn't do it because he was at home.' And I asked mother what that was about. She said that Annette had called and said that there had been a girl killed in our neighborhood."

The lack of preparation became more apparent a few minutes later when Barney asked the witness about first meeting Gary Rogers.

Ron said, "And it was just shortly after that that I went down to the station and gave a lie detector test."

Barney almost choked: "Ronnie, don't—you're not supposed to talk about that."

Any mention of a polygraph in front of the jury was prohibited. Had the state done so, a mistrial would have been in order. No one had bothered to inform Ron. Seconds later he stepped out of bounds again when he described an incident with Dennis Fritz. "I was with Dennis Fritz and we were going down the road and I told him that Dennis Smith had called me back and told me the results of the polygraph test had been inconclusive."

Barney plowed ahead and changed the subject. They talked briefly about Ron's conviction on the forged instrument. Then a few questions about where he was on the night of the murder. Barney finished with a feeble "Did you kill Debbie Carter?"

"No sir. I did not."

"I believe that's all."

In his haste to get his client on and off the stand with as little damage as possible, Barney neglected to rebut most of the allegations from the state's witnesses. Ron could have explained his "dream confession" to Rogers and Featherstone the night after his arrest. He could have explained his jailhouse conversations with John Christian and Mike Tenney. He could have diagrammed the jail and explained to the jury that it was impossible for Terri Holland to hear what she heard without others doing so. He could have flatly denied the statements of Glen Gore, Gary Allen, Tony Vick, Donna Walker, and Letha Caldwell.

Like all prosecutors, Peterson was itching for a shot at the defendant on cross-examination. What he didn't expect was for the defendant to be thoroughly unintimidated. He began by making much of Ron's friendship with Dennis Fritz, now a convicted murderer.

"Isn't it a fact, Mr. Williamson, that you and Dennis Fritz are about the only friends each of you got; isn't that right?"

"Well, let's put it like this," Ron answered coolly. "You framed him, and now you're trying to frame me." The words echoed around the courtroom as Peterson caught his breath.

Changing the subject, he asked if Ron remembered meeting Debbie Carter, something he continually denied. The question was asked again, and Ron blurted, "Peterson, I'm going to make this clear to you one more time."

Judge Jones intervened and instructed the witness to answer the question. Again, Ron denied ever meeting Debbie Carter.

Peterson stomped and strutted around, throwing a few jabs and hitting air. He got into trouble again when he returned to his fiction. "Do you know where you were after ten o'clock on December the 7th?"

Ron: "At home."

Peterson: "Doing what?"

Ron: "After ten o'clock five years ago, I could have been watching television or asleep."

Peterson: "Isn't it a fact you went out that door, went down that alley—"

Ron: "Huh-uh, bud. No way."

Peterson: ". . . went down that alley."

Ron: "No way man."

Peterson: "You and Dennis Fritz."

Ron: "You're—no way. No way."

Peterson: "Walked up to that apartment."

Ron: "No way."

Peterson: "Do you know where Dennis Fritz was that night?"

Ron: "I know he wasn't at Debbie Carter's. That's the way I'll put it."

Peterson: "How do you know he wasn't at Debbie Carter's?"

Ron: "Because you framed him."

Peterson: "How do you know he wasn't at Debbie Carter's?"

Ron: "I'd bet my life on it. Let's put it like that."

Peterson: "Tell us how you know."

Ron: "I just don't—don't ask me any more questions. I'll get down and you can put it to the jury, but I'm telling you you framed him and now you're trying to frame me."

Barney: "Ronnie."

Ron: "My mother knew I was at home. You come harassing me for five years. Now, you can do whatever you want to do to me. I don't care."

Peterson tendered the witness and sat down.

DURING his closing argument, Barney did much to malign the police and their work—the prolonged investigation, the loss of Gore's hair samples, their seeming blindness to Gore as a suspect, Dennis Smith's slipshod fingerprinting at the crime scene, the numerous requests for samples from Ron, the questionable tactics used in taking his dream confession, the failure to provide the defense with Ron's earlier statement, the evershifting opinions from the OSBI gang. The list of errors was long and rich, and Barney referred to the police more than once as the Keystone Kops.

As all good lawyers do, he argued that there was plenty of reasonable doubt and appealed to the jurors to use their common sense.

Peterson argued that there was no doubt whatsoever. The cops, all fine professionals of course, did an exemplary job with their investigation, and Peterson and his team had provided the jury with clear proof of guilt.

Picking up on something he'd heard from Melvin Hett, he played things a bit loose with his terminology. Talking about the hair analysis, he said, "So, over a long period of time Mr. Hett is examining hairs and eliminating, examining and eliminating, along with his other cases. Then in 1985, there's a match."

But Barney was ready. He immediately objected, saying, "If the court please, there hasn't been a match since statehood. We object to him using that term."

The objection was sustained.

Peterson plodded on, summarizing what each of his witnesses said. When he brought up Terri Holland, Ron became tense.

Peterson: "Terri Holland is telling you what she recalls after two years, and her testimony was that she heard this Defendant tell his mother that if she didn't bring him something—"

Ron jumped to his feet and said, "Hold it!"

Peterson: ". . . he ought to kill her just like he killed Debbie Carter."

Ron: "Shut your mouth man, I never said that!"

Barney: "Sit down. Be still now."

The Court: "Mr. Williamson."

Ron: "I did not say that to my mother."

Barney: "Ronnie."

The Court: "Listen to your attorney."

Ron sat down and seethed. Peterson labored on, spinning the testimony of the state's witnesses in a light so favorable Barney was forced to object repeatedly and ask Judge Jones to remind the prosecutor to stay within the facts.

THE JURY retired at 10:15 a.m. on Wednesday. Annette and Renee remained in the courtroom for a while, then left for lunch. It was difficult to eat. After hearing every word of testimony, they were even further convinced their brother was innocent, but it was Peterson's courtroom. Most of the rulings had gone his way. He'd patched together the same witnesses with just as little evidence and got a guilty verdict against Fritz.

They despised the man. He was loud and arrogant and ran over people. They detested him for what he was doing to their brother.

The hours passed. At 4:30 word arrived that the jury had a verdict, and the courtroom filled up quickly. Judge Jones took his place and lectured the spectators against outbursts. Annette and Renee held hands and prayed.

Across the aisle the Carter family held hands, too, and prayed. Their ordeal was almost over.

At 4:40, the jury foreman handed a verdict to the clerk, who glanced at it and passed it on to Judge Jones. He announced the verdict—guilty on all counts. The Carters silently pumped their hands in the air in a show of victory. Annette and Renee wept quietly, as did Peggy Stillwell.

Ron hung his head, shaken but not altogether surprised. After eleven months in the Pontotoc County jail he had become part of a rotten system. He knew Dennis Fritz was an innocent man, yet he'd been convicted by the same cops and same prosecutor in the same courtroom.

Judge Jones was anxious to finish the trial. Without a pause, he ordered the state to begin the penalty phase. Nancy Shew addressed the jury and explained that since the murder was especially heinous, atrocious, and cruel, and since it was committed for the purpose of preventing arrest, and since there was a strong likelihood that Ron would kill again and was thus a continuing threat to society, he should be put to death.

To prove this, the state called four witnesses, four women Ron had encountered before, none of whom had bothered to press criminal charges against him. The first was Beverly Setliff, who testified that on June 14, 1981, seven years earlier, she had seen Ron Williamson outside her house late at night as she was preparing for bed. He yelled, "Hey," and, "I know you're in there and I'm going to get you." She had never seen him before. She locked the doors and he disappeared.

She did not call the police, didn't even think about it, really, and didn't consider filing a complaint until the next day, when she saw a cop at a convenience store and told him about the incident. If a formal report was prepared, she never saw it.

Three weeks later, she saw Ron again, and a friend told her his name. Six years passed. When Ron was arrested, she called the police and told the story of the prowler.

The next witness was Lavita Brewer, the same woman who testified against Dennis Fritz. She told her story again—meeting Ron and Dennis in a bar in Norman, getting in the car with them, becoming frightened, jumping out, calling the police. According to her version, Ron never touched her or threatened her in any manner. She became hysterical in the backseat of Dennis's car because he would not stop and let her out, and the worst thing Ron did during the episode was to tell her to shut up.

She eventually jumped out of the car, fled, called the police, but did not press charges.

Letha Caldwell testified again. She had known Ron Williamson since their junior high days at Byng and had always been friendly with him. During the early 1980s, he and Dennis Fritz began hanging around her house late at night, always drinking. One day she was working in her flower beds and Ron appeared. They had small talk and she kept working, which irritated him. At one point, he grabbed her wrist. She broke free, walked into the house, then realized that her children were inside. He followed her, but didn't touch her again and soon left. She did not report the incident to the police.

The final witness was by far the most damaging. A divorced woman named Andrea Hardcastle told a harrowing tale of an ordeal that lasted over four hours. In 1981, Ron and a friend were at her house, trying to coax her into going out with them. They were headed for the Coachlight. Andrea was keeping three children of her own and two others, so she could not go out. The men left, but Ron soon returned to retrieve a pack of cigarettes. He entered the house uninvited and quickly made a pass at Andrea. It was after ten at night, the children were asleep, and she was frightened. She had no interest in sex. He exploded, striking her repeatedly about the face and head and demanding that she perform oral sex. She refused and, in doing so, realized that the more she talked, the less he hit her.

So they talked. He talked about his baseball career, his failed marriage, his guitar playing, God and religion, his mother. He had gone to high school with her ex-husband, who was a part-time bouncer at the Coachlight. At times he was quiet, peaceful, even tearful, at other times he was erratic, loud, and angry. Andrea worried about the children, all five of them. As he talked, she kept thinking of some way out of the ordeal. He erupted into violent fits, hitting her again and trying to pull off her clothes. He was too drunk to maintain an erection.

At one point, Ron allegedly said that he figured he would have to kill her. Andrea was praying fervently. She decided to play along. She invited him back the next afternoon, when the kids would be gone, and they could have all the sex they wanted. This proposal appealed to him greatly, so he left.

She called her ex-husband and her father, and together they patrolled the streets looking for Ron. They were heavily armed and not shy about roadside justice.

Andrea's face was a mess—cuts, bruises, swollen eyes. Ron wore a ring engraved with the head of a horse, and this caused numerous small puncture wounds around her eyes. The police were called the next day, but she adamantly refused to press charges. Ron lived close by, and she was terrified of him.

Barney was unprepared for her testimony and muddled through a halfhearted cross-examination.

The courtroom was silent when she stepped down from the witness stand. The jurors glared at the defendant. It was hanging time.

Inexplicably, Barney called no witnesses to mitigate the damage and try to save Ron's life. Annette and Renee were sitting in the courtroom, ready to testify. Not one word had been uttered throughout the trial about Ron's mental incompetence. No records had been introduced.

The final words the jurors heard from the witness stand were those of Andrea Hardcastle.

BILL PETERSON begged for the death penalty in his closing argument. And he had some fresh evidence, a new fact or two that had not been proven during the trial. There had been no mention of Ron's horse head ring until Andrea Hardcastle's testimony. Peterson jumped to a few conclusions, expanded the evidence, and decided that Ron had used the same ring when he beat Debbie Carter; thus, her facial injuries most surely were similar to what Andrea Hardcastle's must have been back in January 1981. It was just a wild idea. There was certainly no proof, but then no proof was needed.

Peterson dramatically told the jury, "He left his signature with Andrea Hardcastle, and he underlined it with Debbie Carter." He ended his remarks by saying, "When you come back in here, ladies and gentlemen, I'm going to ask you to say: Ron Williamson, you deserve to die for what you did to Debra Sue Carter."

With perfect timing, Ron blurted, "I did not kill Debbie Carter."

The jury retired but made quick work of the penalty deliberations. In less than two hours, they were back with a sentence of death.

IN A bizarre case of judicial second-guessing, Judge Jones called a hearing the following day to ponder the state's *Brady* violation. Though Barney was exhausted and fed up with the case, he was still indignant that the cops and Peterson had deliberately withheld the 1983 videotape of Ron's polygraph interrogation.

But why bother at this point? The trial was over. The video was of no benefit after the fact.

To no one's surprise, Judge Jones ruled that the suppression of the tape by the authorities was not a *Brady* violation after all. The tape wasn't really hidden; it was handed over after the trial, sort of a delayed submission.

Ron Williamson was on his way to F Cellhouse, the notorious death row at the Oklahoma state prison in McAlester.

CHAPTER 10

Oklahoma is very serious about its death penalty. When the U.S. Supreme Court approved the resumption of executions in 1976, the Oklahoma state legislature rushed into a special session for the sole purpose of enacting death penalty statutes. The following year, the lawmakers debated the innovative idea of death by lethal injection, as opposed to going back to Old Sparky, the state's dependable electric chair. The rationale was that chemicals were more merciful; thus, less likely to attract constitutional attacks of cruel and inhuman punishment; thus, more likely to speed along executions. In the excitement of the moment, with the press watching closely and the voters egging them on, the legislators debated the various ways in which to take human life. Some hardliners wanted hangings and firing squads and such, but in the end lethal injection was approved overwhelmingly, and Oklahoma became the first state to adopt it.

But not the first state to use it. Much to the frustration of lawmakers and police and prosecutors and a wide majority of the public, Oklahoma quickly fell behind the other active death penalty states. Thirteen long years passed without an execution. Finally, in 1990, the waiting ended, and the death chamber was used once again.

Once the dam broke, the flood came. Since 1990, Oklahoma has executed more convicts on a per capita basis than any other state. No place, not even Texas, comes close.

EXECUTIONS in Oklahoma take place at McAlester, a maximum security prison a hundred and twenty miles southeast of Oklahoma City. Death row is there, in an infamous section called the H Unit.

Practice makes perfect, and executions at McAlester are carried out with precision. For the inmate whose time has come, the last day is spent receiving visitors—family members, friends, usually his lawyer. Of course the visits are painful, made even more so by the fact that there can be no physical contact. They chat and cry through a thick wall of glass while talking on a phone. No farewell hugs or kisses from the family, just a gut-wrenching "I love you" through a black receiver. Often the inmate and his visitor will symbolically kiss each other by pressing their lips against the glass. They also imitate touching with their hands.

There is no law that prevents physical contact before an execution. Each state has its own rules, and Oklahoma prefers to keep the rituals as harsh as possible.

If the warden is in a good mood, he allows the inmate to make some phone calls. When the visiting is over, it's time for the last meal, but there is a $15 limit on the menu, and the warden can veto anything on it. Cheeseburgers, fried chicken, catfish, and ice cream are the most popular items requested.

About an hour before his death, the inmate is prepped. He changes clothes and puts on a light blue outfit, much like surgical scrubs. He is secured to a gurney with wide Velcro straps, and as he begins his final ride, there is a pep rally of sorts thrown by his comrades. They shake and kick their cell doors. They rattle the metal bars. They yell and whoop and the racket continues until just after the scheduled moment of execution, then it stops suddenly.

As the inmate is being prepared, the death chamber is waiting and very well organized. Witnesses somberly file into the two viewing rooms—one for the family of the victim, one for the family of the killer. The room for the victims has twenty-four folding chairs, but some are reserved for the press, usually four or five seats, a couple for the lawyers, and a few for the warden and his staff. The local sheriff and prosecutor seldom miss the event.

Behind this room, and behind panels of one-way glass, is the witness room for the family of the killer. It has twelve folding chairs, but often a few are empty. Some inmates do not want their families to watch. Some inmates have no families.

And some victims have no families. Occasionally, their witness room is half-empty, too.

The two rooms are separated, and the two groups are carefully kept away from each other. As the witnesses take their places, they stare at nothing—mini-blinds block out the view of the death chamber.

The gurney enters and is wheeled into place. Technicians are waiting with intravenous tubes, one for each arm. When everything is properly inserted and adjusted, the mini-blinds are raised and the witnesses can see the inmate. One-way glass prevents him from seeing the victim's family, but he can certainly see his own and often acknowledges them. A microphone protrudes from the wall two feet above his head.

A doctor attaches a heart-monitoring device. A deputy warden stands at a small white podium in a corner and records everything in a notebook. Next to him on the wall is a phone, just in case there is late-breaking news on the legal front or a change of heart in the governor's office. In years past a chaplain stood in another corner and read Scripture throughout the execution, but he retired.

The warden steps forward and asks the condemned if he or she has any last words. They often do not, but occasionally one will ask for forgiveness, or proclaim his innocence, or pray, or launch into some bitter denunciation. One sang a hymn. One shook hands with the warden and thanked him and his staff and the entire prison for taking such good care of him during his prolonged visit.

There is a two-minute time limit on the final words, but it is never invoked.

The condemned are always relaxed and low-key. They have accepted their fate and had many years to prepare for this moment. Many welcome it. They prefer death to the horror of living another twenty or thirty years on H Unit.

In a small room behind the gurney, three executioners are hiding. They are not to be seen. Their identities are unknown around the prison. They are not state employees, but freelancers of some variety who were secretly hired by an old warden many years ago. Their arrivals and departures to and from McAlester are mysterious. Only the warden knows who they are, where they come from, and where they get their chemicals. He pays each of them $300 in cash for an execution.

The tubes from the inmate's arms run up and through two two-inch holes in the wall and into the small room where the executioners do their work.

When the formalities are tidied up, and the warden is certain there will be no last-minute phone calls, he nods and the injections start.

First a saline solution is pumped in to open the veins. The first drug is sodium thiopental, and it quickly knocks out the inmate. Another flushing of saline solution, then the second drug, vecuronium bromide, stops the breathing. Another quick flush and the third drug, potassium chloride, stops the heart.

The doctor appears, does a quick check, pronounces death. The mini-blinds close fast, and the witnesses, many of them quite emotional, leave quickly and quietly. The gurney is rolled out. The body is taken to an ambulance. The family must make arrangements to retrieve it, or it goes to a prison cemetery.

Outside the prison gates, two groups hold two very different vigils. The Homicide Survivors sit in front of their RVs and wait for the welcome news that the execution is complete. Nearby is their display, a large three-panel memorial to the victims of the killers. Color photos of children and smiling students; poems to the dead; enlarged headlines announcing some horrific double murder; lots and lots of photos of those butchered by the inhabitants of death row. The memorial is called "Remember the Victims."

Not far away, a Catholic priest leads the other group in a circle of prayer and hymn singing. Some opponents of the death penalty attend every execution, praying not only for those condemned but also for their victims.

The two groups know and respect each other, but they strongly disagree.

When word comes from inside that the execution is over, more prayers are offered. Then the candles are extinguished, and the hymnbooks are put away.

Hugs are exchanged, farewells given. See you at the next execution.

WHEN Ron Williamson arrived at McAlester on April 29, 1988, the H Unit was being discussed but not yet being built. Prison officials wanted a brand-new death row to house their growing inventory of capital inmates, but the legislature wouldn't spend the money.

Ron was taken instead to F Cellhouse, home to eighty-one other condemned men. F Cellhouse, or The Row, as it was commonly called, comprised the bottom two floors of a wing of the old prison house, or Big House, a mammoth four-story building constructed in 1935 and finally abandoned fifty years later. Decades of overcrowding, violence, lawsuits, and riots led to its inevitable closing.

In the vast, empty, and decaying Big House, only F Cellhouse was used, and its sole purpose was to house condemned men in a lockdown environment.

Ron was processed at F Cellhouse. He was given two pairs of khakis, two blue short-sleeve shirts, two white T-shirts, two pairs of white socks, and two pairs of white boxer shorts. All the clothing had been well used. It was clean, but with permanent stains, especially the boxers. The shoes were black leather work shoes, also used. He was also given a pillow, blanket, toilet paper, toothbrush, and toothpaste. During his very brief orientation it was explained that he could purchase other toiletries, along with food and soft drinks and a few other items, at the prison commissary, better known as the canteen, a place he was not allowed to visit. Any money he received from the outside world would go into his account, from which he could purchase his "canteen." A man's canteen was his private little stockpile of goodies, something he protected fiercely in his cell.

When he had changed into his prison clothes and completed the processing, he was led to the wing, or run, where he would spend the next several years waiting for the state to execute him. His hands and ankles were cuffed. As he clutched his pillow, blanket, extra clothes, and other items, the guards opened the huge barred door and the parade began.

Above his head, painted in large black letters, was his address: DEATH ROW.

The run was a hundred feet long and only twelve feet wide, with cells packed together on both sides. The ceiling was eight feet high.

Walking very slowly, Ron and his two guards proceeded down the run. It was a ritual, a brief welcoming ceremony. His neighbors knew he was coming and the catcalling began: "New man on the run!" "New meat!" "Hey, baby!"

Arms hung through the bars of the cell doors, almost within reaching distance. White arms, black arms, brown ones. Lots of tattoos on the arms. Act tough, Ron told himself. Don't show fear. They kicked the doors, yelled, called him names, threw out sexual threats. Always act tough.

He'd seen prisons before, and he'd just survived eleven months in the Pontotoc County jail. Nothing could be worse, he thought.

They stopped at cell 16, and the noise went away. Welcome to The Row. A guard unlocked the door, and Ron entered his new home.

There's an old saying in Oklahoma that refers to someone incarcerated at McAlester—"He's doing time at Big Mac." Ron stretched out on his narrow bunk, closed his eyes, and couldn't believe that he was locked away at Big Mac.

THE CELL was furnished with a set of metal-framed bunk beds, a metal desk with a metal stool that was mounted into the concrete, a stainless-steel toilet/sink combo, a mirror, a set of metal bookcases, and one light-bulb. It was sixteen feet long, seven feet wide, eight feet high. The floor was covered with black and white linoleum tiles. The brick walls were white and had been painted so many times they were smooth.

Thank God there was a window, he thought, and though it provided no view, it did let in light. There were no windows in the Ada jail.

He walked to his door, which was nothing but a set of bars with an opening known as the bean hole for food trays and small packages. He looked into the run and could see three men—the one directly across from him in cell 9, and the ones on each side of him. Ron did not speak, nor did they.

Most new inmates usually said little during the first days. The shock of arriving at a place where they were to live for a few years before being killed was overwhelming. Fear was everywhere: fear of the future, fear of never again seeing what had been lost, fear of not surviving, fear of getting knifed or raped by one of the cold-blooded killers you could hear breathing just a few feet away.

He made his bed and arranged his things. He appreciated the privacy—most death row inmates were single-celled but had the option of a cell mate. There was a constant racket in the run—chatter among the inmates, guards laughing, a loud television, a radio, someone yelling to a friend far down the hall. Ron stayed away from his door, as far from the noise as possible. He slept, read books, and smoked. Everybody smoked on The Row, and the smell of old and new tobacco hung over the run like a thick, pungent fog. There was some ventilation, but it was too old to work. The windows, of course, could not be opened, even though they were covered with thick bars. The drudgery hit hard. There was no daily schedule. No activities to look forward to. One brief hour outside, sometimes. The tedium was numbing.

For men locked up twenty-three hours a day and with very little to do, the undisputed highlight was eating. Three times a day food trays were wheeled along the run and slid through the bean holes. All meals were taken in the cell, alone. Breakfast was at seven, and it was usually scrambled eggs and grits, some bacon on most days, and two or three pieces of toast. The coffee was cold and weak, but treasured nonetheless. Lunch was sandwiches and beans. Dinner was the worst meal—some vile mystery meat with half-cooked vegetables. The portions were ridiculously small, and the food was always cold. It was cooked in another building and pushed over on carts at a very slow pace. Who cared? They were dead men anyway. The food was dreadful, but mealtime was important.

Annette and Renee sent money, and Ron bought food, cigarettes, toiletries, and soft drinks from the canteen. He filled out an order form that listed the few items available, then handed it to the most important man on The Row. The Run Man was a prisoner who had found favor with the guards and was allowed to spend most of his time out of his cell, running errands for the other inmates. He passed along gossip and notes, picked up and delivered laundry and canteen goods, gave advice, occasionally sold drugs.

The exercise yard was sacred ground—a fenced area the size of two basketball courts next to F Cellhouse. For an hour a day, five days a week, each inmate was allowed into "the yard" to get some sun, visit with fellow prisoners, and play basketball or cards or dominoes. The groups were small, usually five or six at a time, and tightly controlled by the inmates themselves. Friends, and only friends, went into the yard together. A new inmate had to be invited before he could feel safe. There were fights and beatings, and the guards watched the yard closely. For the first month, Ron preferred to go out by himself. The Row was full of killers, and he had no business being there.

The only other contact point for prisoners was in the shower. They were allowed three per week, fifteen minutes max, and only two men at a time. If an inmate didn't want, or didn't trust, a shower partner, then he was allowed to bathe alone. Ron showered by himself. There was plenty of hot and cold water, but it didn't mix. It was either scalding or freezing.

TWO OTHER casualties of the Pontotoc County judicial system were on The Row when Ron arrived, though he didn't know it at first. Tommy Ward and Karl Fontenot had been waiting there for almost three years as their appeals were grinding through the courts.

The Run Man handed Ron a note, or a "kite," an unauthorized message that the guards generally ignored. It was from Tommy Ward, saying hello and wishing him well. Ron sent one back and asked for some cigarettes. Though he felt sorry for Tommy and Karl, he was relieved to know that not everyone on The Row was a butcher. He had always believed they were innocent and had thought about them often during his ordeal.

Tommy had spent time with Ron in the jail in Ada and knew he was emotionally unstable. The guards and other inmates there had taunted both of them. Years earlier, in the middle of the night, a voice called out from a dark end of the hall, "Tommy, this is Denice Haraway, please tell them where my body is." He heard the police whispering and other inmates suppressing laughter. Tommy ignored the head games, and they finally left him alone.

Ron could not. "Ron, why did you kill Debbie Carter?" a haunting voice would echo through the Ada jail. Ron would bolt from his bed and begin screaming.

On death row, Tommy battled with his sanity every day. The horror of the place was bad enough for real murderers, but for an innocent man it was literally maddening. He feared for Ron's well-being from the moment he arrived.

One of the guards on The Row knew the details of the Carter murder. Not long after Ron arrived, Tommy heard a guard call out, "Ron, this is Debbie Carter. Why did you kill me?"

Ron, who was quiet at first, began yelling and protesting his innocence. The guards enjoyed his reaction, and the taunting began. The other inmates were also amused and often joined the fun.

A FEW days after Ron arrived, Tommy was suddenly pulled from his cell and draped with chains and cuffs by several gruff and heavy guards. This was something serious, though he had no idea where he was headed. They never tell you.

They marched him away, a skinny little boy surrounded by enough security to protect the president. "Where are we going?" he asked, but the answer was much too important to reveal. He shuffled down the run, out of F Cellhouse, through the dome-like rotunda of the Big House, empty except for the pigeons, and into a conference room in the administration building.

The warden was waiting, and he had bad news.

They kept him shackled and placed in the hot seat, at the end of a long conference table that was jam-packed with assistants and clerks and secretaries and anyone else who wanted to participate in the macabre announcement. The guards stood stone-faced and sentry-like behind him, ready just in case he tried to bolt somewhere when given the news. Everyone around the table was holding a pen and ready to record what was about to happen.

The warden spoke gravely. The bad news was that he had not received a stay of execution, so Tommy's time had come. Yes, it did seem rather early—his appeals were not yet three years old, but sometimes these things happen.

The warden was very sorry, but just doing his job. The big day was two weeks away.

Tommy breathed hard and tried to absorb this. He had lawyers working on his appeals, which, as he'd been told many times, would take years to complete. There was a good chance of a new trial back in Ada.

It was 1988. Oklahoma had not pulled off an execution in more than twenty years. Perhaps they were a bit rusty and didn't know what they were doing.

The warden continued. They would begin making preparations immediately. One important item was what to do with the body.

The body, thought Tommy. My body?

The clerks and assistants and secretaries all frowned at their notepads and scribbled the same words. Why are all these people in here? Tommy asked himself.

Just send me to my mother, I guess, Tommy said, or tried to say.

His knees were weak when he stood. The guards seized him again and marched him back to F Cellhouse. He crawled into his bed and cried, not for himself but for his family and especially for his mother.

Two days later he was informed that there had been a mistake. Some paperwork had been mishandled somewhere along the way. A stay was in place, and Mrs. Ward would not be collecting her son's body anytime soon.

Such false starts were not unusual. Several weeks after her brother left Ada, Annette received a letter from the warden. She assumed it was correspondence of a routine matter. Perhaps she was right, given the trigger-happy mood at McAlester.

Dear Ms. Hudson:

It is with empathy that I must inform you that your brother, Ronald Keith Williamson, Number 134846, is scheduled to be executed on 18 July 1988, at 12:02, A.M., at the Oklahoma State Penitentiary.

Your brother will be moved from his current cell to another cell on the morning prior to the execution date, and at that time his visiting hours will be changed, and will be as follows: 9:00 A.M. to 12 Noon, 1:00 P.M. to 4:00 P.M., and 6:00 to 8:00 P.M.

Visiting during the last 24 hours will be limited to clergymen, Attorney of Record, and two other visitors who have been approved by the Warden. Your brother has the right to have five witnesses present at the execution. These witnesses must be approved by the Warden.

As difficult as it may be, funeral arrangements must be considered, and these arrangements are the responsibility of the family. If this responsibility is not assumed by the family, the State will attend to the burial. Please inform us of your decision in this matter.

If further information is needed, or if I may be of assistance in other ways, please contact me.

Sincerely, James L. Saffle, Warden

The letter was dated June 21, 1988, less than two months after Ronnie arrived at McAlester. Annette knew that appeals were automatic in capital murder cases. Perhaps someone should inform the authorities in charge of the executions.

As unsettling as the letter was, she was able to set it aside. Her brother was innocent and would someday be proven so in a new trial. She adamantly believed this, and would never waiver. She read her Bible, prayed continually, and met often with her pastor.

Still, she had to ask herself what kind of people were running the prison over at McAlester.

AFTER a week or so on The Row, Ron walked to his door one day and said hello to the man in cell 9, directly across the hall, twelve feet way. Greg Wilhoit said hello, and they exchanged a few words. Neither was anxious for a long conversation. The next day Ron said hello again, and they chatted briefly. The next day Greg mentioned that he was from Tulsa. Ron once lived there, with a guy named Stan Wilkins.

"Is he an ironworker?" Greg asked.

Yes, he was, and Greg knew him. The coincidence was amusing and broke the ice. They talked about old friends and places in Tulsa.

Greg was also thirty-four years old, also loved baseball, also had two sisters who were supporting him.

And he was also innocent.

It was the beginning of a deep friendship that helped them both survive their ordeal. Greg invited Ron to attend chapel, a weekly service held off The Row and attended by many capital defendants. Cuffed and shackled, the inmates were herded into a small room where they were led in worship by a saintly chaplain named Charles Story. Ron and Greg seldom missed the services and always sat together.

GREG WILHOIT had been at McAlester for nine months. He was an ironworker, a tough union man with a record of marijuana possessions but nothing violent.

In 1985, Greg and his wife, Kathy, separated. They had two infant daughters and a lot of problems. Greg helped Kathy move into an apartment and stopped by almost every night to see his girls. They were hopeful the marriage could be patched up, but both needed some time alone. They remained sexually active and faithful; neither slept around.

On June 1, three weeks after the separation, a neighbor in Kathy's apartment building became alarmed at the nonstop crying of the two daughters. The neighbor knocked on the door, and when there was no answer, she called the police. Inside, on the floor downstairs, they found Kathy's body. Upstairs, the two toddlers were in their cribs, hungry and frightened.

Kathy had been raped and strangled. The time of death was between 1:00 a.m. and 6:00 a.m. When the police interviewed Greg, he said he was at home, asleep by himself, and thus had no alibi witness. He adamantly denied any involvement in his wife's murder and resented the questioning from the police.

The investigation produced a fingerprint on a phone that had been ripped from the wall and was on the floor near Kathy. The fingerprint matched neither Greg nor his wife. The police found pubic hair and, most important, what appeared to be a bite mark on Kathy's breast. A crime lab expert confirmed that the killer had bitten the breast hard during the attack.

Being the estranged spouse, Greg was soon the leading suspect, though the fingerprint did not match. Melvin Hett with the state crime lab concluded that the pubic hair was not microscopically consistent with Greg's sample. The police asked Greg to submit an impression of his teeth to compare with the bite mark.

Greg did not appreciate being a suspect. He was completely innocent and didn't trust the police. With the help of his parents, he paid $25,000 and retained a lawyer.

The police did not appreciate Greg hiring a lawyer. They obtained a court order requiring him to submit an impression of his teeth. He did, and heard nothing for five months. He was raising his two daughters, working full-time as an ironworker, and hoping the police were history when they arrived one day in January 1986 with an arrest warrant for first-degree murder, punishable by death.

His first lawyer, though well paid and with a good reputation, was far too interested in negotiating a plea bargain. Greg fired him a month before trial, then made the enormous mistake of hiring George Briggs, a washed-up old lawyer at the end of a long, colorful career. His fee was $2,500, a bargain and a red flag.

Briggs was from the old school of country lawyers. You get your witnesses, I'll get mine, and we'll show up at the courthouse and have a good fight. No pretrial discovery. When in doubt, just trust your instincts in court and fly by the seat of your pants.

Briggs was also an alcoholic who was addicted to painkillers that he began taking a few years earlier after a motorcycle accident left him partially brain damaged. On a good day he reeked of booze but could still go through the motions. On a bad day he'd been known to snore in the courtroom and urinate on himself and vomit in the judge's chambers. He was often seen staggering along the hallways of the courthouse. Greg and his parents became alarmed when Briggs drained a few bottles of beer during a lunch.

His drinking and drug addiction were well known to the trial judge and to the Oklahoma state bar association, but virtually nothing was done to either stop Briggs or help him, or protect his clients.

Greg's family located a highly regarded bite expert in Kansas, but Briggs was too busy or too hungover to chat with the man. Briggs interviewed no witnesses and, as far as Greg could tell, did little preparation.

The trial was a nightmare. The state called two bite experts, one of whom had finished dental school less than a year earlier. Briggs had nothing to rebut their testimony. The jury deliberated for two hours and found Greg guilty. Briggs called no mitigating witnesses, and the jury deliberated for one hour and set the punishment at death.

Thirty days later, Greg was taken back to court to receive his sentence of death.

In cell 9, Greg hung newspapers across the bars of his door so no one could see him. He convinced himself that he was not on death row, but rather in his own little cocoon, somewhere else, biding his time reading voraciously and watching his small television. He spoke to no one but the Run Man, who, during his very first chat, asked Greg if he wanted to buy some marijuana. Yes, he did.

At first, Greg did not realize that a few lucky condemned men actually left The Row alive. Occasionally the appeals worked, good lawyers got involved, judges woke up, and miracles happened, but no one had informed him of this. He was sure he would be put to death, and, frankly, he wanted to get it over with.

For six months he left his cell only to shower, quickly and alone. Gradually, though, he made an acquaintance or two and was invited into the yard for an hour of exercise and socializing. Once he began talking, he became instantly disliked. Greg was a rarity on The Row, a man who strongly supported the death penalty. You do the ultimate crime, you pay the ultimate price, he argued loudly. Such opinions were unheard of.

He also developed the irritating habit of watching *David Letterman* at full volume. Sleep is cherished on The Row, and many of the men spend half of each day in another world. When you're sleeping, you're cheating the system. Sleep is your time, not the state's.

Condemned killers do not hesitate to threaten to kill again, and Greg soon heard the rumor that he was a marked man. Every death row has at least one boss and several who want to be. There are factions vying for control. They prey on the weak, often demanding payment for the right to "live" on The Row. When word filtered to Greg that he needed to pay rent, he laughed and sent a message back that he would never pay a dime to anyone for living in such a rat hole.

The Row was ruled by Soledad, the nickname of a killer who'd once spent time in the famous prison in California. Soledad didn't appreciate Greg's pro-death-penalty stance, and he really didn't like David Letterman, and since any boss worthy of respect had to be ready to kill, Greg became the target.

Everyone has enemies on The Row. The feuds are nasty and arise quickly over anything. A pack of cigarettes can provoke an attack in the yard or the shower. Two packs can get you killed.

Greg needed a friend to watch his back.

ANNETTE'S first visit to McAlester was sad and frightening, not that she was expecting anything else. She preferred not to go, but Ronnie had no one but his sisters.

The guards patted her down and checked her purse. Moving through the layers of the Big House was like sinking into the dark belly of a beast. Doors clanged, keys rattled, guards glared as if she had no business there. She was numb, sleepwalking, with a hard knot in her stomach and a racing pulse.

They were from a nice family in a nice house on a shady street. Church on Sundays. A thousand baseball games when Ronnie was a boy. How had it all come to this?

This will become a habit, she admitted to herself. She would hear the same sounds and see the same guards many times in the future. She asked if she could bring stuff—cookies, clothes, cash. No, came the quick answer. Only small change, so she handed the guard a handful of quarters and hoped he passed them on to Ronnie.

The visitation room was long and narrow and split down the center with thick sheets of Plexiglas that were divided by partitions to allow some measure of privacy. All conversations were by phone through a window. No touching whatsoever.

Ronnie eventually showed up. No one was in a hurry at the prison. He looked healthy, maybe even a bit chubby, but then his weight had always gone up and down dramatically.

He thanked her for coming, said he was surviving okay but needed money. The food was awful, and he wanted to buy something to eat at the canteen. He also was desperate for a guitar, and some books and magazines and a small television, which could be purchased through the canteen.

"Get me out of here, Annette," he pleaded over and over. "I didn't kill Debbie Carter and you know it."

She had never wavered in her belief that he was innocent, though some family members now had doubts. She and her husband, Marlon, were both working and raising a family and trying to save a little. Money was tight. What was she supposed to do? The state-funded indigent lawyers were getting themselves organized for his appeals.

Sell your house and hire a big lawyer, he said. Sell everything. Do anything. Just get me out.

The conversation was tense and there were tears. Another inmate arrived for a visit in the booth next to Ronnie. Annette could barely see him through the glass, but she was intrigued by who he was and whom he had killed.

Roger Dale Stafford, Ronnie told her, the famous steak-house murderer. He had nine death sentences, the current record on The Row. He executed six people, including five teenagers, in the rear of a steak house in Oklahoma City in a bungled robbery, then murdered a family of three.

They're all killers, Ronnie kept saying, and all they talk about is killing. It's everywhere on The Row. Get me out!

Did he feel safe? she asked.

Hell no, not living with a bunch of killers. He had always believed in the death penalty, but now he was a die-hard supporter of it. He kept such opinions quiet, though, in his new neighborhood.

There were no time limits on the visits. They eventually said goodbye with sincere promises to write and call. Annette was emotionally drained when she left McAlester.

The calls started immediately. On The Row they put a phone on a cart and rolled it to the cells. A guard punched the numbers, then handed the receiver through the cell door. Since all calls were collect, the guards really didn't care how often they were made. Out of boredom and desperation, Ron was soon yelling for the cart more than anyone else.

He usually began by demanding money, $20 or $30, so he could eat and buy cigarettes. Annette and Renee each tried to send $40 a month, but they had their own expenses and little extra money. They never sent enough, and Ronnie reminded them of this over and over. He was often angry, claiming that they didn't love him or they would get him out. He was innocent, everybody knew it, and there was no one on the outside to free him but his sisters.

The calls were rarely pleasant, though they tried not to fight with him. Ron usually managed, at some point, to remind his sisters how much he loved them.

Annette's husband sent subscriptions to *National Geographic* and the *Ada Evening News*. Ronnie wanted to monitor things back home.

Not long after his arrival at McAlester he heard for the first time about the bizarre confession of Ricky Joe Simmons. Barney knew about the taped confession, but chose not to use it at trial and didn't tell his client. An investigator with the Indigent Defense System took the video of the confession to McAlester and showed it to Ron. He went ballistic. Someone else admitted killing Debbie Carter, and the jury never knew about it!

Surely this news would soon break in Ada, and he wanted to read about it in the local paper.

Ricky Joe Simmons became another obsession, perhaps the principal one, and Ron would fixate on him for many years.

Ron tried to call everybody; he wanted the world to know about Ricky Joe Simmons. His confession was Ron's ticket out, and he wanted someone to step forward and bring the boy to trial. He called Barney, other lawyers, county officials, even old friends, but most refused to accept the collect charges.

Rules were changed and phone privileges were restricted after a couple of death row inmates were caught making calls to the families of their victims, just for the sport of it. On the average, two calls per week were allowed, and every phone number had to be preapproved.

ONCE a week the Run Man pushed a cart of well-used paperback library books through F Cellhouse. Greg Wilhoit read everything that was available—biographies, mysteries, westerns. Stephen King was a favorite, but he really loved the books of John Steinbeck.

He encouraged Ron to read as an escape, and they were soon debating the merits of *The Grapes of Wrath* and *East of Eden*, unusual conversations on The Row. They stood for hours, leaning through the bars of their doors, talking and talking. Books, baseball, women, their trials.

Both were surprised to learn that most death row inmates do not maintain their innocence. Instead, they tend to embellish their crimes when talking among themselves. Death was a constant topic—murders, murder trials, murders yet to be committed.

When Ron continued to claim he was innocent, Greg began to believe him. Every inmate has his trial transcript close by, and Greg read Ron's—all two thousand pages. He was shocked by the trial in Ada. Ron read Greg's transcript and was equally shocked by his trial in Osage County.

They believed each other and ignored the skepticism from their neighbors.

In his early weeks on The Row, the friendship was therapeutic for Ron. Someone finally believed him, someone he could talk to for hours, someone who would listen with an intelligent and sympathetic ear. Away from the cave-like cell in Ada, and able to unload on a friend, his behavior was stable. He didn't rant and pace and scream his innocence. The mood swings were not as dramatic. He slept a lot, read for hours, chain-smoked, and talked to Greg. They went to the exercise yard together, each watching the other's back. Annette sent more money, and Ron purchased a small television from the canteen. She knew how important a guitar was to Ronnie, and she relentlessly went about trying to get one. The canteen didn't stock them. After phone calls and letters she convinced the officials to allow a local music store in McAlester to sell one and send it over.

Trouble started when it arrived. Anxious to impress the others with his talent, Ron played it loudly and sang at full volume. The complaints came with a fury, but Ron didn't care. He loved his guitar and he loved to sing, especially Hank Williams. "Your Cheatin' Heart" echoed up and down the run. The others shouted obscenities. He shouted them right back.

Then Soledad got fed up with Ron's music and threatened to kill him. Who cares? Ron said. I've already got my death sentence.

No EFFORT was made to air-condition F Cellhouse, and when summer arrived, it baked like a sauna. The inmates stripped to their boxers and huddled in front of the small fans sold at the canteen. It was not unusual to wake up before dawn with the sheets soaked with sweat. A few spent the days completely nude.

For some reason, the prison conducted tours of death row. The tourists were usually high school students whose parents and advisers were hoping to scare them away from crime. When the weather was hot, the guards ordered the inmates to get dressed, a tour was coming through. Some complied, others did not.

An Indian nicknamed Buck Naked preferred the native look and was perpetually nude. He had the rare ability to pass gas on demand, and when the tour groups drew near, his favorite trick was to press his rear cheeks against the bars of his door and discharge a thunderous blast of flatulence. This shocked the young students and disrupted their tours.

The guards told him to stop. He refused. His colleagues egged him on, but only during tours. The guards finally hauled him away when visitors arrived. Several others tried imitations but lacked the talent.

Ron just played and sang for the tourists.

ON JULY 4, 1988, Ron awoke in a foul mood and never recovered. It was Independence Day, a time for celebrations and parades and such, and he was locked away in a hellhole for a crime he did not commit. Where was his independence?

He began yelling and cursing and proclaiming his innocence, and when this prompted catcalls up and down the run, he went crazy. He began throwing everything he could find—books, magazines, toiletries, his small radio, his Bible, clothes. The guards watched and told him to settle down. He cursed them and got louder. Pencils, papers, food from the canteen. Then he grabbed his television and slammed it into the brick wall, shattering it. Finally he took his cherished guitar and slammed it repeatedly into the bars of his cell door.

Most death row inmates took a daily dose of a benign antidepressant called Sinequan. It was supposed to calm nerves and help with sleep.

The guards finally convinced Ron to take something stronger, and he became drowsy and quiet. Later in the day, he began cleaning up his cell.

Then he called Annette and, in tears, told her about the episode. She visited him later, and things were not pleasant. He shouted into the phone, accused her of not trying to free him, and again demanded that she sell everything and hire a big-time lawyer who could fix this injustice. She asked him to settle down, stop yelling, and when he didn't, she threatened to leave.

Over time, she and Renee replaced the television, radio, and guitar.

IN SEPTEMBER 1988, a lawyer from Norman by the name of Mark Barrett drove to McAlester to meet his new client. Mark was one of four lawyers who handled the appeals for indigent defendants in capital cases. The Williamson case had been assigned to him. Barney Ward was out of the picture.

Appeals are automatic in capital cases. The necessary notices had been filed, the slow process was under way. Mark explained this to Ron Williamson and listened to his lengthy proclamations of innocence. He was not surprised to hear such talk, and he had not yet studied the transcript of the trial.

To assist his new lawyer, Ron handed over a list of all the witnesses who had lied at his trial, then, in minute detail, described to Mark Barrett the nature and extent of their lies.

Mark found Ron to be intelligent, rational, clearly aware of his predicament and surroundings. He was articulate and spoke at length and in great detail about the lies the police and prosecution had used against him. He was a little panicky, but that was to be expected. Mark had no idea of Ron's medical history.

Mark's father was a minister in the Disciples of Christ denomination, and this bit of background prompted Ron into a long discussion about religion. He wanted Mark to know that he was a devout Christian, had been raised in the church by God-fearing parents, and read his Bible often. He quoted many verses of Scripture and Mark was impressed. One in particular was troubling him, and he asked Mark for his interpretation. They discussed it thoroughly. It was important for Ron to understand the verse, and he was clearly frustrated by his inability to grasp its meaning. Attorney visits had no time limits, and the clients were anxious to stay out of their cells. They talked for over an hour.

Mark Barrett's first impression was that Ron was a fundamentalist, an easy talker, perhaps a bit too slick. As always, he was skeptical of his client's claims of innocence, though his mind was far from closed. He was also handling the appeals for Greg Wilhoit, and he was thoroughly convinced Greg did not kill his wife.

Mark knew there were innocent men on death row, and the more he learned about Ron's case, the more he believed him.

CHAPTER 11

Though Dennis Fritz didn't realize it, twelve months in the dungeon of the county jail had helped prepare him for the severe conditions of prison life.

He arrived at the Conner Correctional Center in June, in the rear of a van loaded with other new inmates, still dazed and in denial and terrified. It was important to look and act confident, and he worked hard at it. Conner had the reputation as the "dump site" of medium security prisons. It was a tough place, tougher than most, and Dennis asked himself over and over how and why he had been randomly assigned to the place.

He was herded through the admissions procedures and given the standard lectures about rules and regulations, then assigned to a two-man cell with bunk beds and a window through which he could see the outdoors. Like Ron, he was thankful for the window. He'd gone for weeks in Ada without seeing sunshine.

His roommate was a Mexican who spoke little English, and that was fine with Dennis. He spoke no Spanish and wasn't in the mood to learn. The first overwhelming challenge was how to find brief moments of privacy with another human always within arm's reach.

Dennis vowed to spend every possible moment working to free himself from his sentence. It would have been easy to give up. The system was so heavily weighted against the inmates, but he was determined to prevail.

Conner was overcrowded and known for its violence. There were gangs, killings, beatings, rapes, drugs everywhere, and guards on the take. He quickly found the safer areas and avoided men he thought were trouble. He treated fear as an asset. After a few months most prisoners unwittingly fell into the routine of the prison and became institutionalized. They lowered their guard, took chances, took safety for granted.

It was a good way to get hurt, and Dennis vowed that he would never forget to be afraid.

The prisoners were awake by 7:00 a.m. and all cell doors were opened. They ate in a large cafeteria and could sit anywhere they wished. The whites took one side, the blacks the other, and the Indians and Hispanics were caught in the middle but leaned toward the darker section. The food for breakfast was not bad—eggs, grits, bacon. Conversation was lively—the men were relieved to have contact with others.

Most wanted to work; anything to stay out of the unit where the cells were. Because Dennis had once taught, he was recruited to teach other inmates in the General Equivalency Diploma program. After breakfast he went to the classroom and taught until noon. His salary was $7.20 a month.

His mother and aunt began sending $50 a month, money they barely scraped together but made a priority. He spent it in the canteen on tobacco, canned tuna, crackers, and cookies. Virtually every inmate smoked and the great currency was cigarettes. A pack of Marlboros was like a pocketful of cash.

Dennis soon found the law library and was pleased to learn that he could study there every day from 1:00 p.m. to 4:00 p.m., without interruption. He had never picked up a law book, but he was determined to master the research. A couple of the law clerks—other inmates who fancied themselves jailhouse lawyers and were quite knowledgeable—befriended him and taught him how to move through the thick treatises and digests. As always, they charged for their advice. The fees were paid in cigarettes.

He began his legal education by reading hundreds of Oklahoma cases, looking for similarities and potential mistakes made during his trial. His appeals would soon start, and he wanted to know as much as his lawyer. He discovered the federal digests and took notes on thousands of cases from throughout the country.

Lockdown was from 4:00 p.m. to 5:00 p.m.; heads were counted, reports made. Dinner was over at 7:30, and from then until the next lockdown at 10:15 the inmates were free to roam around the unit, exercise, play cards or dominoes or basketball. Many chose to just hang out, to sit in groups and talk and smoke and kill time.

Dennis went back to the law library.

His daughter, Elizabeth, was fifteen, and they maintained a lively correspondence. She was being raised by her maternal grandmother in a stable home with plenty of attention. She believed her father to be innocent, but Dennis always suspected she had some doubt. They swapped letters and talked on the phone at least once a week. Dennis would not allow her to visit him, though. He did not want his daughter near the prison. She would not see him dressed like a convict and living behind razor wire.

Wanda Fritz, his mother, traveled to Conner soon after Dennis arrived. Visitation was on Sunday, from 10:00 a.m. to 4:00 p.m., in a room with rows of folding tables and chairs. It was a zoo. Twenty or so inmates were admitted at once, and their families were waiting—wives, children, mothers, and fathers. Emotions were high. The children were often rowdy and loud. The men were not handcuffed and contact was allowed.

Contact was exactly what the men wanted, though excessive kissing and groping were prohibited. The trick was to get a fellow inmate to "jigger," or sidetrack, a guard for a few seconds while rabid sex was accomplished. It was not unusual to see a couple slide between two soft drink machines and somehow copulate. Wives sitting placidly at a table often disappeared quickly, ducking under the table for a quick round of oral sex.

Fortunately, Dennis was able to hold his mother's attention in the midst of such frenzied activity, but the visit was the most stressful time of the week. He discouraged her from returning.

RON SOON began pacing and yelling in his cell. If you weren't crazy when you got to The Row, it didn't take long to lose your mind after you arrived. He stood at his door and screamed, "I am innocent! I am innocent!" for hours, until he became hoarse. With practice, though, his voice strengthened, and he could shout for longer periods of time. "I did not kill Debbie Carter! I did not kill Debbie Carter!"

He memorized the entire transcript of the Ricky Joe Simmons confession, every word, and delivered it at full volume for the benefit of his guards and neighbors. He could also go for hours reciting his trial transcript, pages and pages of the testimony that had sent him to death row. The other inmates wanted to choke him, but at the same time they marveled at his memory.

But they were not impressed at two in the morning.

Renee received a strange letter from another inmate. It read, in part:

Dear Renee:

Praise the Lord! This is Jay Neill, #141128. I am writing this on behalf, and at the request of your brother Ron. Ron lives caddycorner to my cell. At times Ron goes through very difficult stages on a daily basis. I am under the impression that he is on some form of medication to attempt to stabilize and modify his behavior. At best though, the limitation of the types of medication they will distribute here only works in a marginal capacity at best. Ron's biggest defeat is his low self-esteem. And I believe the people here at O.S.P. tell him he is below par in an I.Q. Scale. His worst times come between 12 am and 4 am.

At times, spaced periodically he screams different things at the top of his lungs. This has disturbed many convicts in the vicinity. At first they tried to reason with him, then to tolerate. But even that has worn thin with many around him. (Due to the sleepless nights for sure.)

I am a Christian and I pray daily for Ron. I talk to him and listen to him. He loves both you and Annette very much. I am his friend. I have acted in the capacity of a buffer between Ron and the people his yelling bothers by getting up and talking to him until he is calm.

God bless you and your family.

Sincerely, Jay Neill

Neill's friendship with anyone on The Row was always doubtful, and his conversion to Christianity was often the topic of conversation. His "friends" were skeptical. Before prison, he and his boyfriend longed to move to San Francisco to enjoy a more open lifestyle. Since they had no money, they decided to rob a bank, an undertaking with which they had no experience. They picked one in the town of Geronimo, and after they entered it loudly and announced their intentions, things fell apart. In the chaos of the robbery, Neill and his partner fatally stabbed three bank tellers, shot one customer to death, and wounded three others. In the midst of the bloodbath, Neill ran out of bullets, something he realized as he put his revolver to the head of a small child and pulled the trigger. Nothing happened—the child was unharmed, at least physically. The two killers escaped with about $20,000 in cash and were soon in San Francisco, where they went on a shopping spree—full-length mink coats, lovely scarves, and such. They threw money around in gay bars and had a decadent time for slightly more than twenty-four hours. Then they were hauled back to Oklahoma, where Neill was eventually executed.

On The Row, Neill liked to quote Scripture and deliver mini-sermons, but few listened.

ON DEATH ROW, medical attention was not a priority. Every inmate said that the first thing you lose is your health, then your sanity. Ron was seen by a prison doctor who had the benefit of his previous prison records and mental health history. It was noted that he had a long history of drug and alcohol abuse, certainly not a surprise on F Cellhouse. He suffered from depression and had been bipolar for at least ten years. There was some schizophrenia and personality disorder.

He was prescribed Mellaril again, and it settled him down.

Most of the other inmates thought Ron was simply "playing the nut role," pretending to be crazy in hopes of somehow walking away from The Row.

Two doors down from Greg Wilhoit lived an old inmate named Sonny Hays. No one was certain how long Sonny had been waiting, but he had arrived there before anyone else. He was pushing seventy, in terrible health, and refused to see or speak to anyone. He covered his cell door with newspapers and blankets, kept his lights off, ate only enough to stay alive, never showered, shaved, or cut his hair, never had visitors, and refused to meet with his lawyers. He neither sent nor received mail, made no phone calls, bought nothing from the canteen, ignored his laundry, and had no television or radio. He never left his dark, little dungeon, and days could pass with no sound from within.

Sonny was completely insane, and since a mentally incompetent person cannot be executed, he was simply rotting away and dying on his own terms. Now there was a new crazy man on The Row, though Ron had a hard time convincing others. He was just playing the nut role.

One episode, though, got their attention. Ron managed to clog his toilet and flood his cell with two inches of water. He stripped naked and began doing belly flops into the pool from his top bunk, yelling incoherently as he did so. The guards finally managed to secure and sedate him.

ALTHOUGH there was no air-conditioning on F Cellhouse, there was a heating system, and winter brought the reasonable expectation of having warm air pumped through the ancient vents. It didn't happen. The cells were frigid. Ice often formed on the inside of the windows during the night, and the heavily bundled inmates stayed in bed as long as possible.

The only way to sleep was to layer on all available clothing—both sets of socks, boxers, T-shirts, khakis, work shirts, and anything else a prisoner might be able to afford from the canteen. Extra blankets were luxuries and were not furnished by the state. The food, which was cold in the summertime, was barely edible in winter.

THE CONVICTIONS of Tommy Ward and Karl Fontenot were reversed by the Oklahoma Court of Criminal Appeals because their confessions were used against each other at trial, and since neither testified, each was denied the right to confront the other.

Had separate trials been given, the constitutional problems would have been avoided.

Had the confessions been suppressed, of course, there would have been no convictions.

They were taken off The Row and sent back to Ada. Tommy was retried in the town of Shawnee, in Pottawatomie County. With Bill Peterson and Chris Ross prosecuting once again, and with the judge permitting the jury to see the taped confession, Tommy was again found guilty and rewarded with another death sentence. During his retrial, his mother was driven to the courthouse each day by Annette Hudson. Karl was retried in the town of Holdenville, in Hughes County. He, too, was found guilty and given a death sentence.

Ron was ecstatic at their reversals, then dismayed at their subsequent convictions. His own direct appeal was slowly inching through the system. His case had been reassigned within the Appellate Public Defender's Office. Due to the increasing number of capital cases, more lawyers were hired. Mark Barrett was overworked and needed to unload a case or two. He was also anxiously awaiting a ruling from the Court of Criminal Appeals in Greg Wilhoit's case. That court was notoriously tough on defendants, but Mark was convinced Greg would get a new trial.

Ron's new lawyer was Bill Luker, and his brief argued vigorously that Ron had not received a fair trial. He attacked the representation of Barney Ward and claimed Ron had received "ineffective assistance of counsel," usually the first argument in a capital case. Chief among Barney's sins was his failure to raise the issue of Ron's mental incompetence. None of his medical records were in evidence. Luker researched Barney's mistakes, and the list became long.

He assailed the methods and tactics of the police and the prosecutor, and his brief grew lengthy. He also challenged the rulings of Judge Jones: allowing Ron's dream confession to be heard by the jury, ignoring the numerous *Brady* violations by the prosecution, and in general failing to protect Ron's right to a fair trial.

The vast majority of Bill Luker's clients were clearly guilty. His job was to make sure they received a fair hearing on appeal. Ron's case was different, though. The more he researched and the more questions he asked, the more Luker became convinced that it was an appeal he could win.

Ron was a very cooperative client with strong views that he was ready to share with his lawyer. He called frequently and wrote rambling letters. His comments and observations were generally helpful. At times, his recall of the details of his medical history was astounding.

He dwelled on the confession of Ricky Joe Simmons, and considered its exclusion from his trial a major travesty. He wrote Luker:

Dear Bill:
    You know I think Ricky Simmons killed Debbie. He must have or he wouldn't have confessed to it. Now, Bill, I've been going through

physical hell. I think it's only fair for Simmons to pay for what he did and for me to go free. They don't want to release his confession to you because they know you'd put it in my brief and immediately win me a new trial. So for God sakes tell them son of a bitches you want his confession.

Your Friend, Ron

WITH plenty of free time, Ron developed an active correspondence, especially with his sisters. They knew how important the letters were, and they found time to write back. Money was usually an issue. He was unable to eat the prison food and preferred to buy whatever he could from the canteen. He wrote to Renee and said, in part:

Renee:

I know Annette sends me a little money. But my misery is increasing. I've got Karl Fontenot here and he doesn't have anyone sending him anything. Could you please send me a little extra, even if it's $10.00.

Love Ronnie

Just before his first Christmas on The Row, he wrote Renee and said, in part:

Renee:

Hey, thanks for sending the money. It'll go for specific needs. Mainly guitar strings and coffee.

I got 5 Christmas cards this year, including yours. Christmas can give some good feelings.

Renee, the $20 really came at a good time. I had just borrowed some money to buy some guitar strings from a friend of mine and I was going to pay him back out of the $50 a month Annette sends. That would have cut me a little short. I know $50 may sound like a lot, but I've been giving, sharing with a guy here whose mother can't afford to send anything. She did send him $10 but that's the first money he's received since Sept when I moved near him. I give him coffee, cigarettes, etc. Poor fellow.

Today's Friday, so you all will be opening gifts tomorrow. I hope everybody gets what they need. Kids sure grow up fast. I'm gonna start crying if I don't get myself together.

Tell everybody I love them, Ronnie

IT WAS difficult to think of Ronnie having "good feelings" during the holidays. The tedium of death row was horrible enough, but to be cut off from his family brought a level of pain and desperation he could not handle. Early in the spring of 1989 he began slipping badly. The pressure, the drudgery, the sheer frustration of being sent to hell for a crime he did not commit, consumed him, and he fell apart. He began cutting his wrists and attempting suicide. He was very depressed and wanted to die. The wounds were superficial but left scars. There were several episodes of this, and he was watched closely by the guards. When the wrist cutting didn't work, he managed to start a fire with his mattress and let it drip over his extremities. The burns were treated and eventually healed. More than once, he was put on a suicide watch.

On July 12, 1989, he wrote to Renee:

Dear Renee:

I'm going through so much suffering. I've burned some tissue and got several second and third degree burns. The pressure here is immense. Never getting to go anywhere when the suffering is intolerable, Renee, I've had headaches, I've banged into the concrete, I've gotten down on the floor and banged my head against the concrete. I've hit myself in the face til I was so sore the next day from the punches. Everybody here is stuck here like sardines. I know for a fact this is the most suffering I've ever had to endure. The magic to the problem and its solution is money. I'm talking about never having anything to eat that's worth a shit. This food is like living on K-rations on some damn God-forbidden island. People here are poor but I've been so hungry that I've had to ask for a morsel to stop the craving. I've lost weight. There's so much suffering here.

Please help me. Ron

IN ONE prolonged depressive bout, Ron stopped communication with everyone and withdrew completely until the guards found him curled into a fetal position on his bed. He would respond to nothing.

Then, on September 29, Ron cut his wrists again. He was taking his medications sporadically, was talking nonstop about suicide, and was finally deemed to be a threat to himself. He was moved out of F Cellhouse and transferred to Eastern State Hospital in Vinita. Upon his admission, his chief complaint was, "I have suffered unjustified abuse."

At Eastern State he was first seen by a staff physician, a Dr. Lizarraga, who saw a thirty-six-year-old with a history of drugs and alcohol, unkempt, unshaven, with long graying hair and a mustache, in shabby prison dress, with burn marks on his legs and scars on his arms, scars he made sure the doctor noticed. He freely admitted many of his misdeeds but adamantly denied killing Debbie Carter. The injustice from which he was suffering had caused him to lose hope and want to die.

For the next three months, Ron was a patient at Eastern State. His medication was stabilized. He was seen by various doctors—a neurologist, a psychologist, several psychiatrists. It was noted more than once that he was unstable emotionally, had a low tolerance for frustration, was self-centered with low self-esteem, was detached at times, and had a tendency to explode quickly. The mood swings were wild and remarkable.

He was demanding, and over time became aggressive with the staff and other patients. This aggression could not be tolerated, and Ron was discharged and sent back to death row. Dr. Lizarraga prescribed lithium carbonate, Navane, and Cogentin, a drug used primarily to treat symptoms of Parkinson's disease but sometimes used to reduce shakiness and restlessness caused by tranquilizers.

BACK AT Big Mac, a prison guard by the name of Savage was brutally attacked by Mikell Patrick Smith, a death row inmate generally regarded as the most dangerous killer in the prison. Smith rigged a knife, or a "shank," to the end of a broom handle and thrust it through the bean hole as the guard was serving him lunch. The shank went into his chest and heart, but Officer Savage miraculously survived.

Two years earlier, Smith had stabbed a fellow inmate.

The attack occurred not on death row but on D Cellhouse, where Smith was being held for disciplinary reasons. Nonetheless, the prison officials decided that a new, state-of-the-art death row facility was required. The attack was well publicized and prompted funding for the new unit.

Plans were drawn up for H Unit, which from the outset was designed to "maximize security and control, while providing inmates and staff with a safe, modern environment in which to live and work." It would have two hundred cells on two floors, running along four quads.

From the beginning, the design of H Unit was driven by the prison staff. In the tense atmosphere following the attack on Officer Savage, the staff was given enormous input into the creation of a "noncontact" facility. Early in the design phase, thirty-five prison employees met with the Tulsa architects hired by the Department of Corrections.

Though no death row inmate had ever escaped from McAlester, the designers of H Unit adopted the dramatic plan of putting the entire unit underground.

AFTER two years on death row, Ron's mental health was seriously deteriorating. His noise—yelling, screaming, cursing at all hours of the day and night—grew worse. His behavior grew even more desperate. His temper would explode over nothing, and he would launch into a fit of cursing and throwing things. In another fit he would spit for hours into the hall; he once spat on a guard. But when he began throwing his feces through the bars, it was time to take him away.

"He's slingin' shit again," a guard yelled, and everybody ducked for cover. When things were clear, they rushed him and hauled him away, back to Vinita for another round of evaluation.

He spent a month at Eastern State in July and August 1990. He was again seen by Dr. Lizarraga, who diagnosed the same problems as before. After three weeks, Ron began demanding to be returned to death row. He was concerned about his appeal and felt that he could work on it better at McAlester, where at least they had a law library. His medications had been adjusted, he seemed to be stabilized, and so he was sent back.

After thirteen years of frustration, Oklahoma finally managed to untangle the appeals process and schedule an execution. The unlucky inmate was Charles Troy Coleman, a white man who'd killed three people and had been on death row for eleven years. He was the leader of a small faction that was usually stirring up trouble on The Row, and many of his neighbors were not upset by the prospect of Chuck finally getting the needle. Most of the men, though, knew that when the killings finally started, there would be no turning back.

The Coleman execution was a media event, and the press converged outside Big Mac. There were candlelight vigils and interviews with victims, protesters, ministers, anyone who happened to walk by. As the hours passed, the excitement increased.

Greg Wilhoit and Coleman had become friends, though they argued bitterly over the death penalty. Ron was still in favor of it, though he swayed back and forth. He was not fond of Coleman, who, not surprisingly, had become frustrated with Ron's noisy presence.

The Row was quiet and heavily secured the night Coleman was executed. The circus was outside the prison, where the press counted down the minutes as if a New Year were approaching. Greg was in his cell, watching it all on television. Just after midnight, the news arrived— Charles Troy Coleman was dead.

Several inmates clapped and cheered; most sat quietly in their cells. Some were in prayer.

Greg's reaction was completely unexpected. He was suddenly overcome with emotion and bitter at those who cheered the news. His friend was gone. The world was not now a safer place. Not a single future murderer would be deterred; he knew killers and what prompted them to act. If the victim's family was pleased, then they were far from closure. Greg had been raised in a Methodist church and now studied the Bible every day. Didn't Jesus teach forgiveness? If killing was wrong, then why was the state allowed to kill? By whose authority was the execution carried out? He'd been hit with these arguments before, many times, but now they resonated from a different source.

The death of Charles Coleman was a dramatic revelation for Greg. At that moment he flipped 180 degrees, never to return to his eye-for-an-eye beliefs.

Later, he offered these thoughts to Ron, who confessed that he shared many of them. The next day, though, Ron was an ardent supporter of the death penalty who wanted Ricky Joe Simmons dragged in off the streets of Ada and shot on the spot.

THE PROSECUTION of Ron Williamson was vindicated on May 15, 1991, when the Oklahoma Court of Criminal Appeals unanimously affirmed his conviction and death sentence. The court, in an opinion written by Judge Gary Lumpkin, found several mistakes with the trial, but the "overwhelming evidence" against the defendant far outweighed any of the trifling errors committed by Barney, the cops, Peterson, and Judge

Jones. The court spent little time discussing exactly what evidence had been so overwhelming.

Bill Luker called Ron with the bad news, and he took it well enough. Ron had studied the briefs, talked to Bill many times, and been cautioned against optimism.

ON THE same date, Dennis Fritz received the same news from the same court. Again, the justices found several mistakes in his trial but were evidently swayed by the "overwhelming evidence" against Dennis.

He had not been impressed with the brief filed by his appellate lawyer, and he was not surprised when his conviction was upheld. After three years in the prison library Dennis believed that he knew the statutes and cases better than his attorney.

He was disappointed but did not give up. Like Ron, he had other arguments to make in other courts. Quitting was not an option. But unlike Ron, Dennis was now on his own. Since he was not on death row, there were no indigent lawyers available for him.

BUT THE Court of Criminal Appeals was not always a rubber stamp for the prosecution. Much to Mark Barrett's delight, he received the news on April 16, 1991, that a new trial had been ordered for Greg Wilhoit. The court found it impossible to ignore the miserable job done by George Briggs in defending Greg and ruled that he did not receive adequate representation.

When you're on trial for your life, hire either the best lawyer in town or the worst. Greg had unwittingly hired the worst, and now he had a new trial.

When an inmate was to be removed from his cell and taken off The Row for any reason, there was never an explanation. Guards simply showed up with orders to get dressed, quickly.

Greg knew he'd won his appeal, though, and when the guards arrived at his cell door, the big day had come. "Pack your stuff," one of them said, and it was time to leave. In a couple of minutes he stuffed his entire collection of assets into one cardboard box, then walked away with his escorts. Ron had been moved to the other end of the run, and there was no chance of a farewell. As Greg left McAlester, his thoughts were of the friend he was leaving behind.

When he arrived at the jail in Osage County, a bail hearing was quickly arranged by Mark Barrett. With a capital murder charge still pending and a trial date yet to be set, Greg was not exactly a free man. Instead of the usual exorbitant bond that was impossible to make, the judge set bail at $50,000, a sum Greg's parents and sisters quickly covered.

After five years in jail, four on death row, Greg was free, never to return to a prison cell.

CONSTRUCTION of H Unit had begun in 1990. Virtually everything was made of concrete—floors, walls, ceilings, bunks, bookshelves. To eliminate the chance of shanks being produced, no metal was included in the plans. There were plenty of bars and some glass, but not in the cells. Everything there was concrete.

When the structure was complete, it was covered with dirt. Energy efficiency was the official reason. Natural light and ventilation were extinguished.

When H Unit opened in November 1991, the prison celebrated its new, state-of-the-art death house by throwing a party. Big shots were invited. Ribbons were cut. The prison band was forced to play a few tunes. Tours were given—the future inhabitants were still over in the Big House, a quarter of a mile away. Guests were given the opportunity to pay to sleep one night on a brand-new concrete bunk in the cell of their choice.

After the party, and to work out the kinks, some medium security prisoners were moved in first and watched closely to see what mischief they could create. When H Unit proved sturdy, functional, and escape-proof, it was time to send in the bad boys from F Cellhouse.

The complaining and bitching started immediately. There were no windows, no chance of outside light, no hope of fresh air. Double-celling was implemented, and the cells were too small for two men. The concrete bunks were too hard and only thirty-six inches apart. A stainless-steel toilet/sink was wedged between them, so that a bowel movement was a shared event. The layout of the pods was such that most of the daily chatter—the lifeblood for the prisoners—was cut off. As a non-contact facility, H Unit was designed not only to keep the guards away from inmates but to isolate the prisoners themselves. The food was worse than on F Cellhouse. The yard, the most cherished area at the old place, was nothing but a concrete box much smaller than a tennis court. Its walls were eighteen feet tall, and the entire area was covered with a thick grate that blocked out whatever light could penetrate the sun dome. It was impossible to see green grass.

The new concrete had not been sealed or painted. Concrete dust was everywhere. It piled up in the corners of the cells. It clung to the walls, settled on the floors, hung in the air, and of course was inhaled by the inmates. Attorneys visiting their clients often left coughing and rasping because of the dust.

The state-of-the-art ventilation system was "closed," meaning there was no outside circulation at all. This was tolerable until the power went out, which happened often while the bugs were being worked out of the system.

Leslie Delk, an indigent defense lawyer assigned to Ron Williamson, discussed the problems in a letter to a colleague who had sued the prison:

> The food situation is horrible and almost every client I have has
> lost weight. One client has lost 90 pounds in 10 months. I have

communicated this with the prison, but of course they tell me he is fine, etc. One thing discovered on a recent trip to the infirmary was that the food is brought over from the old prison where it is prepared behind the walls. When it arrives at H-Unit, there are inmates—shock incarceration guys, I think—that serve it up. These guys are told that they can have whatever is left, so the portions the death row inmates are now receiving are about half of what the rest of the prison receives. It is my understanding that there is little or no DOC supervision of the food as it is put on the trays for the death row guys. All my clients have complained that the food is always cold now, and that it is so poorly prepared that the men are sick from it and the quantities are so low that most people are forced to purchase food from the canteen so they can get enough to eat. This is of course the prison store that charges whatever they want for the foods they offer. (Usually much higher than we could purchase from a grocery store.) Also many of my clients have no family to help support them so they go without.

H Unit was a shock to the inmates. After hearing rumors for two years about a new, modern $11 million facility, they were stunned when they moved into an underground prison with less space and more restrictions than F Cellhouse.

Ron hated H Unit. His roommate was Rick Rojem, a resident of The Row since 1985 and a calming influence. Rick was a Buddhist who spent hours in meditation and also enjoyed playing the guitar. Privacy was impossible in their cramped cell. They rigged a blanket from the ceiling and between the beds in a lame effort to withdraw into their own worlds.

Rojem was worried about Ron. He had lost interest in reading. His mind and conversation could not stay on one subject. He was medicated at times, but far from getting proper treatment. He would sleep for hours, then pace around the tiny cell for an entire night, mumbling incoherently or chanting about one of his delusions. Then he would stand at the door and scream in agony. Since they were together twenty-three hours a day, Rick was watching his cell mate go insane, and he couldn't help him.

Ron lost ninety pounds after moving into H Unit. His hair turned gray, and he looked like a ghost. Annette was waiting one day in the visitors' room when she saw the guards lead a wiry old man with long, stringy gray hair and a beard into the room. Who is that? she thought. Her brother.

She said, "When I saw them bring this man with long hair and just a skinny, horrible, emaciated-looking man that they brought to visit me that I would not have recognized if I met him on the street, I came home, and I wrote the warden asking him to have Ron checked for AIDS because he looked so gauntish, and knowing the stories you hear about prisons, I asked them to check him for AIDS."

The warden wrote back and assured her Ronnie did not have AIDS. She fired off another letter and complained about the food, the high prices in the canteen, and the fact that the profits from the canteen went into a fund to help buy exercise equipment for the guards.

In 1992, a psychiatrist named Ken Foster was hired by the prison and soon met Ron Williamson. He found him to be disheveled, disoriented, out of touch with reality, thin, gray, frail, emaciated, in poor physical condition. It was obvious to Dr. Foster, as it should have been to the prison officials, that something was wrong.

Ron's mental condition was even worse than his physical. His outbursts and explosions were far beyond normal prison clamor, and it was no secret among the guards and staff that he had lost contact with reality. Dr. Foster witnessed several bouts of the maniacal screaming and noted three general themes: (1) that Ron was innocent, (2) that Ricky Joe Simmons had confessed to the murder and should be prosecuted, and (3) that Ron was in great physical pain, usually in his chest, and he was afraid he was about to die.

Though his symptoms were obvious and extreme, the records reviewed by Dr. Foster indicated that Ron had been receiving no mental health treatment for a long time. The denial of medication for a person as sick as Ron normally results in the onset of psychotic symptoms.

Dr. Foster wrote, "The psychotic reaction and the accompanying deterioration are worsened when a person is under the multiple stresses which accompany being in a death row environment and having the knowledge that you are scheduled to die. The GAF scale, as set forth in authoritative mental health manuals, considers imprisonment a 'catastrophic' stressor."

It was impossible to speculate how much worse the catastrophe might be for an innocent person.

Dr. Foster decided Ron needed better medications in a better environment. Ron would always be mentally ill, but improvements were possible, even for a death row inmate. However, Dr. Foster soon learned that helping sick and condemned prisoners was a very low priority.

He spoke to James Saffle, a regional director with the Department of Corrections, and to Dan Reynolds, the warden at McAlester. Both were familiar with Ron Williamson and his problems, and both had more important things to worry about.

Ken Foster, though, proved to be a rather stubborn, independent sort who disliked bureaucratic decisions and actually wanted to help his patients. He kept reporting to Saffle and Reynolds and made sure they knew the details of Ron's serious mental and physical problems. He insisted on meeting with Reynolds at least once a week to review the status of his patients; Ron was always mentioned. And he spoke daily to a deputy warden, gave the routine updates, and made sure the summaries were passed on to the warden.

Repeatedly, Dr. Foster explained to those who ran the prison that Ron was not getting the medicines he needed and that he was deteriorating mentally and physically because of inadequate treatment. He was especially incensed that Ron would not be transferred to the Special Care Unit, or SCU, a building within view of H Unit.

Inmates who exhibited serious mental problems were routinely moved into the SCU, the only facility at McAlester designed for such treatment. However, the DOC had a long-standing policy that denied death row inmates access to the SCU. The official reason was vague, but many capital defense lawyers suspected the policy was in place to help speed along executions. If a severely disturbed death row inmate was properly evaluated, he might be found to be incompetent, thus thwarting a trip to the chamber.

The policy had been challenged many times but remained intractable.

Ken Foster challenged it again. He explained repeatedly to Saffle and Reynolds that he could not adequately treat Ron Williamson without placing him at the SCU, where he could monitor his condition and regulate his medication. Often his explanations were pointed, heated, and intense. But Dan Reynolds proved stubbornly resistant to the idea of moving Ron and saw no need to improve his treatment. Don't bother with death row inmates, Reynolds said. They're going to die anyway.

Dr. Foster's appeals on behalf of Ron became so bothersome that Warden Reynolds locked him out of the prison.

When the lockout ended, Dr. Foster resumed his efforts to move Ron to the SCU. It took four years.

AFTER his direct appeal was over, Ron's case entered "post-conviction relief," the next stage in which he was allowed to present evidence that was not offered at trial.

As was the practice at that time, Bill Luker transferred the file to Leslie Delk, with the Appellate Public Defender's Office. Her first priority was obtaining better medical treatment for her client. She saw Ron once on F Cellhouse and realized he was a very sick man. After he was transferred to H Unit, she became alarmed at his eroding condition.

Though Delk was not a psychiatrist or psychologist, she had received extensive training in the detection and nature of mental illness. Part of her job as a capital defense attorney was to observe such problems and try to get adequate treatment. She relied on the opinions of mental health experts, but it was difficult with Ron because a proper examination was impossible. As part of the noncontact policy at H Unit, no one could sit in the same room with the prisoner, not even his lawyer. A psychiatrist trying to examine Ron had to do so through a sheet of glass while talking to him on the phone.

Delk arranged for a Dr. Pat Fleming to do a psychological evaluation of Ron, as required in post-conviction proceedings. Dr. Fleming made three attempts but was unable to complete her assessment. Her patient was agitated, delusional, noncooperative, and hallucinating. The staff informed Dr. Fleming that such behavior was not at all unusual. It was obvious that he was a very disturbed man who was in no condition to assist his attorney or function in any meaningful way. She was severely restricted in her attempt to evaluate Ron because she was not allowed a confidential visit in which she could sit in the same room to question, observe, and administer tests.

Dr. Fleming met with the staff physician on H Unit and detailed her concerns. Later, she was assured that Ron had been seen by mental health professionals from within the prison, but she saw no improvement. She strongly recommended a commitment to Eastern State Hospital for an extended period to stabilize Ron and properly evaluate him.

Her recommendation was denied.

Leslie Delk hammered away at the prison officials. She met with the correctional staff, the medical staff, and the various wardens to lodge her complaints and demand better treatment. Promises were made, then ignored. Benign efforts were made—slight changes in Ron's medications—but he received no significant treatment. She documented her frustrations with a series of letters to the prison officials. She visited Ron as often as possible, and when she was certain his condition could not worsen, it did. Leslie worried that he might die at any time.

WHILE the medical staff struggled to treat Ron, the correctional staff was having great fun at his expense. For amusement, some of the prison guards enjoyed playing with the new intercom on H Unit. Each cell had a two-way speaker to the control room, yet another smart toy to keep the guards as far away from the inmates as possible.

But it wasn't far enough.

"Ron, this is God," a haunting voice called into Ron's cell deep in the night. "Why did you kill Debbie Carter?" A pause, then the guards would snicker as they heard Ron screaming through his door, "I didn't kill anybody! I am innocent!" His deep, raspy voice rattled through the southwest quad and disrupted the quiet. The seizure would last an hour or so, upsetting the other inmates but greatly humoring the guards.

When things were quiet, the voice returned. "Ron, this is Debbie Carter. Why did you kill me?"

His tormented screams would go on and on.

"Ron, this is Charlie Carter. Why did you kill my daughter?"

The other inmates begged the guards to stop it, but they were having too much fun. Rick Rojem believed that two of the more sadistic guards, in particular, lived for the fun of mistreating Ron. The abuse went on for months.

"Just ignore them," Rick pleaded with his cell mate. "If you ignore them, they'll quit."

Ron couldn't grasp this idea. He was determined to convince everyone around him that he was innocent, and bawling it at the top of his lungs seemed the appropriate way. Often, when he couldn't scream any longer, when he was physically spent or too hoarse to continue, he would stand with his face close to the speaker and whisper incoherently for hours.

Leslie Delk finally heard of the fun and games and fired off a letter on October 12, 1992, to the manager of H Unit. It read, in part:

Also, I had mentioned to you that I had been hearing from different folks that Ron was being harassed through the intercom by certain guards who apparently find it humorous to taunt the "crazies" and get them to react. I am continuing to hear about this problem and most recently heard that Officer Martin walked up to the door of Ron's cell and started harassing him and taunting him (I believe that the content of these usually revolve around "Ricky Joe Simmons" and "Debra Sue Carter"). From what I understand, Officer Reading stepped in to get Officer Martin to quit his behavior but had to repeatedly tell him to quit harassing Ron before Martin actually stopped.

I have heard Officer Martin's name from several different sources now as being one of the people who routinely harass Ron and so I would like to know if you could investigate this matter and take appropriate action. Maybe it would be [beneficial] for you to have some training sessions for your guards who have to deal with those inmates who are mentally ill.

Not all of the guards were cruel. A female guard stopped by Ron's cell late one night for a chat. He looked awful and said he was starving, said he hadn't eaten for days. She believed him. She left and returned a few minutes later with a jar of peanut butter and a loaf of stale bread.

In a letter to Renee, Ron said he enjoyed the "feast" immensely and there wasn't a crumb left over.

KIM MARKS was an investigator with the Oklahoma Indigent Defense System who ultimately spent more time on H Unit with Ron than anyone else. When she was first assigned his case, she reviewed the trial transcripts, reports, and exhibits. She was a former newspaper reporter, and her curiosity drove her to at least question Ron's guilt.

She made a list of potential suspects, twelve in all and most with criminal backgrounds. Glen Gore was number one, for all the obvious reasons. He was with Debbie the night she was murdered. They had known each other for years; thus, he could gain access to her apartment without force. He had a wretched history of violence against women. He had pointed the finger at Ron.

Why had the cops shown so little interest in Gore? The deeper Kim probed into the police reports and the trial itself, the more she became convinced that Ron's protests were well grounded.

She visited him many times on H Unit and, like Leslie Delk, watched him completely unravel. She approached each visit with a mix of curiosity and apprehension. Never had she seen an inmate age as rapidly as Ron. His dark brown hair was grayer with each visit, and he was not yet forty. He was gaunt and ghostlike, due in no small part to the lack of sunshine. His clothes were dirty and fit badly. His eyes were hollow and deeply troubled.

A major part of her job was to determine if the client had mental problems, then attempt to find not only adequate treatment but also expert witnesses. It was obvious to her, and obvious to any layperson, that he was mentally ill and suffering greatly from his condition. Early on, she was stiff-armed by the DOC policy of keeping death row inmates out of the Special Care Unit. Like Dr. Foster, Kim would fight that battle for years.

She located and reviewed the 1983 videotape of Ron's second polygraph. Though at that time he'd already been diagnosed as depressed and bipolar, and perhaps schizophrenic, he was coherent, under control, and able to present himself as a normal person. But nine years later, there was nothing normal about him. He was delusional, out of touch with reality, and consumed with obsessions—Ricky Joe Simmons, religion, the liars at his trial, lack of money, Debbie Carter, the law, his music, the massive lawsuit he would one day file against the state, his baseball career, the abuses and injustices to which he was being subjected.

She talked to the staff and heard their reports of his ability to scream for an entire day, then she got a good dose of it. Because of the peculiarities of the layout of H Unit, the women's restroom had a vent that carried sounds from the southwest quad, where Ron was housed.

On a trip to the restroom, she was stunned to hear him bellowing like a madman.

It rattled her, and, working with Leslie, she pushed even harder to force the prison to provide better treatment. They tried to get an exception to move him to the SCU. They tried to have him evaluated at Eastern State.

Their efforts were futile.

IN JUNE 1992, Leslie Delk, as part of the post-conviction process, filed an application for a hearing to determine mental competency in the district court of Pontotoc County. Bill Peterson filed an objection, and the court denied the request.

This denial was immediately appealed to the Court of Criminal Appeals, where it was upheld.

In July, she filed an extensive application for post-conviction relief. Her claims were based primarily on the voluminous records of Ron's mental health, and she argued that his lack of competency should have been addressed at trial. Two months later, post-conviction relief was denied, and Leslie appealed again to the Oklahoma Court of Criminal Appeals.

Not surprisingly, she lost again. The next step was a routine and hopeless appeal to the U.S. Supreme Court. A year later it issued a perfunctory denial. Other routine filings were made, more routine denials were entered, and when all state remedies were exhausted on August 26, 1994, the execution of Ron Williamson was set by the Court of Criminal Appeals for September 27, 1994.

He had been on death row for six years and four months.

AFTER two years of freedom, Greg Wilhoit was dragged back into a courtroom to once again face charges of murdering his wife.

After he left McAlester, he settled in Tulsa and tried to reestablish something close to a normal life. It was not easy. He carried emotional and psychological scars from his ordeal. His daughters, now eight and nine years old, were being raised by some friends from church, two schoolteachers, and their lives were quite stable. His parents and sisters were supportive, as always.

His case had gathered some attention. His trial lawyer, George Briggs, had mercifully passed away, but not before having his license to practice revoked by the state. Several prominent criminal lawyers contacted Greg and wanted to represent him. Lawyers are attracted to cameras like ants to a picnic, and Greg was amused to see so much interest in his case.

But it was an easy choice. His pal Mark Barrett had won his release, and Greg was confident he would now win his freedom.

During his first trial, the most damaging evidence was the testimony of the state's two bite-mark experts. Both told the jury that the wound on Kathy Wilhoit's breast had been left there by her estranged husband. The Wilhoit family found a leading bite-mark expert, Dr. Thomas Krauss of Kansas. Dr. Krauss was stunned at the discrepancies between Greg's dental impression and the actual wound. The two were drastically different.

Mark Barrett then sent the bite mark to eleven nationally renowned experts, many of whom usually testified on behalf of the prosecution. They included the FBI's top bite-mark consultant and the expert who testified against Ted Bundy. The verdict was unanimous—all twelve bite-mark experts concluded that Greg Wilhoit had to be excluded. The comparisons were not even close.

At an evidentiary hearing, an expert for the defense identified twenty major discrepancies between Greg's teeth and the bite mark, and testified that each one conclusively excluded Greg.

But the prosecutor pushed on and insisted on a trial, which quickly became a farce. Mark Barrett successfully excluded the state's bite-mark experts, then destroyed the credibility of the DNA man called by the state.

After the prosecution rested, Mark Barrett made a forceful motion to dismiss the evidence presented by the state and direct a verdict in favor of Greg Wilhoit. Then the judge called for a recess, and they went to lunch. When they returned, and when the jury was back and the courtroom was settled, the judge, in a rare move, announced that the motion would be granted. The case was dismissed.

"Mr. Wilhoit," he said, "you are now a free man."

After a long night of celebrating with his family and friends, Greg Wilhoit raced to the airport the next morning and flew to California, never to return to Oklahoma unless it was to visit his family or fight the death penalty. Eight years after Kathy's murder, he was finally a free man.

By chasing the wrong suspect, the police and prosecutors had allowed the real killer's trail to grow cold. He has yet to be found.

THE NEW death chamber on H Unit was working just fine. On March 10, 1992, Robyn Leroy Parks, male black, age forty-three, was executed for the 1978 murder of a gas station attendant. He had been on The Row for thirteen years.

Three days later, Olan Randle Robison, male white, age forty-six, was executed for murdering a couple after he broke into their rural home in 1980.

Ron Williamson was to be the third man strapped to a gurney on H Unit and offered the opportunity to say a few final words.

ON AUGUST 30, 1994, Ron was greeted at his cell door by a menacing squad of frowning guards who wanted to take him somewhere. He was cuffed at the ankles and wrists, and a belly chain linked all the hardware together. This was something serious.

As usual, he was gaunt, dirty, unshaven, and unstable, and the guards gave him as much room as possible. Officer Martin was one of the five.

Ron was led out of H Unit, into a van, and driven the short distance to the administrative offices at the front of the prison. Surrounded by his entourage, he was taken to the warden's office, to a room with a long conference table where many people were waiting to witness something dramatic. Still shackled and guarded closely by his sentries, he was seated at one end of the table. The warden was at the other, and he began the meeting by introducing Ron to the numerous staff members seated around the table, all looking rather glum.

A real pleasure to meet you all.

Ron was then handed a "notification," which the warden began reading:

> You have been sentenced to die for the crime of murder at 12:01 a.m. on Tuesday September 27, 1994. The purpose of this meeting is to inform you of the rules and procedures to be followed for the next thirty days and to discuss certain privileges you may be afforded.

Ron became upset and said that he hadn't killed anyone. Maybe he'd done some bad things in his life, but murder wasn't one of them.

The warden kept reading, and Ron again insisted that he did not kill Debbie Carter.

The warden and the unit manager chatted with him for a few minutes and calmed him down. They were not there to judge him, they said, but they were just following the rules and procedures.

But Ron had a video of Ricky Simmons confessing to the crime, and he wanted to show it to the warden. Again he denied killing Debbie, and he rambled on about somehow getting on television in Ada to profess his innocence. He mentioned his sister going to college in Ada.

The warden continued reading:

> On the morning prior to the date of execution, you will be placed in a special cell where you will remain until the time of execution. While in this cell and until the time of execution you will be under constant surveillance by Correctional Officers.

Ron interrupted again, yelling that he did not kill Debbie Carter.

The warden plowed on, reading pages of rules regarding visitors, personal belongings, and funeral arrangements. Ron tuned him out and became subdued.

"What should we do with your body?" the warden asked.

Ron was emotional and confused and unprepared for such a question. Finally he managed to suggest that they just ship him to Annette.

When he had no questions and claimed he understood it all, he was marched back to his cell. The countdown began.

HE FORGOT to call Annette. Two days later she was riffling through her mail when she came across an envelope from the Department of Corrections in McAlester. Inside was a letter from a deputy warden:

Ms. Hudson:

It is with empathy that I must inform you that your brother, Ronald Keith Williamson (#134846) is scheduled to be executed at the Oklahoma State Penitentiary at 12:01 a.m. on Tuesday, September 27, 1994.

Visiting during the day prior to the execution date will be limited to Clergymen, Attorney of Record, and two other persons who have been approved by the Warden.

As difficult as it may be, funeral arrangements must be considered, and these arrangements are the responsibility of the family. If this responsibility is not assumed by the family, the State will attend to the funeral. Please inform me of your decision.

Sincerely, Ken Klingler

Annette called Renee with the horrible news. Both were distraught and worked hard to convince each other that it couldn't be true. Other conversations followed, and they decided that they would not bring his body back to Ada. It would not be put on display at Criswell's funeral home for the town to gawk at. Instead, they would have a private service and burial in McAlester, by invitation only. Only a few close friends and a few family members would attend.

They were informed by the prison that they would be allowed to witness the execution. Renee said she couldn't do it. Annette was determined to be there at the end.

The news swept through Ada. Peggy Stillwell was watching the local TV station when she heard the rather surprising report that an execution date had been set for Ron Williamson. Though this was good news, she was angry because no one had informed her. She had been promised that she would be allowed to witness the execution, and she certainly wanted to. Perhaps someone would call in a few days.

Annette kept to herself, and tried to deny it was happening. Her visits to the prison had become less frequent, and shorter in duration. Ronnie was out of his mind and would either yell at her or pretend she wasn't there. Several times she had left after seeing him for less than five minutes.

CHAPTER 13

Once the Oklahoma courts were finished with Ron's case and the
date of execution was set, his attorneys hustled to federal court
and began the next stage of appeals. The proceedings are known as
habeas corpus—Latin for "you should have the body." A writ for habeas
corpus required that an inmate be brought before the court to determine
the legality of his detention.

His case was assigned to Janet Chesley, a lawyer with the Indigent
Defense System in Norman. Janet had extensive experience with habeas
work and was accustomed to the frenetic pace of filing last-minute motions and appeals while watching the clock race toward an execution.
She met with Ron, explained the process, and assured him he would get
a stay. In her work such conversations were not unusual, and her clients,
though understandably jittery, always came to trust her. The execution
date was serious, but no one was put to death until the habeas appeals
had been exhausted.

But Ron was different. The formal pronouncement of a date with death had pushed him even deeper into insanity. He was counting the days, unable to believe Janet's promises. The clock had not stopped. The death chamber was waiting.

A week went by, then two. Ron spent much time in prayer and Bible study. He also slept a lot and stopped screaming. His drugs were being liberally dispensed. The Row was quiet, and waiting. The other inmates missed nothing and wondered if the state would really execute someone as insane as Ron Williamson.

Three weeks went by.

THE U.S. District Court for the Eastern District of Oklahoma is in Muskogee. In 1994, there were two judges, neither of whom was particularly fond of habeas corpus appeals or jailhouse lawsuits. They came in by the truckload. Every prisoner had issues and complaints; most claimed innocence and abuse. The death row boys had real lawyers, some from big firms working pro bono, and the briefs were thick and creative and had to be reckoned with. The general population prisoners were usually represented by themselves, with no shortage of advice from the writ writers who held sway in the law libraries and sold their opinions for cigarettes. If the inmates weren't filing habeas appeals, they were filing lawsuits over bad food, cold showers, mean guards, tight handcuffs, lack of sunlight. The list was long.

Most prisoner suits lacked merit and were dismissed outright, then sent to the Tenth Circuit Court of Appeals in Denver, home base for the sprawling federal district that included Oklahoma.

The habeas corpus appeal filed by Janet Chesley was randomly assigned to Judge Frank Seay, a Jimmy Carter appointee who took the bench in 1979. Judge Seay was from Seminole, and prior to his federal appointment he had served for eleven years as the trial judge in the Twenty-second District, which included Pontotoc County. He was familiar with the courthouse there, and the town and its lawyers.

In May 1971, Judge Seay had driven to the village of Asher and delivered a high school commencement speech. One of the seventeen graduates was Ron Williamson.

After fifteen years on the bench, Judge Seay had little patience with the habeas corpus appeals that landed in his office. The Williamson petition arrived there in September 1994, just a few days before the execution. He suspected—in fact he knew—that the death penalty lawyers often waited until the last possible moment to file their petitions so that he, and other federal judges, would be forced to grant stays while the paperwork got sorted out. He often wondered what the poor convict was going through, sweating the hours on death row while his lawyers engaged in a bit of brinksmanship with a federal judge.

But it was good lawyering, and though Judge Seay understood it, he still didn't like the process. He'd granted a few stays, but never a new trial in a habeas corpus matter.

As always, the Williamson petition was first read by Jim Payne, a U.S. magistrate in the federal court office. Payne was known to have conservative leanings and a similar dislike for habeas work, but he was also highly regarded because of his innate fairness. It had been his duty for many years to plow through each habeas corpus filing and search for valid claims, which, though rare, did exist often enough to keep the reading interesting.

To Jim Payne, the job was crucial. If he missed something buried in the voluminous briefs and transcripts, then an innocent man might be executed.

Janet Chesley's petition was so well written that it captured his attention in the first paragraph, and by the time he finished it, he had some doubts about the fairness of Ron's trial. Her arguments centered on the issues of inadequate defense counsel, mental competency, and the unreliability of hair evidence.

Jim Payne read the petition at home, at night, and when he returned to the office the following morning, he met with Judge Seay and recommended a stay. Judge Seay had great respect for his magistrate, and after a long discussion about the Williamson petition he agreed to stop the execution.

After watching the clock and praying fervently for twenty-three days, Ron was informed that his execution had been delayed indefinitely. His brush with death had taken him to within five days of getting the needle.

JIM PAYNE passed the habeas petition on to his law clerk, Gail Seward, who read it and agreed that an in-depth review was called for. He then gave it to the office rookie, a law clerk by the name of Vicky Hildebrand, who, because of her complete lack of seniority, had been assigned the unofficial title of "death penalty clerk." Vicky had been a social worker before law school, and she had quickly and quietly assumed the role as the token bleeding heart in Judge Seay's moderate-to-conservative office.

Williamson was her first habeas case involving the death penalty, and as she read his petition, she was captivated by the opening paragraph:

> This case is a bizarre one about a dream that turned into a nightmare for Ronald Keith Williamson. His arrest came nearly 5 years after the crime—after Mr. Williamson's alibi witness was dead—and was based almost entirely on the "confession," related as a dream, of a seriously mentally ill man, Ron Williamson.

Vicky read on, and was soon struck by the paucity of credible evidence offered at his trial and by the haphazard strategies of his defense. When she finished it, she had strong doubts about Ron's guilt.

And she immediately asked herself if she had the nerves for such a job. Would every habeas petition be so persuasive? Was she going to believe every death row inmate? She confided in Jim Payne, who devised a plan. They would draft Gail Seward, more of a centrist, and get her opinion. Vicky spent an entire Friday copying the lengthy trial transcript—three copies, one for each member of the conspiracy. Each spent the entire weekend reading every word of Ron's trial, and when they huddled early on Monday morning, the verdict was unanimous. From the right, left, and center, all agreed that justice had not been served. Not only were they certain the trial had been unconstitutional; they also believed Ron might very well be innocent.

They were intrigued by the reference to *The Dreams of Ada*. Janet Chesley's petition made much of the dream confession Ron had allegedly made. He had been reading the book shortly after his arrest, and had it in his cell when he gave his own jailhouse dream to John Christian. Published seven years earlier, the book was out of print, but Vicky found copies in used bookstores and libraries. The three read it quickly, and their suspicions of the authorities in Ada were greatly magnified.

Since Judge Seay was known to be rather abrupt when dealing with habeas matters, it was decided that Jim Payne would approach him and break the ice on the Williamson case. Judge Seay listened carefully, then got an earful from Vicky and Gail. The three felt strongly that a new trial was in order, and after hearing them out, the judge agreed to study the petition.

He knew Bill Peterson and Barney Ward and most of the gang down in Ada. He considered Barney an old pal but had never cared for Peterson. Frankly, he was not surprised at the sloppy trial and flimsy evidence. Strange things happened in Ada, and Judge Seay had heard for years that the cops had a bad reputation. He was particularly bothered by the lack of control Judge Ronald Jones had exerted over the proceedings. Bad police work and slanted prosecutions were not unusual, but the trial judge was supposed to guarantee fairness.

Nor was he surprised that the Court of Criminal Appeals had seen nothing wrong with the trial.

When he became convinced that justice had not been served, he and his staff launched into a thorough review of the case.

DENNIS FRITZ had lost contact with Ron. He had written one letter to his old friend, but it went unanswered.

Kim Marks and Leslie Delk drove to Conner to interview Dennis in connection with their investigation. They brought the Ricky Joe Simmons video and played the confession. Dennis, like Ron, was angry that someone else had confessed to the murder they were convicted of committing, yet this information had not been available at his trial. He developed a correspondence with Kim Marks, and she kept him posted on the developments in Ron's case.

As a fixture in the law library, Dennis heard all the legal gossip and knew the latest rulings from around the country. He and his fellow jailhouse lawyers missed nothing in the field of criminal procedure. DNA testing was first mentioned in the early 1990s, and he read everything he could find on the subject.

In 1993, a segment of *Donahue* was devoted to four men who had been exonerated by DNA testing. The show found a wide audience, especially in the prisons, and served as a catalyst for the innocence movement across the country.

One group that had already gained attention was the Innocence Project, founded in 1992 by two New York lawyers, Peter Neufeld and Barry Scheck. They set up shop in the Benjamin N. Cardozo School of Law as a nonprofit legal clinic where students handled the case work while staff attorneys supervised. Neufeld had a long history of legal activism in Brooklyn. Scheck was an expert on forensic DNA and became famous as one of the attorneys for O.J. Simpson.

Dennis watched the Simpson trial closely, and when it was over, he considered the possibility of contacting Barry Scheck.

AFTER receiving numerous complaints about H Unit, in 1994 Amnesty International conducted a thorough evaluation of the place. It found many violations of international standards, including treaties adopted by the United States and minimum rules set forth by the United Nations. The violations included cells that were too small, inadequately furnished, unlit, unventilated, windowless, and without access to natural light. Not surprisingly, the exercise yards were found to be unduly restrictive and much too small. Many inmates skipped their one hour a day so they could have the privacy of the cell without their roommate. Other than a high school diploma course, there were no educational programs, nor were the inmates allowed to work. Religious services were restricted. Isolation of individual prisoners was too severe. The food service needed a thorough review.

In conclusion, Amnesty International found that conditions on H Unit amounted to cruel, inhuman, or degrading treatment in violation of international standards. The conditions, when "applied over a period of time, can have a detrimental effect on the physical and mental health of prisoners."

The report was issued, but was not binding on the prison. It did add fuel to some of the prisoner lawsuits that had been filed.

AFTER a three-year hiatus, the death chamber machinery cranked up again. On March 20, 1995, Thomas Grasso, male white, age thirty-two, was executed after only two years on The Row. Though it had been difficult, Grasso was able to stop his appeals and get things over with.

Next came Roger Dale Stafford, the infamous steak-house murderer, who had one of the more notable executions. Mass murders in big cities draw more press, and Stafford went out in a blaze of glory. He'd spent fifteen years on death row, and his case was used by police and prosecutors and especially politicians as a prime example of the flaws in the appeals process.

On August 11, 1995, a bizarre execution took place. Robert Brecheen, a forty-year-old white male, barely made it to the death chamber. The day before, he swallowed a handful of painkillers that he had somehow smuggled in and stockpiled. His suicide was to be his final effort at telling the state to go to hell, but the state prevailed. Brecheen was found unconscious by the guards and rushed to the hospital, where his stomach was pumped and he was stabilized enough to get hauled back to H Unit for a proper killing.

JUDGE SEAY directed his staff through a tedious evaluation of every aspect of the Williamson case. They pored over the transcripts, which included the preliminary hearing and every other court appearance. They cataloged Ron's lengthy medical records. They studied the police files and reports from the OSBI experts.

The workload was divided among Vicky Hildebrand, Jim Payne, and Gail Seward. It became a group project, with no shortage of ideas and eagerness. The trial was rotten, a clear miscarriage of justice had occurred, and they wanted to correct it.

Judge Seay had never trusted hair evidence. He had once presided over a federal death penalty case in which the star witness was to be the FBI's top hair expert. His qualifications were beyond reproach and he'd testified many times, but Judge Seay was not impressed. The expert didn't testify and was sent away.

Vicky Hildebrand volunteered for the research on hair evidence. For months she read dozens of cases and studies and became convinced that it was all junk science. It was so wildly unreliable that it should never be used in any trial, a conclusion Judge Seay had long since reached.

Gail Seward concentrated on Barney Ward and the mistakes he made at trial. Jim Payne tackled the *Brady* issues. For months the team worked on little else, putting Williamson aside only to tend to pressing matters. There was no deadline on their work, but Judge Seay was a taskmaster who didn't tolerate an idle docket. They worked nights and weekends. They read and edited each other's work. As they peeled away more layers, they found more mistakes, and as the trial errors piled up, their enthusiasm increased.

Jim Payne had daily briefings with Judge Seay, who, as expected, offered no shortage of comments. He read the team's initial drafts, did his editing, sent them back for more work.

As it became obvious that a new trial would be ordered, the case began to bother Judge Seay. Barney was an old friend, an old warrior past his prime who would be deeply hurt by the criticism. How would Ada react to the news that their former judge had taken sides with the notorious killer Ron Williamson?

The team knew that their work would be scrutinized at the next level, at the Tenth Circuit Court of Appeals in Denver. What if they got reversed? Were they convinced enough in their cause? Could they argue so persuasively that the Tenth Circuit would be convinced?

For almost a year, the team labored under the guidance of Judge Seay. Finally, on September 19, 1995, one year after the execution had been stayed, he issued a writ of habeas corpus and granted a new trial.

The opinion accompanying the order was exhaustive, one hundred pages long, and a masterpiece of judicial analysis and reasoning. In clear yet scholarly language, Judge Seay threw the book at Barney Ward, Bill Peterson, the Ada Police Department, and the OSBI, and though he held his fire on the unfortunate officiating by Judge Jones, he left little guesswork as to how he felt about it.

Ron deserved a new trial for many reasons, chief among them ineffective assistance of counsel. Barney's mistakes were numerous and harmful. They included the failure to raise the issue of his client's mental competency; failure to thoroughly investigate and present evidence against Glen Gore; failure to flesh out the fact that Terri Holland had also testified against Karl Fontenot and Tommy Ward; failure to inform the jury that Ricky Joe Simmons had confessed to the murder and had even done so on a videotape that Barney actually possessed; failure to attack Ron's confessions and suppress them before trial; and failure to call mitigating witnesses during the penalty phase.

Bill Peterson and the cops were faulted for hiding the 1983 video of Ron's second polygraph; using confessions obtained by questionable means, including Ron's dream confession; calling to the stand and putting under oath jailhouse snitches; presenting a case with almost no physical evidence; and sitting on exculpatory evidence.

Judge Seay analyzed the history of hair evidence and ruled, rather dramatically, that it was too unreliable and should be banned from all courts. He criticized the OSBI experts for their mishandling of the samples in the Fritz and Williamson investigation.

Bill Peterson, Judge Jones, and Judge John David Miller were faulted for not stopping the proceedings and inquiring into Ron's mental health.

Judge Jones was wrong for holding a *Brady* hearing on exculpatory materials *after the trial was over*! His denial of Barney's request for a forensic expert to rebut the testimony from the OSBI gang was reversible error in itself.

With the precision of a surgeon, Judge Seay cut through every aspect of the trial and laid bare the mockery of Ron's conviction. Unlike the Oklahoma Court of Criminal Appeals, a tribunal that had examined the case twice, Judge Seay saw a bad conviction and questioned everything.

At the end of his opinion, he added something unusual—an epilogue. He wrote:

> While considering my decision in this case, I told a friend, a layman, I believed the facts and the law dictated that I must grant a new trial to a man who had been convicted and sentenced to death.
>
> My friend asked, "Is he a murderer?"
>
> I replied simply, "We won't know until he receives a fair trial."
>
> God help us, if ever in this great country we turn our heads while people who have not had fair trials are executed. That almost happened in this case.

As a courtesy, Judge Seay sent a copy of his opinion to Barney Ward, with a note saying he was sorry but he had no choice. Barney would never speak to him again.

Though Vicky Hildebrand, Gail Seward, and Jim Payne felt strongly about their work, they were still somewhat apprehensive when it was made public. Giving a new trial to a death row inmate was not popular in Oklahoma. Ron's case had consumed their lives for a year, and though they were sure of themselves, they did not want Judge Seay and his office criticized.

"PROSECUTORS Vow to Fight Order for New Trial," read the headline in the *Ada Evening News* on September 27, 1995. On one side of it was a high school photo of Ron Williamson, on the other was one of Bill Peterson. The report began:

> An angry Bill Peterson said that he would be "more than happy" to make an appearance before the United States Supreme Court, if necessary, in order to overturn a recent federal judge's ruling which has ordered a new trial for convicted Pontotoc County murderer Ronald Keith Williamson.

Fortunately, at least for Peterson, he would not get the chance to go to Washington and argue the case. He went on to say that he had been assured by the state's attorney general that he, himself, would personally handle the "immediate" appeal to the Tenth Circuit in Denver. He was quoted as saying:

> I'm flabbergasted, bumfuzzled, angry, confused and a lot of other things. To have had this case go through so many appeals and so much scrutiny without ever having anyone question the conviction, and then for this opinion to come down, it simply doesn't make any sense.

He neglected to say, and the reporter neglected to point out, that all death penalty convictions go the habeas corpus route and end up in federal court, where, sooner or later, an opinion of some sort is delivered.

But Peterson was on a roll. He continued:

> This case has been considered by the U.S. Supreme Court on two occasions. And, on both occasions, the Court reaffirmed the convictions and denied the requests for rehearings.

Not exactly. The U.S. Supreme Court never considered the merits of Ron's case; in fact, by denying certiorari, the Court refused to hear the case and sent it back to Oklahoma. This was standard practice.

Peterson saved his tallest tale for the end. Judge Seay had cited, in a footnote to his opinion, Robert Mayer's book *The Dreams of Ada* and made a reference to the number of convictions based on dream confessions coming out of the same courtroom. Peterson was upset that the book had been mentioned in a court ruling and said, evidently with a straight face:

> It is simply not true that any of these three men—Williamson, Fontenot, or Ward—were convicted based on dream confessions.

THE STATE of Oklahoma appealed Judge Seay's ruling to the Tenth Circuit Court of Appeals in Denver. Though Ron was pleased with the turn of events and the prospect of a new trial, he was still in prison, surviving day by day as the process dragged on.

He was not, however, fighting alone. Kim Marks, his investigator, Janet Chesley, his lawyer, and Dr. Foster were relentless in their efforts to obtain proper treatment. For almost four years, the prison had refused to admit Ron to its Special Care Unit, where better medications and better conditions were available. The SCU was within view of H Unit, an easy walk, but officially off-limits to death row inmates.

Kim Marks reported this description of her client:

> I was so frightened, not of him, but for him. I insisted that we try and get somebody higher up in the penal system to get some help, because his hair had grown out to his shoulders, he had yellow streaks in them where he'd been pulling, because you could see the nicotine stains completely down his fingers and on his hands, not just on the tips; his teeth were literally rotting out of his mouth. I think he had been twisting them. His skin was gray, because he had, obviously, not bathed in weeks; he was skin and bones; his shirt looked like it hadn't been washed, much less hung up or ironed, in months; and he was pacing; he could barely talk, and every time he did talk spit would fly from his mouth. He was not making any sense whatsoever, and I was really afraid we were going to lose him, that he would die in prison from physical health problems related to his mental health problems.

Janet Chesley, Kim Marks, and Ken Foster badgered the various wardens who came and went at McAlester, as well as deputy wardens and assistants. Susan Otto, the director of the Federal Public Defender's Office and Janet's supervisor, managed to pull some strings at the Department of Corrections. Finally, in February 1996, James Saffle, then a higher ranking official with DOC, agreed to meet with Kim and Janet. As the meeting began, Saffle announced that he had authorized Ron Ward, the current warden at McAlester, to make an exception for Ron Williamson and to transfer him immediately to the SCU.

Ron Ward's memo to the director of the SCU admitted that the unit was officially off-limits for death row inmates. It read, in part:

> I am authorizing an exception to the Standard Operating Procedures for the Special Care Unit of the Oklahoma Penitentiary which states:

"Any OSP inmate except those on Death Row are eligible for Special Care Unit Services."

What was behind this change of heart? Two weeks earlier, a prison psychologist sent a confidential memo to a deputy warden concerning Ron Williamson. Among other comments, the psychologist gave some valid reasons for moving Ron to the SCU:

> In our team discussion we agreed that Mr. Williamson was psychotic and would likely benefit from major adjustment to his medication. We also noted that he has steadfastly refused even to consider or discuss any such adjustment.
> As you know, the Special Care Unit has the latitude to force medicate when need be.

The H Unit staff was tired of Ron and needed a break. The memo went on:

> There is little doubt that Mr. Williamson's condition is deteriorating week by week. I have noticed it, and H-Unit staff have brought it up regularly. Earlier today, Mike Mullens made emphatic mention of this deterioration and of the adverse effect the inmate's psychotic outbursts were having on our Southwest Quad.

But the best reason to move Ron was to speed up his execution. The memo concluded:

> In my opinion, as things stand now with Mr. Williamson, his psychosis has reached a level that would probably render him less than competent to be executed. A period at our SCU could well restore him to an appropriate level of competence.

Ron was walked over to the SCU, admitted, and given a nicer cell with a window. Dr. Foster changed his medications and monitored their intake. Though Ron was far from healthy, he was quiet and not in constant pain.

He was also extremely fragile, his mania barely under control. Progress was made, then suddenly, on April 25, after three months in the SCU, Ron was abruptly pulled out and taken back to H Unit for two weeks. There was no medical authorization for the transfer; Dr. Foster was unaware of it. No reason was given. When he was returned to the SCU, he had regressed considerably. Dr. Foster sent a memo to the warden and described the damage the sudden transfer had inflicted on the patient.

Coincidentally, Ron's sudden transfer on April 25 just happened to occur the day before another execution. On April 26, Benjamin Brewer was put to death for stabbing a twenty-year-old coed in Tulsa in 1978. Brewer had been on death row for over seventeen years.

Even though he was at the SCU, Ron was still a death row inmate. He couldn't be allowed to miss the drama of another killing at H Unit.

Janet Chesley suspected the sudden transfer had something to do with the legal maneuverings. The state of Oklahoma had appealed Judge Seay's ruling to the Tenth Circuit in Denver, and oral arguments were scheduled. To prevent her from arguing that her client was so mentally incompetent that he had been moved to the Special Care Unit, Ron was moved back to H Unit. She erupted when she first heard of the transfer. She berated the prison officials and the attorneys for the state who were handling the appeals. Finally, she promised not to mention during her oral argument that Ron was in the SCU.

He was moved back, but the damage was painfully clear.

DENNIS FRITZ heard the good news that Ron had prevailed at the federal level and would get another trial. Dennis had not been so lucky. Since he was not under a death sentence, he had no lawyer and was forced to file his own habeas corpus petition. He had lost at the district court level in 1995 and was appealing to the federal Tenth Circuit.

Ron's retrial was bittersweet for Dennis. He was dejected because he was convicted by the same witnesses and the same set of facts, yet his habeas appeal had been turned down. At the same time, he was very pleased that Ronnie would get another day in court.

In March 1996, he finally wrote the Innocence Project and requested their help. A student volunteer wrote back and sent a questionnaire. In June, the student requested Dennis's lab work—the analysis of his hair, blood, and saliva. Dennis had it neatly filed away in his cell, and he quickly sent it to New York. In August, he sent his appellate briefs, and in November he sent his entire trial transcript. Later that month, he received the wonderful news that the Innocence Project had officially taken his case.

Letters went back and forth, weeks and months passed. The Tenth Circuit denied his appeal, and when the Supreme Court refused to hear his case in May 1997, Dennis went through his own bout of depression. His appeals were over. All those wise judges sitting in their black robes and plowing through their thick law books had seen nothing wrong with his trial. Not a single one detected the obvious—an innocent man was wrongly convicted.

The future of life in prison that he had so strongly refused to believe was now a possibility.

In May, he sent four letters to the Innocence Project.

In 1979, in the small town of Okarche, just north of Oklahoma City, two men, Steven Hatch and Glen Ake, broke into the home of the Reverend Richard Douglass. In the ensuing ordeal, Douglass and his wife were shot and killed. Their two young children were also shot and left for dead; somehow they survived. The killing was done by Glen Ake, who was convicted and sentenced to death, then given a new trial because the judge had denied him access to a mental health expert. His appeal, *Ake v. Oklahoma*, was a landmark decision. At his second trial, he received a life sentence, which he is still serving.

Steven Hatch's participation in the killings was greatly in doubt and hotly disputed, but he nonetheless received the death penalty. On August 9, 1996, Hatch was strapped to the gurney and rolled into the death chamber on H Unit. Present in the witness room were the two Douglass children, adults by then.

Glen Ake, the unquestioned gunman, got life. Steven Hatch, who killed no one, was executed.

In 1994, a twenty-year-old American Indian named Scott Dawn Carpenter robbed a store in Lake Eufaula and murdered the owner. After only two years on death row, he was able to stop his appeals and get the needle.

On April 10, 1997, the Tenth Circuit Court of Appeals in Denver affirmed Judge Seay. The court took exception to his ban on hair evidence, but agreed that Ron Williamson had been wrongly convicted.

With a new trial in order, Ron's case was moved to the Capital Trial Division of the Indigent Defense System, where the new director, Mark Barrett, supervised a team of eight lawyers. Because of the complexity of the case, and because of his experience with Ron, he assigned the case to himself. The initial truckload of materials he received filled sixteen boxes.

In May 1997, Mark and Janet Chesley drove to McAlester to see the client. Janet's role was to reintroduce Mark to Ron. They had last seen each other in 1988, shortly after Ron arrived in F Cellhouse and Mark was assigned his first appeal.

Though he knew Janet and Kim Marks and most of the indigent appellate lawyers, and though he'd heard many rumors and tales of Ron and his adventures on death row, Mark was still startled at his condition. In 1988, Ron was thirty-five years old, weighed 220 pounds, and had an athletic build, confident walk, dark hair, and a baby face. Nine years later, he was forty-three and could easily have passed for sixty-five. After a year in the SCU, he was still gaunt, pale, disheveled, ghostlike, and obviously very sick.

But he was able to remain engaged through a long conversation about his case. He rambled at times, and drifted off into monologues that made no sense whatsoever, but for the most part he knew what was going on and where his case was headed. Mark explained that DNA testing would compare Ron's blood, hair, and saliva samples with the hair and semen found at the crime scene, and that the conclusion would be certain, guaranteed, foolproof. DNA doesn't lie.

Ron showed no hesitation; in fact he was eager to have the testing done.

"I am innocent," he said over and over. "And I have nothing to hide."

MARK BARRETT and Bill Peterson agreed that Ron should be evaluated to determine his mental competency. They also agreed on DNA testing. Peterson pushed hard for DNA because he was convinced it would finally nail Ron.

The testing would have to wait, however, because Mark Barrett's austere budget wouldn't allow it. The cost was initially expected to be about $5,000, money that would not be available for a few months. It would eventually cost much more than the first estimate.

Instead, Mark went to work on the competency hearing. He and his rather lean staff compiled Ron's medical records. They located a psychologist who reviewed the records, interviewed Ron, and was willing to travel to Ada to testify.

After two trips to the Oklahoma Court of Criminal Appeals, a one-year layover in Judge Seay's office, a two-year stop at the Tenth Circuit in Denver, two useless but required visits to the U.S. Supreme Court in Washington, and a truckload of routine filings back and forth among all these various courts, the matter of the state of Oklahoma versus Ronald Keith Williamson had now returned home.

It was back in Ada, ten years after four cops surrounded him, shirtless and shaggy and tinkering with a lawn mower with only three wheels, and arrested him for murder.

CHAPTER 14

Tom Landrith was a third-generation native of Pontotoc County. He attended Ada High School and played on two state championship football teams. College and law school were at the University of Oklahoma, and when he passed the bar, he settled into his hometown and joined a small firm. In 1994, he ran for district court judge and easily defeated G. C. Mayhue, who had defeated Ronald Jones in 1990.

Judge Landrith was well acquainted with Ron Williamson and the Carter murder, and when the Tenth Circuit affirmed Judge Seay, he knew the case was headed back to Ada, to his courtroom. Typical of a small town, he had represented Ron on a drunk-driving charge in the early 1980s; they briefly played on the same softball team; Landrith played high school football with Johnny Carter, Debbie's uncle; and Landrith and Bill Peterson were old friends. During Ron's murder trial in 1988, Landrith had slipped into the courtroom several times out of curiosity. Of course, he knew Barney well.

It was Ada, and everybody knew everybody.

Landrith was a popular judge, folksy and funny, but strict in his courtroom. Though he had never been fully convinced Ron was guilty, he was not convinced he was innocent, either. Like most folks in Ada, he had always felt the guy had a loose screw or two. But he was anxious to see Ron, and to make sure his retrial was conducted fairly.

The murder was fifteen years old and still unsolved. Judge Landrith had great sympathy for the Carters and their ordeal. It was time to settle the matter.

ON SUNDAY, July 13, 1997, Ron Williamson left McAlester, never to return. He was driven by two Pontotoc County deputies to Eastern State Hospital in Vinita. The sheriff, Jeff Glase, told a newspaper reporter that the prisoner behaved himself.

"They didn't report any trouble out of him whatsoever," Glase said. "But when you're in shackles, leg irons and a straight jacket, there's not really much you can do to cause a lot of trouble."

It was Ron's fourth admission to Eastern State. He was placed in the "pretrial program," to be evaluated and treated so that he could one day stand trial.

Judge Landrith set a trial date for July 28, but then postponed it pending an evaluation of Ron by the doctors at Eastern State. Though Bill Peterson did not object to the evaluation, he left little doubt as to his opinion of Ron's competency. In a letter to Mark Barrett, he said, "My personal opinion is that he was competent under Oklahoma law and that his disruptions in court were merely a show of anger at the time he was tried and convicted." And, "He functioned reasonably well in jail."

Bill Peterson liked the idea of DNA testing. He had never wavered in his belief that Williamson was the killer, and now it could be proven with real science. He and Mark Barrett swapped letters and quibbled over the details—which lab, who pays for what, when to start the testing—but both agreed that the testing would take place.

Ron was stabilized and doing better. Anyplace, even a mental hospital, was an improvement over McAlester. Eastern State had several units, and he was placed in a heavily secured one, complete with bars on the windows and plenty of razor wire to look at. The rooms were small, old, and not very nice, and the secured unit was overflowing with patients. Ron was lucky to have a room; others slept in beds in the hallways.

He was immediately examined by Dr. Curtis Grundy and found to be incompetent. Ron appreciated the nature of the charges against him but was unable to assist his attorneys. Dr. Grundy wrote to Judge Landrith and said that with proper treatment Ron might become competent enough to stand trial.

Two months later, Dr. Grundy evaluated him again. In a detailed, four-page report sent to Judge Landrith, Dr. Grundy determined that Ron (1) was able to appreciate the nature of the charges against him, (2) was able to consult with his lawyer and rationally assist in the preparation of his defense, and (3) was mentally ill and required further treatment—"he should continue to receive psychiatric treatment throughout his trial participation for the purpose of maintaining his competence to stand trial."

Additionally, Dr. Grundy determined that Ron was harmless, saying, "Mr. Williamson does not appear to pose an immediate, significant threat to himself or others should he be released without further inpatient treatment. He currently denies experiencing suicidal and homicidal ideation or intent. He has not displayed aggressive behavior towards himself or others during this hospitalization. The current assessment of his dangerousness is based upon his placement in a structured, secure setting and may not be applicable to unstructured environments."

JUDGE LANDRITH set the competency hearing for December 10, and Ron was moved back to Ada. He checked into the Pontotoc County jail, said hello to his old pal John Christian, and was placed in his old cell. Annette was soon there to see him, with food, and she found him upbeat, hopeful, and very happy to be "home." He was excited about a new trial and the prospect of proving his innocence. He rambled on incessantly about Ricky Joe Simmons, with Annette constantly asking him to change the subject. He could not.

The day before the hearing, he spent four hours with Dr. Sally Church, a psychologist hired by Mark Barrett to testify about his competency. Dr. Church had already met with him twice and reviewed the extensive records of his medical history. She had little doubt that he was incompetent to stand trial.

Ron, though, was determined to prove he was ready for a trial. For nine years he had dreamed of the chance to again confront Bill Peterson and Dennis Smith and Gary Rogers and all the liars and snitches. He'd killed no one, and he was desperate to finally prove it. He liked Mark Barrett, but he was angry that his own lawyer was trying to prove he was crazy.

Ron just wanted a trial.

JUDGE LANDRITH scheduled the hearing in a smaller courtroom, down the hall from the main one, where Ron had been convicted. On the morning of the tenth, every seat was taken. Annette was there, as were several reporters. Janet Chesley and Kim Marks were waiting to testify. Barney Ward was absent.

The last time Ron made the short walk from the jail to the courthouse in handcuffs he had been sentenced to die. He was thirty-five then, still a young man with dark hair and a stocky build and nice suit. Nine years later, he made the walk again, a white-haired, ghostlike old man in prison garb and unsteady on his feet. When he walked into the courtroom, Tom Landrith was shocked at his appearance. Ron was very happy to see "Tommy" up there on the bench in a black robe.

When Ron nodded and smiled, the judge noticed that most of his teeth were gone. His hair was streaked yellow from the nicotine on his hands.

Appearing for the state to contest Ron's claims of incompetence was Bill Peterson, who was irritated by the very notion and disdainful of the proceedings. Mark Barrett was assisted by Sara Bonnell, a lawyer from Purcell who would hold the "second seat" in Ron's retrial. Sara was an experienced criminal lawyer, and Mark relied heavily on her.

They wasted no time in proving their case. Ron was the first witness and within seconds had everybody thoroughly confused. Mark asked him his name, then they had the following exchange:

Mark: "Mr. Williamson, there's a person other than yourself who you believe committed this crime?"

Ron: "Yes there is. His name is Ricky Joe Simmons of 323 West 3rd Street, at the time of September 24th, 1987, confession to the Ada Police Department. That's the address he listed he was living at. I received verification there were some Simmons living at that address, along with Ricky Joe Simmons. There was a Cody and a Debbie Simmons living there."

Mark: "And you tried to get the word out about Ricky Simmons?"

Ron: "I have told a lot of people about Mr. Simmons. I've wrote to Joe Gifford, I wrote to Tom and Jerry Criswell at the funeral home, and knowing that if they bought a monument here in Ada, they would have bought it from Joe Gifford, because he's the only monument works. And Forget-Me-Not Florist handled the floral arrangements. I wrote to them. I wrote to some people at the Solo Company, where his former, his former employer. I wrote to the glass plant, his former employer, and to the decedent's former employer."

Mark: "Let's back up a minute. Why was it important for you to write the monument company?"

Ron: "Because I know Joe Gifford. When I was growing up, I mowed his yard, as a kid, with Burt Rose, my next-door neighbor. And knowing that, if Mr. Carter and Ms. Stillwell bought a monument here in Ada, Oklahoma, they bought it from Joe Gifford, because he is the only monument works here. I grew up by Gifford Monument works."

Mark: "Why would you write to Forget-Me-Not Florist?"

Ron: "Because, knowing, if they bought flowers here in Ada, Ms.

Stillwell is from Stonewall, Oklahoma, knowing that if they bought flowers here in Ada, they possibly could have bought from Forget-Me-Not Florist."

Mark: "How about the funeral home?"

Ron: "The funeral home is, Criswell Funeral Home is the funeral home, I read from Bill Luker's brief, stating that they are the people responsible for handling the funeral and burial arrangements for the decedent."

Mark: "And it was important for you to let them know Ricky—"

Ron: "Yes, he was an extremely dangerous man, and I asked for some support in getting him arrested."

Mark: "That's because of handling funeral arrangements for Ms. Carter?"

Ron: "That is correct."

Mark: "Did you also write to the manager of the Florida Marlins?"

Ron: "I wrote to the third base coach of the Oakland Athletics, who later became, yes, the manager of the Florida Marlins."

Mark: "And did you ask him to keep some sort of information he gave you under his hat?"

Ron: "No, I told him the whole story about the Del Monte catsup bottle that Simmons said that Dennis Smith, holding up a Del Monte catsup bottle in his right hand on the witness stand, and Ricky Joe Simmons saying he raped the decedent with a catsup bottle, I wrote to Rene and told him that that's the most shocking piece of evidence I've ever seen in the forty-four years I've been alive."

Mark: "But you know that the Florida Marlins manager told some other people about it, is that right?"

Ron: "Probably so, because Rene Lachemann is a good friend of mine."

Mark: "So, is there something you've heard that makes you believe this?"

Ron: "Oh, yes, because I used to listen to Monday night football and I listened to the World Series, and I've been listening to some reports on television, and through the media, that that Del Monte catsup bottle has become infamous."

Mark: "Okay, you hear them talking—"

Ron: "Oh, yes, definitely so."

Mark: "On Monday night—"

Ron: "Definitely so."

Mark: "And during the World Series—"

Ron: "It's a cheering pep squad sick ordeal I have to go through, but it's, nonetheless, necessary for me to get Simmons confessed that he did, in fact, rape, rape by instrumentation and rape by forcible sodomy and murder Debra Sue Carter at her home at 1022½ East 8th Street, December the 8th, 1982."

Mark: "Do you also hear Debra Carter's name mentioned during—"

Ron: "Yes I do."

Mark: "Is this during Monday night football also?"

Ron: "I hear Debra Sue Carter's name continually."

Mark: "You don't have a TV in your cell, do you?"

Ron: "I hear other people's television. I have heard them at Vinita. I had a television on death row. I definitely hear that I am associated with this horrible crime and I am doing my very dead level best to clear my name of this stinking mess."

Mark paused so everyone could catch a breath. Spectators exchanged looks. Others were frowning, trying not to make eye contact with anyone. Judge Landrith was writing something on his legal pad. The lawyers were scribbling, too, though putting sensible words together was not easy at the moment.

From a lawyer's perspective, it was extremely difficult to examine an incompetent witness because no one, including the witness, knew what answers were likely to spew forth. Mark decided to just let him talk.

In attendance for the Carter family was Christy Shepherd, Debbie's niece, who had grown up not far from the Williamsons. She was a licensed health counselor who'd spent years working with severely mentally ill adults. After a few minutes of listening to Ron, she was convinced. Later that day she told her mother and Peggy Stillwell that Ron Williamson was a very sick man.

Also watching, but for different reasons, was Dr. Curtis Grundy, Bill Peterson's chief witness.

The questioning continued, though questions were unnecessary. Ron either ignored them or gave a quick answer before returning to Ricky Joe Simmons and rambling on until the next question cut him off. After ten minutes on the stand, Mark Barrett had heard enough.

Annette followed her brother and testified about his unstable thoughts and his obsession with Ricky Joe Simmons.

Janet Chesley testified in detail about her representation of Ron and her efforts to get him moved into the Special Care Unit at McAlester. She, too, described his nonstop ramblings about Ricky Joe Simmons, and said that he was unable to assist with his defense because he talked of nothing else. Ron was improving, in her opinion, and she was hopeful he would one day be able to get his new trial. But that day was still far away.

Kim Marks covered much of the same territory. She had not seen Ron in several months and was pleased with his improved appearance. In vivid detail, she described Ron on H Unit and said she often thought he might die. He was progressing mentally but was still unable to focus on anything but Ricky Joe Simmons. He was not ready for a trial.

Dr. Sally Church was the final witness for Ron. In the long and colorful history of Ron Williamson's court proceedings, she was, incredibly, the first expert to testify about his mental health.

He was bipolar and schizophrenic, two of the most difficult disorders to treat because the patient does not always understand what the medications do. Ron often stopped taking his pills, and that was common with the two disorders. Dr. Church described the effects, treatments, and potential causes of bipolar disorder and schizophrenia.

During her examination of Ron, the day before at the county jail, he asked her if she heard a television in the distance. She wasn't sure. Ron certainly did, and on the television show they were talking about

Debbie Carter and the catsup bottle. It happened like this: He had written to Rene Lachemann, a former player and coach with Oakland, and told him about Ricky Simmons and Debbie Carter and the catsup bottle. Ron believed that Rene Lachemann for some reason had mentioned this to a couple of sports announcers who began talking about it on the air. The story spread—*Monday Night Football*, the World Series, and so on—until now it was all over the tube.

"Can't you hear them in there?" Ron yelled at Dr. Church. "They're yelling Catsup!, Catsup!, Catsup!"

She concluded her testimony with the opinion that Ron was unable to assist his attorney and prepare for trial.

During the recess for lunch, Dr. Grundy asked Mark Barrett if he could meet with Ron alone. Mark trusted Dr. Grundy and had no objection. The psychiatrist and the patient/inmate met in the witness room at the jail.

When court convened after lunch, Bill Peterson stood and sheepishly announced:

> Yeah, Judge, I visited with our witness [Grundy] over the recess, and
> I think the State of Oklahoma would be willing to stipulate that . . .
> competency is obtainable, but at this particular point in time, Mr.
> Williamson is not competent.

After watching Ron in court and chatting with him for fifteen minutes during lunch, Dr. Grundy did an about-face and changed his opinion. Ron was simply not ready for a trial.

Judge Landrith ruled Ron to be incompetent and wanted him back in thirty days for another look. As the hearing was winding down, Ron said, "Could I ask a question?"

Judge Landrith: "Yes sir."

Ron: "Tommy, I've known you and I knew your dad, Paul, and I'm telling you in honest truth, I don't know how this Duke Graham and this Jim Smith business, you know, how it correlates to Ricky Joe Simmons.

I don't know that. And if that's about my competency, let me get down here within thirty days and let's get Simmons arrested, put him on the witness stand show this videotape and try to get a confession from him as to what he actually did."

Judge Landrith: "I understand what you're saying."

If "Tommy" did, in fact, understand, he was the only one in the courtroom who did so.

Against his wishes, Ron was returned to Eastern State for more observation and treatment. He preferred to remain in Ada to speed things along toward his trial, and he was irritated with his lawyers for wanting him at Vinita. Mark Barrett was desperate to get him out of the Pontotoc County jail before more snitches appeared on the scene.

Then a dentist at Eastern State examined a sore in the roof of his mouth, did a biopsy, and discovered cancer. The growth was encapsulated and easily removed. The surgery was successful, and the doctor told Ron that had it gone untreated, say at the county jail or at McAlester, the cancer would have spread to his brain.

Ron called Mark and thanked him for the stay at Eastern State. "You saved my life," Ron said, and they were friends again.

In 1995, the state of Oklahoma drew a blood sample from every prison inmate, began analyzing them, and entered the results into its new DNA data bank.

The evidence from the Carter investigation was still locked away at the OSBI lab in Oklahoma City. The blood, fingerprints, semen, and hair samples from the crime scene, along with the numerous prints and blood, hair, and saliva samples taken from the witnesses and suspects, were all in storage.

The fact that the state had possession of everything did not comfort Dennis Fritz. He didn't trust Bill Peterson and the Ada police, and he certainly didn't trust their cohorts at the Oklahoma State Bureau of Investigation. Hell, Gary Rogers was an OSBI agent.

Fritz waited. Throughout 1998, he corresponded with the Innocence Project, tried to be patient, and waited. Ten years in prison had taught him patience and perseverance, and he had experienced the cruelty of false hope.

A letter from Ron helped. It was a rambling, seven-page hello on Eastern State letterhead, and Dennis chuckled as he read it. His old friend had not lost his wit or his fight. Ricky Joe Simmons was still loose, and, damn it, Ron intended to nail him.

To keep his own sanity, Dennis stayed in the law library, poring over cases. He made a hopeful discovery—his habeas corpus appeal had been filed in the U.S. District Court for the Western District of Oklahoma. Pontotoc County was in the Eastern District. He compared notes with the other law clerks and the combined wisdom was that the Western District did not have jurisdiction over him. He rewrote his petition and brief, and re-filed in the proper court. It was a long shot, but it energized him and gave him another fight.

In January 1999, he talked by phone to Barry Scheck. Scheck was at war on many fronts; the Innocence Project was swamped with wrongful conviction cases. Dennis expressed his concern with the state having control of all the evidence, and Barry explained that that was usually the case. Relax, he said, nothing will happen to the samples. He knew how to protect the evidence from tampering.

Scheck's fascination with Dennis's case was simple: the police had failed to investigate the last man seen with the victim. It was an enormous red flag, and it was all Scheck needed to take the case.

ON JANUARY 26 and 27, 1999, at a company called Laboratory Corporation of America (LabCorp), near Raleigh, North Carolina, the semen samples from the crime scene—the torn panties, the bedsheets, and the vaginal swabs—were tested against the DNA profiles of Ron Williamson and Dennis Fritz. A DNA expert from California, Brian Wraxall, had been hired by the attorneys for Ron and Dennis to monitor the testing.

Two days later, Judge Landrith delivered the news that Mark Barrett and many others had been dreaming of. The results of the DNA tests had been analyzed and confirmed at LabCorp, and the semen from the crime scene excluded Ron Williamson and Dennis Fritz.

As always, Annette was in close contact with Mark Barrett and knew the testing was under way, somewhere. She was at home when the phone rang. It was Mark, and his first words were "Annette, Ron is innocent." Her knees buckled and she almost fainted. "Are you sure, Mark?"

"Ron is innocent," he said again. "We just got the lab results."

She couldn't talk for crying and promised to call him back later. She sat down, and for a long time she wept and she prayed. She thanked God over and over for his goodness. Her Christian faith had sustained her through the nightmare of Ron's ordeal, and now the Lord had answered her prayers. She hummed a few hymns, cried some more, then began calling family and friends. Renee's reaction was almost identical.

They made the four-hour drive to Vinita the next day. Waiting there were Mark Barrett and Sara Bonnell—a little celebration was in order. As Ron was brought into the visitors' room, Dr. Curtis Grundy happened by and was invited to hear the good news. Ron was his patient, and they had developed a close relationship. After eighteen months at Vinita, Ron was stable, making slow progress, and putting on weight.

"We have some great news," Mark said, addressing his client. "The lab results are back. The DNA proves you and Dennis are innocent."

Ron was instantly overcome with emotion and reached for his sisters. They hugged and wept, and then instinctively broke into "I'll Fly Away," a popular gospel hymn they had learned as children.

MARK BARRETT immediately filed a motion to dismiss the charges and turn Ron loose, and Judge Landrith was anxious to address the issue. Bill Peterson objected and wanted further testing on the hair. A hearing was scheduled for February 3.

Bill Peterson opposed the motion, but he could not do so quietly. Before the hearing, he was quoted in the *Ada Evening News* as saying: "DNA testing of the hair samples, which was not available in 1982, will prove they were responsible for Carter's murder."

The statement rattled Mark Barrett and Barry Scheck. If Peterson was cocky enough to make such public claims at such a late hour, was it possible that he knew something they didn't? Did he have access to the hair taken from the crime scene? Could the samples be switched?

There were no empty seats in the main courtroom on February 3. Ann Kelley, a reporter for the *Ada Evening News*, was fascinated by the case and was covering it thoroughly. Her front-page reports were being widely read, and when Judge Landrith settled behind his bench, the room was crowded with policemen, courthouse employees, family members, and local lawyers.

Barney was there, seeing nothing but hearing more than anyone. He was thick-skinned and had learned to live with Judge Seay's opinion from 1995. He would never agree with it, but he couldn't change it. Barney had always believed that his client had been framed by the police and Peterson, and it was wonderful watching their flimsy case unravel in the spotlight.

The lawyers argued for forty-five minutes, then Judge Landrith wisely decided to complete the testing of the hair before making a final decision. Do it fast, he told the lawyers.

To his credit, Bill Peterson promised, on the record and in open court, to agree to a dismissal if Williamson and Fritz were excluded by DNA testing of the crime scene hair.

ON FEBRUARY 10, 1999, Mark Barrett and Sara Bonnell drove to the Lexington Correctional Center to see Glen Gore, in what was supposedly a routine interview. Though Ron's retrial had not been scheduled, they were preparing for it anyway.

Gore surprised them by saying he had been expecting a visit. He was reading the newspapers, keeping up with events. He had read about Judge Seay's opinion back in 1995 and knew that another trial was somewhere in the future. They chatted for a while about that possibility, and the conversation shifted to Bill Peterson, a man Gore despised because he put him in prison for forty years.

Barrett asked Gore why he testified against Williamson and Fritz.

It was all Peterson, he said. Peterson threatened him, said he'd go after him if he didn't help nail Williamson and Fritz.

"Would you be willing to take a polygraph on this?" Mark asked.

Gore said he had no problem with a polygraph, and added that he had offered to take one for the police, but it never happened.

The lawyers asked Gore if he would give them a saliva sample for DNA, and he said it wasn't necessary. The state already had his DNA— all prisoners were required to submit samples. As they talked about DNA, Mark Barrett told Gore that Fritz and Williamson had been tested. Gore already knew this.

"Could your DNA be on her?" Barrett asked.

Probably, Gore said, because he had danced with her five times that night. Dancing wouldn't do it, Mark said, and went on to explain the basics of leaving a DNA trail. Blood, saliva, hair, sweat, semen. "They have DNA from the semen," Mark said.

Gore's expression changed dramatically, and he was obviously bothered by this information. He called time and left to go find his legal adviser. He returned with Reuben, a jailhouse lawyer. While he was away, Sara Bonnell asked a guard for a Q-tip.

"Glen, would you give a saliva sample?" Sara asked, holding the Q-tip. Gore grabbed the Q-tip, snapped it in two, cleaned both ears, then dropped the two halves into his shirt pocket.

"Did you have sex with her?" Mark asked.

Gore wouldn't respond.

"Are you saying you never had sex with her?" Mark asked again.

"I'm not saying that."

"If you did, that semen is going to match up to your DNA."

"I didn't do it," Gore said. "I can't help you."

He and Reuben stood, and the interview was over. As they were leaving, Mark Barrett asked Gore if they could meet again. Sure, said Gore, but it might be better if they met at his job site.

Job site? Mark thought he was serving a forty-year prison sentence.

Gore explained that during the day he worked in Purcell, Sara Bonnell's hometown, in the Public Works Department. Catch him over there, and they could have a longer talk.

Mark and Sara agreed, though both were taken aback by Gore's outside employment.

That afternoon Mark called Mary Long, who was then in charge of the DNA-testing section of the OSBI, and suggested that they find Gore's DNA in the prison data bank and compare it with the semen samples from the crime scene. She agreed to do so.

DENNIS FRITZ was locked in his cell for the 4:15 p.m. count. He heard the familiar voice of a prisoner counselor in the hall, beyond his metal door. The voice yelled, "Hey, Fritz, you're a free man!" Then something about "DNA."

Dennis couldn't get out of his cell, and the counselor disappeared. His cell mate heard it, too, and they spent the rest of the night talking about what it meant.

It was too late to call New York. Dennis suffered through the night, slept little, and tried unsuccessfully to throttle his excitement. When he reached the Innocence Project early the next morning, the news was confirmed. DNA testing had excluded Dennis and Ron from the semen found at the crime scene.

Dennis was euphoric. Almost twelve years after he was arrested, the truth was finally known. The proof was ironclad and irrefutable. He would be vindicated and exonerated and set free. He called his mother, and she was overcome with emotion. He called his daughter, Elizabeth, now twenty-five years old, and they celebrated. They had not seen each other in twelve years, and they talked about how sweet the reunion would be.

To SAFEGUARD the crime scene hair and also the samples given by Fritz and Williamson, Mark Barrett arranged for an expert to examine the hair and to microscopically photograph it with an infrared camera.

Less than three weeks after the hearing on the motion to dismiss, LabCorp completed the first-stage testing and sent back an inconclusive report. Mark Barrett and Sara Bonnell drove to Ada for a meeting in the chambers of the judge. Tom Landrith was anxious to get the answers that only DNA could provide.

Because of the complexities of DNA testing, various labs were being used to test different hairs. And because of the distrust between the prosecution and the defense, different labs were necessary. A total of five labs were eventually involved in the case.

The lawyers discussed this with Judge Landrith, and again he pressed them to do it as fast as possible.

After the hearing, Mark and Sara walked downstairs in the courthouse to Bill Peterson's office. In correspondence and in hearings, he was growing increasingly hostile. Perhaps they could thaw things a bit with a friendly visit.

Instead, they heard a tirade. Peterson was still convinced Ron Williamson had raped and murdered Debbie Carter, and his evidence had not changed. Forget the DNA. Forget the experts from the OSBI. Williamson was a bad guy who'd raped women in Tulsa and hung out in bars and roamed the streets with his guitar and lived close to Debbie Carter. Peterson vehemently believed that Gary Allen, Fritz's neighbor, had actually seen Ron Williamson and Dennis Fritz in the yard the night of the murder washing off blood with a water hose while laughing and cursing. They had to be guilty! Peterson ranted on and on, working harder to reassure himself than to convince Mark and Sara.

They were dumbfounded. The man was thoroughly incapable of admitting a mistake or grasping the reality of the situation.

THE MONTH of March seemed like a year for Dennis Fritz. The euphoria vanished, and he struggled to get through each day. He was obsessed with the possibility of hair samples being switched by Peterson or someone at the OSBI. With the semen issue put to rest, the state would be desperate to salvage its case with the only evidence it had left. If he and Ron were cleared by DNA testing of the hair, then they would walk and the bogus prosecution would be exposed. Reputations were on the line.

Everything was out of his control, and Dennis was overcome with stress. He feared a heart attack and visited the prison clinic, complaining of heart palpitations. The pills they gave him did little to help.

The days dragged on, then April arrived.

THE EXCITEMENT faded for Ron, too. The extreme euphoria crashed into another round of severe depression and anxiety, and he became suicidal. He called Mark Barrett often, and his lawyer kept reassuring him. Mark accepted every call, and when he wasn't in the office, he made sure someone there talked to the client.

Ron, like Dennis, was terrified of the authorities cooking the test results. Both were in prison because of the state's experts, people who still had access to the evidence. It wasn't difficult to imagine a scenario in which the hair could be compromised in an effort to protect people and cover up an injustice. Ron had made no secret of his desire to sue everybody in sight once he was set free. People in higher places had to be nervous.

Ron called as often as he was permitted, usually once a day. He was paranoid and offered all sorts of nightmarish plots.

At one point, Mark Barrett did something he had never done before, and would probably never do again. He guaranteed Ron that he would get him out of prison. If the DNA fell through, then they would go to trial, and Mark guaranteed an acquittal.

Comforting words from an experienced lawyer, and Ron was calm for a few days.

"HAIR SAMPLES Don't Match" was the headline of the Sunday edition of the Ada paper on April 11. Ann Kelley reported that LabCorp had tested fourteen of seventeen hairs taken from the crime scene and they "were in no way consistent with Fritz or Williamson's DNA makeup." Bill Peterson said:

> At this point we don't know who the hairs belong to. We haven't tested them against anybody but Fritz and Williamson. There was no question in my mind when we started the whole DNA process that these two men were guilty. I wanted it [physical evidence] sent off for the purpose of getting these two guys. When we got the results on the semen samples, I was so surprised my jaw dropped to the floor.

The final report was due from the lab the following Wednesday, April 14. Judge Landrith scheduled a hearing for April 15, and there was speculation that the two men might be set free. Fritz and Williamson would both be in court on the fifteenth.

And Barry Scheck was coming to town! Scheck's fame was growing enormously as the Innocence Project pulled off one DNA exoneration after another, and when word circulated that he would be in Ada for yet another one, the media circus began. State and national news companies called Mark Barrett, Judge Landrith, Bill Peterson, the Innocence Project, the Carter family, all the major players. Excitement built quickly.

Would Ron Williamson and Dennis Fritz really walk free on Thursday?

DENNIS FRITZ had not heard the results of the hair tests. On Tuesday, April 13, he was in his cell when a guard appeared from nowhere and barked, "Pack your shit. You're leaving."

Dennis knew he was going back to Ada, hopefully for his release. He packed quickly, said good-bye to a couple of friends, and hurried away. There to drive him back to Ada was none other than John Christian, a familiar face from the Pontotoc County jail.

Twelve years in jail and prison had taught Dennis to treasure his privacy and his freedom, and to appreciate the little things, like open spaces and forests and flowers. Spring was everywhere, and as he headed back to Ada, he smiled through the window at the farms and rolling hills and countryside.

His thoughts were random. He did not know of the latest test results, nor was he certain why he was headed back to Ada. There was a chance he would be released, and there was also the chance that a last-minute hitch would derail things. Twelve years earlier, he'd almost been released during his preliminary hearing when Judge Miller realized the state had so little proof. Then the cops and Peterson produced James Harjo, and Dennis went to trial, then to prison.

He thought of Elizabeth and how wonderful it would be to see and hold her. He couldn't wait to get out of Oklahoma.

Then he was scared again. He was so close to freedom, yet he was still wearing handcuffs and headed for a jail.

Ann Kelley and a photographer were waiting for him. He smiled as he entered the jail and was eager to talk to the reporter. "This case should never have been prosecuted," he said for the newspaper. "The evidence they had against me was insufficient and if the police had done an adequate investigation of all the suspects this may never have happened." He explained the problems with the indigent defense system. "When you don't have any money to defend yourself, you're at the mercy of the judicial system. Once in the system, it's almost impossible to get out, even if you are innocent."

He spent a quiet night in his old haunt, dreaming of freedom.

The quietness of the jail was disrupted the next day, April 14, when Ron Williamson arrived from Vinita, wearing prison stripes and grinning at the cameras. The word was out that they would be released the following day, and the story had caught the attention of the national press.

Ron and Dennis had not seen each other in eleven years. Each had written to the other only once, but when they were reunited, they hugged and laughed and tried to grasp the reality of where they were and what was happening. The lawyers arrived, and they talked to them for an hour. NBC's *Dateline* was there with a camera recording everything. Jim Dwyer with the *New York Daily News* had arrived with Barry Scheck.

They were packed in the small interview room on the east side of the jail, facing the courthouse. At one point, Ron stretched out on the floor, looked through the glass door, and rested his head in his hand. Finally someone asked, "Hey, Ron, what are you doing?"

"Waiting on Peterson," he said.

The courthouse lawn was crawling with reporters and cameras. One happened to catch Bill Peterson, who agreed to an interview. When Ron saw the prosecutor in front of the courthouse, he yelled at the door, "You fat rascal! We beat you, Peterson!"

Dennis's mother and daughter surprised him at the jail. Though he and Elizabeth had maintained an active correspondence, and she had sent him many photos, he was unprepared for what he saw. She was a beautiful, elegant, very mature young lady of twenty-five, and he wept uncontrollably as he hugged her.

There were many tears at the jail that afternoon.

RON AND Dennis were placed in separate cells, lest they start killing again.

Sheriff Glase explained, "I'm going to keep them apart. I just don't feel right putting two convicted murderers in the same cell together—and until the judge says so, that's what they are."

Their cells were side by side, and so they talked. Dennis's cell mate had a small television, and from news reports he heard firsthand that they would be released the following day. Dennis relayed all this to Ron.

To no one's surprise, Terri Holland was back in jail, another layover in her astonishing career as a petty criminal. She and Ron exchanged words, but nothing particularly unpleasant. As the night wore one, Ron lapsed into his old habits. He began yelling about his freedom and injustices, shouting obscenities at the female inmates, and talking loudly to God.

CHAPTER 15

The exonerations of Ron Williamson and Dennis Fritz brought national attention to Ada. By daybreak on April 15, the courthouse was surrounded by news vans, satellite trucks, photographers, cameramen, and reporters. The townsfolk drifted over, curious at the commotion and anxious to see more. So much jockeying had gone on for seats in the courtroom that Judge Landrith was forced to improvise a lottery system for the reporters and a one-line live feed out of his office window for the news trucks.

A collection of cameras was waiting outside the jail, and when the two defendants emerged, they were surrounded. Ron was wearing a coat and tie, dress shirt, and slacks that Annette had hurriedly bought for him, and he had new shoes that were too small and killing his feet. Dennis's mother had brought him a suit, but he preferred the street clothes he'd been allowed to wear during his last years in prison. They quickly made their final walk in handcuffs, smiling and bantering with the reporters.

Annette and Renee arrived early and took their usual seats, front row behind the defense table. They held hands and prayed, cried, and managed a laugh or two. It was too early to celebrate. They were joined by their children, other relatives, and some friends. Wanda and Elizabeth Fritz sat nearby, also holding hands and whispering excitedly. The courtroom filled up. The Carter family sat across the aisle, once more dragged into court to suffer through another hearing as the state floundered in its efforts to solve their crime and find justice. Seventeen years after Debbie's murder, and her first two accused and convicted killers were about to walk.

The seats were soon filled, and the crowd began stacking up along the walls. Judge Landrith had agreed to allow cameras, and he herded the photographers and reporters into the jury box, where folding chairs were brought in and wedged against each other. Cops and deputies were everywhere. Security was tight. There had been anonymous phone calls and threats against Ron and Dennis. The courtroom was packed and tension was high.

Lots of cops were present, though Dennis Smith and Gary Rogers were somewhere else.

The lawyers arrived—Mark, Sara, and Barry Scheck for the defendants, Bill Peterson, Nancy Shew, and Chris Ross for the state. There were smiles and handshakes. The state was "joining" in the motion to dismiss, to set the boys free. This was a joint effort to right a wrong, a rare example of the community coming together at a crucial hour to properly address an injustice. One big happy family. Everyone should be congratulated and take pride in the system that was working so beautifully.

Ron and Dennis were brought in, and their handcuffs were removed for the last time. They sat behind their lawyers, a few feet away from their families. Ron stared straight ahead and saw little. Dennis, though, looked at the crowd and saw glum, hard faces. Most of those present did not seem too happy with the prospect of their release.

Judge Landrith assumed the bench, welcomed everyone, and quickly got down to business. He asked Peterson to call his first witness. Mary

Long, now the head of the DNA unit at the OSBI, took the stand and began with an overview of the testing process. She talked about the different labs that had been used to analyze the hair and semen from the crime scene and the samples from the suspects.

Ron and Dennis began to sweat. They had thought the hearing would take only a few minutes, time enough for Judge Landrith to dismiss the charges and send them home. As the minutes crept by, they began to worry. Ron began to fidget and grumble, "What's going on?" Sara Bonnell scribbled notes to assure him things were fine.

Dennis was a nervous wreck. Where was the testimony leading? Could there be another surprise? Every trip to that courtroom had been a nightmare. Sitting in it now evoked harrowing memories of lying witnesses and stone-faced jurors and Peterson demanding the death penalty. Dennis made the mistake of again glancing around the courtroom, and again did not see many supporters.

Mary Long turned to the important material. Seventeen hairs taken from the crime scene were tested—thirteen pubic, four scalp. Ten of the hairs were found on the bed or in the bedding. Two came from the torn panties, three from the washcloth in the victim's mouth, and two from under her body.

Only four of the seventeen could be matched with a DNA profile. Two belonged to Debbie, and none came from Ron or Dennis. Zero.

Long then testified that the semen samples taken from the bedding, the torn panties, and the victim had been tested earlier, and, of course, Ron and Dennis had been excluded. She was then excused from the witness stand.

IN 1988, Melvin Hett testified that of the seventeen hairs, thirteen were "microscopically consistent" with the hair of Dennis, and four with Ron's samples. There was even a "match." Also, in his third and final report, filed after Dennis's trial had started, Hett excluded Glen Gore from any of the hair. His expert testimony was the only direct "credible" proof the state offered against both Ron and Dennis, and had much to do with their convictions.

DNA TESTING revealed that one scalp hair found under the body and one pubic hair found in the bedding had been left behind by Glen Gore. Also, the semen recovered by a vaginal swab during the autopsy was tested. Its source was Glen Gore.

Judge Landrith knew this but had kept it confidential until the hearing. With his approval, Bill Peterson announced the Gore findings to a shocked courtroom.

Peterson said, "Your Honor, this is a very trying time for the criminal justice system. This murder happened in 1982, it was tried in 1988. At that particular time we had evidence that was presented to a jury that convicted Dennis Fritz and Ron Williamson by evidence that was, in my opinion, at that particular time, overwhelming."

Without refreshing memories as to what, exactly, the overwhelming proof had been eleven years earlier, he rambled on about how DNA now contradicted much of what he had once believed. Based on the evidence he had left, he could not prosecute the two defendants. He asked that the motion to dismiss be granted, then sat down.

At no time did Peterson offer any conciliatory comments, or words of regret, or admissions of errors made, or even an apology.

At the least, Ron and Dennis were expecting an apology. Twelve years of their lives had been stolen by malfeasance, human error, and arrogance. The injustice they had endured could easily have been avoided, and the state owed them something as simple as an apology.

It would never happen, and it became an open sore that never healed.

Judge Landrith made a few comments about the injustice of it all, then asked Ron and Dennis to stand. He announced that all charges were thereby dismissed. They were free men. Free to go. There was applause and cheering from a few of the spectators; most, though, were not in the mood to celebrate. Annette and Renee hugged their children and relatives and had another good cry.

Ron bolted from the defense table, past the jury box, out a side door, down the stairs to the front steps of the courthouse, where he paused and filled his lungs with cool air. Then he lit a cigarette, the first of a million in the free world, and waved it jubilantly at a camera. The photo was printed in dozens of newspapers.

A few minutes later he was back. He and Dennis, their families and lawyers, huddled in the courtroom and posed for photos and answered questions from a horde of reporters. Mark Barrett had called Greg Wilhoit and asked him to fly back to Oklahoma for the big day. When Ron saw Greg, they embraced like the brothers they were.

"How do you feel, Mr. Williamson?" a reporter asked.

"About what?" Ron shot back, then said, "I feel like my feet are killing me. These shoes are too small." The questions went on for an hour, even though a press conference was planned for later.

Peggy Stillwell was helped from the courtroom by her daughters and sisters. She was overwhelmed and in shock; the family had not been warned of the news of Glen Gore. They were back at the murder scene now, waiting for another trial, no closer to justice. And they were confused; most of the family still believed Fritz and Williamson were guilty, but how did Gore figure in?

Ron and Dennis finally began their exit, every step of it duly preserved and recorded. The mob crept down the stairs and out the front door. They paused for a second, free men now, and soaked in the sun and chilly air.

They were liberated, free, exonerated, yet no one had offered an apology, an explanation, or even a dime in compensation—not a shred of aid of any type.

IT WAS time for lunch. Ron's favorite place was Bob's Barbecue, north of town. Annette called ahead and reserved several tables; several would be needed because the entourage was growing by the minute.

Though he had only a few teeth left, and though it would otherwise have been difficult to eat with so many cameras in his face, Ron devoured a plateful of pork ribs and wanted more. Never one to savor his food, he did manage to savor the moment. He was polite to everyone, thanked all the strangers who stopped by to encourage him, hugged those who wanted a hug, chatted with every reporter who wanted a story.

He and Dennis couldn't stop smiling, even with mouths full of barbecue.

THE DAY before, Jim Dwyer, a reporter for the *New York Daily News*, and Alexandra Pelosi of NBC's *Dateline*, drove to Purcell to find Glen Gore and ask him some questions. Gore knew things were heating up over in Ada and that he was rapidly becoming the prime suspect. But, remarkably, the prison staff did not.

Gore heard that some out-of-towners were looking for him, and assumed they were lawyers or law enforcement types, people he'd rather avoid. Around noon, he walked away from his job cleaning ditches in Purcell and escaped. He found some woods and walked several miles, then stumbled upon a highway and hitchhiked in the general direction of Ada.

When Ron and Dennis heard of Gore's escape, they howled with laughter. He must be guilty.

AFTER a long lunch, the Fritz-Williamson group drove to the lodge in Wintersmith Park in Ada for a press conference. Joined by their lawyers, Ron and Dennis sat behind a long table and faced the cameras. Scheck talked about the Innocence Project and its work to free those wrongly convicted. Mark Barrett was asked how the injustice occurred in the first place, and he gave a long history of the misguided prosecution—the five-year delay, the lazy and suspicious police work, the snitches, the junk science. Most of the questions were directed at the two brand-new ex-onerees. Dennis said he planned to leave Oklahoma, go back to Kansas City, and spend as much time as possible with Elizabeth, and in due course he would figure out the rest of his life. Ron had no immediate plans, except to get out of Ada.

Their panel was joined by Greg Wilhoit and Tim Durham, another Oklahoma exoneree from Tulsa. Tim spent four years in prison for a rape he did not commit before the Innocence Project secured his release with DNA testing.

AT THE federal courthouse in Muskogee, Jim Payne, Vicky Hildebrand, and Gail Seward quietly suppressed their deep satisfaction. There was no celebration—their work on the Williamson matter was now four years removed, and they were knee-deep in other cases—but they nonetheless paused to savor the moment. Long before DNA erased the mysteries, they had found the truth the old way with brains and sweat and, in doing so, had saved the life of an innocent man.

Judge Seay wasn't smug, either. The vindication was sweet, but he was much too busy with other matters. He had simply done his job, that was all. Though every other judge along the way had failed Ron Williamson, Frank Seay understood the system and knew its flaws. The truth was often hard to find, but he was willing to search for it and he knew where to look.

MARK BARRETT had asked Annette to find a place for the press conference, and perhaps a little reception, something nice in the way of a homecoming for Ron and Dennis. She knew just the place—the fellowship hall of her church, the same church in which Ronnie grew up, the same church where she had played both the piano and the organ for the past forty years.

The day before, she had called her pastor to ask permission and arrange the details. He hesitated, stuttered a bit, then finally said he needed to poll the elders. Annette smelled trouble and headed for the church. When she arrived, the pastor said that he had called the elders, and it was their opinion, and his as well, that the church should be off-limits for such an event. Annette was stunned and asked why.

There could be violence, he explained. There were already reports of threats against Ron and Dennis, and things might get out of control. The town was buzzing about the release, with most folks unhappy with it. There were some tough guys on the Carter side, and, well, it just wouldn't work.

"But this church has been praying for Ronnie for twelve years," she reminded him.

Yes, indeed, and we will continue to do so, he said. But there are a lot of people who still think he's guilty. It's too controversial. The church could be tainted. The answer is no.

Annette became emotional and ran from his office. He tried to console her, but she would have none of it.

She left and called Renee. Within minutes Gary Simmons was driving to Ada, some three hours from their home near Dallas. Gary drove straight to the church and confronted the pastor, who held his ground. They argued for a long time, but resolved nothing. The church was standing firm; it was simply too risky.

"Ron will be here Sunday morning," Gary said. "Will you recognize him?"

"No," the pastor said.

THE CELEBRATION resumed at Annette's house where dinner was served and friends filtered in and out. After the dishes were done, everyone gathered in the sunroom, where an old-fashioned gospel sing-along erupted. Barry Scheck, a Jewish guy from New York, heard music he'd never heard before, and gamely tried to sing along. Mark Barrett was there; it was a proud and remarkable moment for him, and he didn't want to leave. Sara Bonnell, Janet Chesley, and Kim Marks all sang along. Greg Wilhoit and his sister Nancy were there. The Fritz family—Dennis, Elizabeth, and Wanda—sat close together and joined in the fun.

"That night everyone stayed around for the celebration party at Annette's house," Renee said. "There was lots of food, singing, laughter. Annette was playing the piano, Ronnie playing the guitar, and the rest of us joining and singing a variety of songs. Everyone was singing, clapping, having such a good time. Then, at ten o'clock, there was silence as the news came on the television. We were all sitting in the sunroom, wall-to-wall people, waiting to hear the news we had longed to hear for so many years announcing to the town that my little brother, Ronald Keith Williamson, was not only free but innocent! Although it was such a joyous occasion and we were all so relieved, we could see the sickness in Ronnie's eyes from the many years of being tormented and abused."

They celebrated again at the TV news report. When it was over, Mark Barrett and Barry Scheck and some of the crowd said their good nights. Tomorrow would be a very long day.

Later in the evening, the phone rang and Annette answered it. An anonymous caller said the Ku Klux Klan was in the area and looking for Ronnie. One of the great rumors of the day was that someone on the Carter side had bought a contract for a hit on Ron and Dennis, and that the KKK was now in the business of hired killings. There were remnants of Klan activity in southeastern Oklahoma, but it had been decades since the group had been suspected of murder. They normally didn't target white people, but in the heat of the moment the Klan was considered the nearest organized gang that might be able to pull off such a hit.

The call was chilling nonetheless, and Annette whispered the message to Renee and Gary. They decided to take the threat seriously but try to keep it from Ronnie.

"The happiest night of our lives soon became the most terrifying night of our lives," Renee said. "We decided to call the Ada police. They informed us they would be sending no one and there was nothing they could do unless something happened. How could we be so naive to think they would protect us? In a panic, we all ran through the house, closing blinds, locking windows and doors. It was obvious no one was going to sleep because everyone's nerves were on edge. Our son-in-law was worried about his wife and new baby being in such danger. We gathered around and prayed and asked the Lord to calm our nerves and for the angels to surround our house and protect us. We all made it through the night unharmed. The Lord once again honored our prayers. Looking back on the night it's almost humorous to think our first thought was to call the Ada police."

ANN KELLEY of the *Ada Evening News* had a full day covering the events. That night she received a call from Chris Ross, assistant district attorney. Ross was upset and complained that the prosecutors and police were being vilified.

No one was telling their side of the story.

EARLY the next morning, at the beginning of their first full day of freedom, Ron and Dennis, along with their lawyers, Mark Barrett and Barry Scheck, drove to the local Holiday Inn, where an NBC camera crew was setting up. They appeared live on the *Today* show, with Matt Lauer doing the interview.

The story was gaining momentum, and most of the reporters were still in Ada, looking for anyone remotely connected to the case or the people involved in it. The Gore escape was a wonderful subplot.

The group—exonerees, families, lawyers—drove to Norman and stopped at the offices of the Oklahoma Indigent Defense System for another party. Ron said a few words and thanked those who had worked so hard to protect him and eventually free him. Afterward, they hurried to Oklahoma City to film a segment of *Inside Edition*, and then one for a show called *Burden of Proof*.

Lawyers Scheck and Barrett were trying to arrange a meeting with the governor and top legislators to lobby for legislation that would facilitate DNA testing and provide compensation for those wrongfully convicted. The group went to the state capitol to shake hands and twist arms and hold another press conference. The timing was perfect; they had the national media following them. The governor was working hard and too busy, so he sent forth a top aide, a creative type who seized upon the idea of having Ron and Dennis meet with the members of the Oklahoma Court of Criminal Appeals. It was unclear what this meeting was expected to produce, but resentment was certainly a possibility. It was Friday afternoon, though, and the judges were likewise hard at work. Only one ventured out of her chambers to say hello, and she was harmless. She had not been on the court when it reviewed and affirmed the convictions of Fritz and Williamson.

Barry Scheck left town and headed back to New York. Mark stayed in Norman, his home, and Sara drove to Purcell. There was a lull in the frenzy, and everybody needed a break. Dennis and his mother stayed in Oklahoma City at Elizabeth's home.

Riding back to Ada, with Annette behind the wheel, Ron sat in the front seat for a change. No handcuffs. No prison stripes. No armed deputy watching him. He soaked in the countryside, the farms and scattered oil rigs and gentle rolling hills of southeast Oklahoma.

He couldn't wait to leave.

"It was almost like we had to reacquaint ourselves with him since he'd been out of our lives for so long," Renee said. "The next day after he was released we had such a good day with him. I told him to bear with us, that we had a lot of questions and were very curious about what his life had been like on death row. He was very sweet about it and graciously answered our questions for a few hours. One of the questions I asked him was, 'What are all those scars on your arms?' He said, 'I would be so depressed that I would sit and cut myself.' We asked him what his cell was like, was the food edible, etcetera. But after many questions he looked at all of us and said, 'I'd rather not talk about it anymore. Let's talk about something else.' And we honored his wishes. He would sit outside on the patio at Annette's house and sing and play his guitar. Sometimes we could hear him from inside, and it was all I could do to hold back the tears listening to him and thinking about what he had been through. He would go to the refrigerator and just stand there with the door open looking at what he might want to eat. He was amazed at all the food in the house and especially knowing he could eat any and all he wanted. He stood at the kitchen window in awe and commented about all the nice cars we were driving, some he had never heard of. He commented one day while riding in the car how different it was to see people walking and running and going about their busy everyday lives."

Ron was excited about returning to church. Annette had not told him about the incident with the pastor, nor would she ever. Mark Barrett and Sara Bonnell were invited; Ron wanted them there with him. The entire Williamson entourage arrived for the Sunday worship hour in a rush and stormed down to the very front row. Annette was behind the organ, as always, and when she began the first rather rowdy hymn Ron jumped to his feet, clapping and singing and smiling, truly filled with the spirit.

During the announcements, the pastor made no mention of Ron's return, but during the morning prayer he did manage to say that God loved everyone, even Ronnie.

Annette and Renee boiled with anger.

A Pentecostal worship service is not for the timid, and as the music cranked up and the choir began rocking and the congregation got loud, a handful of church members made their way over to Ron for a hello, a hug, a welcome back. Damned few. The rest of the good Christian folks glared at the murderer in their midst.

Annette left the church that Sunday, never to return.

The Sunday edition of the Ada newspaper ran a front-page story with the headline "Prosecutor Defends His Work on High Profile Case." There was a lawyerly photo of Bill Peterson, behind a podium, in court, in action.

For obvious reasons, he was not doing too well in the aftermath of the exonerations and felt compelled to share his resentment with the people of Ada. He was not getting his fair share of the credit for protecting Ron and Dennis, and the lengthy story, by Ann Kelley, was nothing but an embarrassing tantrum by a badly beaten prosecutor who should have avoided reporters.

It began:

> Pontotoc County District Attorney Bill Peterson claims Dennis Fritz and Ron Williamson's defense attorneys are wrongly taking credit for the DNA tests that freed their clients from prison.

As Ann Kelley fed him all the rope he needed to hang himself, Peterson recalled in detail the history of the DNA testing in the Carter case. At every possible opportunity, he took cheap shots at Mark Barrett and Barry Scheck while never missing a chance to pat himself on the back. DNA testing was his idea!

He managed to avoid the obvious. Not once did he admit that he wanted DNA testing so he could nail Ron and Dennis in their coffins. He was so convinced of their guilt that he happily went along with the testing. Now that the test results had gone the other way, he was demanding credit for being such a fair guy.

The bratlike finger-pointing went on for paragraphs. He dropped vague, sinister hints about other suspects and gathering more evidence. The story read:

> He [Peterson] said if new evidence is found linking Fritz and Williamson to Carter's murder, double jeopardy would not apply and they could be tried again.
>
> Peterson said the investigation into Carter's murder has been reopened for some time and Glen Gore is not the only suspect.

The story ended with two appalling quotations from Peterson. The first was:

> I did the right thing in 1988 when I tried them. By recommending their convictions be dismissed, I did what was legally, morally, and ethically the right thing to do with the evidence I now have against them.

Left unsaid, of course, was the fact that his highly ethical and utterly moral consent to the dismissal came almost five years after Ron was almost executed, and four years after Peterson publicly rebuked Judge Seay for ordering a new trial. By seizing the high ethical ground at the eleventh hour, Peterson lamely helped to ensure that Ron and Dennis spent only twelve years in prison as innocent men.

The most reprehensible part of the story was the next quotation. It was also highlighted and placed in the center of the front page. Peterson said:

> Innocent has never crossed my lips in regards to Williamson and Fritz. This doesn't prove their innocence. It just means I can't prosecute them with the evidence I now have.

Ron and Dennis were emotional and shaky enough after only four days of freedom, and the story terrified them. Why would Peterson want to try them again? He had convicted them once, and they had no doubt he could do it again.

New evidence, old evidence, zero evidence. It didn't matter. They'd just suffered twelve years behind bars for killing no one. But in Pontotoc County, evidence was not a factor.

The story infuriated Mark Barrett and Barry Scheck, and both drafted lengthy rebuttals to fire off to the paper. But they wisely waited, and after a few days realized few people were listening to Peterson.

ON SUNDAY afternoon, Ron and Dennis and their supporters drove to Norman, at the request of Mark Barrett. With fortuitous timing, Amnesty International was throwing its annual outdoor rock concert to raise money. There was a nice crowd gathered at an outdoor amphitheater. The weather was warm and sunny.

Between songs, Mark Barrett spoke, then introduced Ron, Dennis, Greg, and Tim Durham. Each took a few minutes and shared his experiences. Though they were nervous and not accustomed to public speaking, they found the courage and spoke from their hearts. The audience adored them.

Four men, four average white guys from good families, all chewed up and abused by the system and locked away for a combined total of thirty-three years. Their message was clear: until the system is fixed, it could happen to anyone.

After speaking, they lounged around the amphitheater, listening to the music, eating ice cream, basking in the sun and the freedom. Bruce Leba showed up from nowhere and bear-hugged his old buddy. Bruce had not attended Ronnie's trial, nor had he written him in prison. He felt guilty for this neglect, and he apologized sincerely to his best friend from high school. Ron was quick to forgive him.

He was willing to forgive everyone. The intoxicating smell of freedom smothered old grudges and fantasies of retribution. Though he had dreamed of a massive lawsuit for twelve years, it was all history now. He did not want to relive the nightmares.

THE MEDIA could not get enough of their stories. Ron especially took the spotlight. Because he was a white man from a white town who'd been knocked around by white cops and charged by a white prosecutor and convicted by a white jury, he became a large and willing subject for reporters and journalists. Such abuse might be common for the poor and the minorities, but not for small-town heroes.

The promising baseball career, the ugly slide into insanity on death row, the near brush with execution, the bumbling cops who couldn't see the obvious killer—the story was rich and layered.

Interview requests poured into Mark Barrett's office from around the world.

AFTER six days in the bush, Glen Gore turned himself in. He contacted an Ada lawyer, who called the prison and made the arrangements. As he was making preparations to surrender, he was very specific in his desire to avoid being handled by the authorities in Ada.

He shouldn't have worried. The gang that couldn't shoot straight wasn't clamoring to get Gore back in Ada for another trial. Time was needed to heal badly wounded egos. Peterson and the police were posturing behind their official stance that the investigation had been reopened, that they were plowing ahead with new enthusiasm to find the killer, or perhaps killers. Gore was but one player in this effort.

The prosecutor and the police could never admit they were wrong, so they clung to the hopeless belief that maybe they were right. Maybe another drug addict would stumble into the police station and confess, or implicate Ron and Dennis. Maybe a fine new snitch would appear.

Maybe the cops could pinch another dream confession from a witness or suspect.

It was Ada. Good, solid police work might turn up all sorts of new leads.

Ron and Dennis had not been excluded.

CHAPTER 16

The daily rituals of Yankee Stadium vary slightly when the team is out of town. Without the urgency of crowds and cameras and without the expectation of another pristine playing surface, the old house creaks slowly to life, so that by late morning the groundskeepers in their khaki shorts and ash T-shirts are tending the field at a languid pace. Grantley, the chief grass cutter, tinkers with a spiderlike Toro mower, while Tommy, the clay specialist, packs and levels the dirt behind home plate. Dan pushes a smaller mower across the thick bluegrass along the first-base line. Sprinklers erupt at orchestrated intervals around the outfield warning track. A tour guide huddles with a group behind the third-base dugout and points to something in the distance, beyond the scoreboard.

The fifty-seven thousand seats are empty. Sounds echo softly around the place—the muffled engine of a small mower, the laughter of a groundskeeper, the distant hissing of a spray washer cleaning seats in the upper deck, the 4 train rumbling by just beyond the right-field wall, the pecking of a hammer near the press box. For those who maintain the house that Ruth built, the off days are cherished, wedged between the nostalgia of Yankee greatness and the promise of more to come.

Some twenty-five years after he was expected to arrive, Ron Williamson stepped up from the bench in the Yankee dugout and onto the brown crushed-shell warning track that borders the field. He paused to take in the enormity of the stadium, to soak in the atmosphere of baseball's holiest shrine. It was a brilliantly blue clear spring day. The air was light, the sun was high, the grass so flat and green it could have been a fine carpet. The sun warmed his pale skin. The smell of freshly cut grass reminded him of other fields, other games, old dreams.

He was wearing a Yankee cap, a souvenir from the front office, and because he was a celebrity at the moment, in New York for a segment on *Good Morning America* with Diane Sawyer, he was wearing his only sport coat, the navy blazer Annette had hurriedly purchased two weeks earlier, and his only tie and pair of slacks. The shoes had changed, though. He'd lost interest in clothes. Though he'd once worked in a haberdashery and offered ready opinions about what others wore, he didn't care now. Twelve years of prison garb does that to you.

Under the cap was a bowl-cut mess of bright gray hair, thick and disheveled. Ron was now forty-six but looked much older. He adjusted the cap, then stepped onto the grass. He was six feet tall, and though his body showed the damage of twenty years of abuse and neglect, there were still hints of the great athlete. He strolled across foul territory, stepped over the dirt base path, and headed for the mound, where he stood for a moment and gazed up at the endless rows of bright blue seats. He gently put his foot on the rubber, then shook his head. Don Larsen had pitched the perfect game from this exact spot. Whitey Ford, one of his idols, had owned this mound. He looked over his left shoulder, out to right field, where the wall seemed too close, where Roger Maris had placed so many fly balls just far enough to clear the fence. And far away in deep center, beyond the wall he could see the monuments of the greatest Yankees.

Mickey was out there.

Mark Barrett stood at home plate, also wearing a Yankee cap, and wondered what his client was thinking. Release a man from prison, where he'd spent twelve years for nothing, with no apologies because no one has the guts to admit wrongdoing, no farewells, just get the hell out of here and please go as quietly as possible. No compensation, counseling, letter from the governor or any other official; no citation for public service. Two weeks later he's in the midst of a media storm, and everybody wants a piece of him.

Remarkably, Ron was holding no grudges. He and Dennis were too busy soaking up the richness of their emancipation. The grudges would come later, long after the media went away.

Barry Scheck was near the dugout, watching Ron and chatting with the others. A die-hard Yankee fan, he had made the phone calls that set up the special visit to the stadium. He was their host in New York for a few days.

Photos were taken, a camera crew filmed Ron on the mound, then the little tour continued along the first-base line, drifting slowly as their guide rambled on about this Yankee and that one. Ron knew many of the stats and stories. No baseball had ever been hit completely out of Yankee Stadium, the guide was saying, but Mantle got close. He bounced one off the facade in right center, right up there, he said as he pointed to the spot, about 535 feet from home plate. "But the one in Washington was further," Ron said. "It was 565 feet. Pitcher was Chuck Stobbs." The guide was impressed.

A few steps behind Ron was Annette, following along, as always, sweating the details, making the tough decisions, cleaning up. She was not a baseball fan, and at that moment her primary concern was keeping her brother sober. He was sore at her because she had not allowed him to get drunk the night before.

Their group included Dennis, Greg Wilhoit, and Tim Durham. All four exonerees had appeared on *Good Morning America*. ABC was covering the expenses for the trip. Jim Dwyer was there from the *New York Daily News*.

They stopped in center field, on the warning track. On the other side was Monument Park, with large busts of Ruth and Gehrig, Mantle and DiMaggio, and dozens of smaller plaques of other great Yankees. Before renovation, this little corner of near-sacred ground had actually been in fair territory, the guide was saying. A gate opened and they walked through the fence, onto a brick patio, and for a moment it was easy to forget they were in a baseball stadium.

Ron stepped close to the bust of Mantle and read his short biography. He could still quote the career stats he had memorized as a kid.

Ron's last year as a Yankee had been 1977, at Fort Lauderdale, Class A, about as far away from Monument Park as a serious ballplayer could get. Annette had some old photos of him in a Yankee uniform, a real one. In fact, it had once been worn by a real Yankee in this very ballpark. The big club simply handed them down, and as the old uniforms made their sad little trek down the minor-league ladder, they collected the battle scars of life in the outposts. Every pair of pants had been stitched in the knees and rear end. Every elastic waistband had been downsized, enlarged, smudged with markers on the inside so the trainers could keep them straight. Every jersey was stained with grass and sweat.

1977, Fort Lauderdale Yankees. Ron made fourteen appearances, pitched thirty-three innings, won two, lost four, and got knocked around enough so that the Yankees had no trouble cutting him when the season was mercifully over.

The tour moved on. Ron paused for a second to sneer at the plaque of Reggie Jackson. The guide was talking about the shifting dimensions of the stadium, how it was bigger when Ruth played, smaller for Maris and Mantle. The film crew tagged along, recording scenes that would never survive editing.

It was amusing, Annette thought, all this attention. As a kid and a teenager, Ronnie had craved the spotlight, demanded it, and now forty years later cameras were recording every move.

Enjoy the moment, she kept telling herself. A month earlier he'd been locked up in a mental hospital, and they were not sure he would ever get out.

They slowly made their way back to the Yankee dugout and killed some time there. As Ron absorbed the magic of the place for a few final minutes, he said to Mark Barrett, "I just got a taste of how much fun they were having up here."

Mark nodded but could think of nothing to say.

"All I ever wanted to do was play baseball," Ron said. "It's the only fun I've ever had."

He paused and looked around, then said, "You know, this all sort of washes over you after a while. What I really want is a cold beer."

The drinking began in New York.

FROM Yankee Stadium, the victory lap stretched to Disney World, where a German television company paid for three nights of fun for the entire entourage. All Ron and Dennis had to do was tell their story, and the Germans, with typical European fascination with the death penalty, recorded every detail.

Ron's favorite part of Disney World was Epcot, at the German village, where he found Bavarian beer and knocked back one stein after another.

They flew to Los Angeles for a live appearance on the *Leeza* show. Shortly before airtime, Ron sneaked away and drained a pint of vodka. Without most of his teeth, his words were not crisp to begin with, and no one noticed his slightly thick tongue.

As the days passed, the story lost some of its urgency, and the group—Ron, Annette, Mark, Dennis, Elizabeth, and Sara Bonnell—headed home.

The last place Ron wanted to be was Ada.

He stayed with Annette and began the difficult process of trying to adjust. The reporters eventually went away.

Under Annette's constant supervision, he was diligent with his medications and stable. He slept a lot, played his guitar, and dreamed of becoming famous as a singer. She did not tolerate alcohol in her home, and he seldom left it.

The fear of being arrested and sent back to prison consumed him and forced him to instinctively glance over his shoulder and jump at any loud noise. Ron knew the police had not forgotten about him. They still believed he was somehow involved in the murder. So did most folks in Ada.

He wanted to get out, but had no money. He was unable to hold a job and never talked about employment. He hadn't had a driver's license in almost twenty years and wasn't particularly interested in studying a driver's manual and taking tests.

Annette was arguing with the Social Security Administration in an effort to collect the back payments for his disability. The checks stopped when he went to prison. She finally prevailed, and the lump sum award was $60,000. His monthly benefits of $600 were reinstated, payable until his disability was removed, an unlikely event.

Overnight, he felt like a millionaire and wanted to live on his own. He was also desperate to leave Ada, and Oklahoma, too. Annette's only child, Michael, was living in Springfield, Missouri, and they hatched the plan to move Ron there. They spent $20,000 on a new, furnished, two-bedroom mobile home, and moved him in.

Though it was a proud moment, Annette was worried about Ron living by himself. When she finally left him, he was sitting in his new recliner watching his new television, a very happy man. When she returned three weeks later to check on him, he was still sitting in his recliner with a disheartening collection of empty beer cans piled around it.

When he wasn't sleeping, drinking, talking on the phone, or playing his guitar, he was loitering at a nearby Wal-Mart, his source for beer and cigarettes. But something happened, an incident, and he was asked to spend his time elsewhere.

In those heady days of being on his own, he became fixated on repaying all those who'd loaned him money over the years. Saving money seemed like a ridiculous idea, and he began giving it away. He was moved by appeals on television—starving children, evangelists about to lose their entire ministries, and so on. He sent money.

His telephone bills were enormous. He called Annette and Renee, Mark Barrett, Sara Bonnell, Greg Wilhoit, the Indigent Defense System lawyers, Judge Landrith, Bruce Leba, even some prison officials. He was usually upbeat, happy to be free, but by the end of every conversation he was ranting about Ricky Joe Simmons. He was not impressed by the DNA trail left by Glen Gore. Ron wanted Simmons arrested immediately for the "rape, rape by instrumentation and rape by forcible sodomy and murder [of] Debra Sue Carter at her home at 1022½, East 8th Street, December the 8th, 1982!!" Every conversation included at least two recitations of this detailed demand.

Oddly enough, Ron also called Peggy Stillwell, and the two developed a cordial relationship by phone. He assured her he had never met Debbie, and Peggy believed him. Eighteen years after losing her daughter, she was still unable to say good-bye. She confessed to Ron that for years she'd had a nagging suspicion that the murder was not really solved.

As a general rule he avoided bars and loose women, though one episode burned him. Walking down the street, tending to his own business, a car with two ladies stopped and he got in. They went out for a round of barhopping, the night grew long, and they retired to his trailer, where one of his companions found his stash of cash under his bed. When he later discovered the theft of $1,000, he swore off women altogether.

Michael Hudson was his only friend in Springfield, and he encouraged his nephew to buy a guitar and taught him a few chords. Michael checked on him regularly and reported to his mother. The drinking was getting worse.

The booze and his medications did not mix well, and he became extremely paranoid. The sight of a police car provoked serious attacks of anxiety. He refused to even jaywalk, thinking the cops were always watching. Peterson and the Ada police were up to something. He taped newspapers over the windows, padlocked his doors, then taped them, too, from the inside. He slept with a butcher's knife.

Mark Barrett visited him twice and slept over. He was alarmed at Ron's condition, his paranoia and drinking, and he was particularly worried about the knife.

Ron was lonely, and terrified.

DENNIS FRITZ wasn't jaywalking, either. He returned to Kansas City and moved in with his mother in the little house on Lister Avenue. When he had last seen it, the house had been surrounded by a dejected SWAT team.

Months after their release, Glen Gore had not been charged. The investigation was plodding along in some direction, and as Dennis understood things, he and Ron were still suspects. Dennis flinched at the sight of a police car. He watched his back whenever he left the house. He jumped when the phone rang.

He drove to Springfield to visit Ronnie and was startled by the extent of his drinking. They tried to laugh and reminisce for a couple of days, but Ronnie was drinking too much. He wasn't a mean drunk, or an emotional one, just a loud and unpleasant one. He would sleep until noon, wake up, pop a top, have a beer for breakfast and lunch, and start playing his guitar.

They were driving around one afternoon, drinking beer and enjoying their freedom. Ron was playing his guitar. Dennis was driving very carefully. He did not know Springfield, and the last thing he wanted was trouble with the cops. Ron decided they should stop at a certain nightclub where he would somehow talk his way into a gig that night. Dennis thought this was a bad idea, especially since Ron was not familiar with the club and didn't know the owner or bouncers. A heated argument ensued, and they made their way back to the trailer.

Ron dreamed of being onstage. He wanted to perform for thousands and sell albums and become famous. Dennis was reluctant to tell him that with his scratchy voice and damaged vocal chords, and marginal talent with the guitar, it was nothing more than a dream. He did, however, press Ron to cut back on the booze. He suggested that Ron mix in a nonalcoholic beer every now and then with his daily onslaught of Budweiser and lay off the hard stuff. He was getting fat, and Dennis urged him to exercise and stop smoking.

Ron listened but kept drinking, real beer. After three days, Dennis left for Kansas City. He returned a few weeks later with Mark Barrett, who was passing through. They drove Ron to a coffeehouse where he took to the tiny stage with his guitar and sang Bob Dylan songs for tips. Though the crowd was small and more interested in eating than listening, Ron was performing and quite happy.

To STAY busy and earn something, Dennis found a part-time job grilling hamburgers for minimum wage. Since he'd kept his nose in law books for the past twelve years, he found the habit hard to break. Barry Scheck encouraged him to consider law school, and even promised to help with the tuition. The University of Missouri–Kansas City was nearby, with a law school and flexible classes. Dennis began studying for the admissions test but was soon overwhelmed.

He was suffering from post-traumatic stress of some variety, and at times the pressure was debilitating. The horror of prison was always there—nightmares and flashbacks and fears of being arrested again. The murder investigation was ongoing, and with the Ada cops running loose, there was always the chance of the midnight knock on the door, or maybe even another assault from a SWAT team. Dennis eventually sought professional help, and slowly he began putting his life together. Barry Scheck was talking about a lawsuit, a massive claim against those who'd created and carried out the injustice, and Dennis focused on the idea.

There was a new fight on the horizon, and he geared up for it.

RON's life was headed in the opposite direction. He was acting strange, and the neighbors noticed. Then he began carrying the butcher's knife through the mobile home park, claiming that Peterson and the Ada cops were after him. He was protecting himself, and not going back to prison.

Annette received an eviction notice. When Ronnie refused to answer her calls, she obtained a court order to have him picked up for a mental evaluation.

He was in his trailer, doors and windows taped and covered, drinking a beer and watching television, when he suddenly heard words squawk from a bullhorn, "Come out with your hands up!" He peeked outside, saw the cops, and thought his life was over, again. He was going back to death row.

The police were as afraid of him as he was of them, but both sides eventually found common ground. Ron was taken not to death row but instead to a mental hospital for evaluation.

The trailer, less than a year old but quite a mess, was sold. When he was released from the hospital, Annette searched for a place to put him. The only bed she could find was in a nursing home outside of Springfield. She drove to the hospital, packed him up, and moved him into the Dallas County Care Center.

The daily structure and regular care were at first welcome. His pills were taken on time, and alcohol was forbidden. Ron felt better, but soon grew weary of being surrounded by old and frail seniors in wheelchairs. He began complaining and was soon unbearable, so Annette found another room in Marshfield, Missouri. It, too, was filled with sad old folks. Ron was only forty-seven. What the hell was he doing in a nursing home?

He asked this question over and over, and Annette finally decided to bring him back to Oklahoma.

He would not return to Ada, not that anyone wanted him to. In Oklahoma City, Annette found a bed at the Harbor House, an old motel that had been converted into a home for men who were transitioning from one phase of life to something that was hopefully better. No alcohol was allowed, and Ron had been sober for months.

Mark Barrett visited him several times at Harbor House and knew Ron couldn't stay there very long. No one could. Most of the other men were zombielike and scarred worse than Ron.

MONTHS passed and Glen Gore was not charged with murder. The new investigation was proving to be as fruitful as the old one, eighteen years earlier.

The Ada police, the prosecutors, and the OSBI had infallible DNA proof that the source of the crime scene semen and hair was Glen Gore, but they just couldn't solve the murder. More proof was needed.

Ron and Dennis had not been ruled out as suspects. And though they were free men and thrilled to be so, there was always a dark cloud hanging over them. They talked weekly and sometimes daily to each other, and to their lawyers. After a year of living in fear, they decided to fight back.

Had Bill Peterson, the Ada police, and the state of Oklahoma apologized for the injustice and closed the books on Ron Williamson and Dennis Fritz, the authorities would have taken the honorable course and ended a sad story.

Instead, they got themselves sued.

IN APRIL 2000, co-plaintiffs Dennis Fritz and Ron Williamson filed suit against half the state of Oklahoma. The defendants were the city of Ada,

Pontotoc County, Bill Peterson, Dennis Smith, John Christian, Mike Tenney, Glen Gore, Terri Holland, James Harjo, the state of Oklahoma, the OSBI, OSBI employees Gary Rogers, Rusty Featherstone, Melvin Hett, Jerry Peters, and Larry Mullins, and the Department of Corrections officials Gary Maynard, Dan Reynolds, James Saffle, and Larry Fields.

The lawsuit was filed in federal court as a civil rights case, alleging violations under the Fourth, Fifth, Sixth, Eighth, and Fourteenth amendments to the Constitution. It was randomly assigned to none other than Judge Frank Seay, who would later recuse himself.

The lawsuit claimed that defendants (1) failed to provide the plaintiffs with a fair trial by fabricating evidence and withholding exculpatory evidence; (2) conspired to falsely arrest and maliciously prosecute the plaintiffs; (3) engaged in deceitful conduct; (4) intentionally inflicted emotional distress; (5) acted negligently in prosecuting the plaintiffs; and (6) initiated and maintained a malicious prosecution.

The claim against the prison system alleged that Ron was mistreated while on death row and that his mental illness was ignored by officials who were repeatedly put on notice.

The lawsuit demanded $100 million in damages.

Bill Peterson was quoted in the Ada newspaper as saying, "In my opinion it's a frivolous lawsuit to attract attention. I'm not worried about it."

He also reaffirmed that the investigation into the homicide "continues."

The lawsuit was filed by Barry Scheck's firm and a Kansas City lawyer named Cheryl Pilate. Mark Barrett would join the team later when he left the Indigent Defense System and entered private practice.

CIVIL suits for wrongful convictions are extremely difficult to win, and most exonerees are shut out from the courthouse. Being wrongfully convicted does not automatically give one the right to sue.

A potential plaintiff must claim and prove that his civil rights were violated, that his constitutional protections were breached, and that this resulted in a wrongful conviction. Then, the difficult part: virtually everyone involved in the legal process that led to the bad conviction is cloaked with immunity. A judge is immune from a wrongful conviction lawsuit regardless of how poorly he handled the trial. A prosecutor is immune as long as he does his job—that is, as long as he prosecutes. If, however, he gets too involved in the investigation, then he might become liable. And a policeman is immune unless it can be shown that his actions were so wrong that any reasonable law enforcement officer would have known that he was violating the Constitution.

Such lawsuits are ruinously expensive to maintain, with the plaintiff's attorneys forced to front tens, even hundreds, of thousands of dollars in litigation costs. And they are almost too risky to file because recovery is such a long shot.

Most wrongfully convicted people, like Greg Wilhoit, never receive a dime.

RON's next stop, in July 2001, was the Transition House in Norman, a well-established facility that offered men a structured environment, counseling, and training. Its goal was to rehabilitate its patients to the point of allowing them to live on their own, with supervision from counselors. The ultimate goal was assimilation back into the community as productive and stable citizens.

Phase one was a twelve-month program in which the men lived in dorms with roommates and plenty of rules. One of the first training exercises was to teach them how to use transit buses and move around the city. Cooking, cleaning, and personal hygiene were also taught and emphasized. Ron could scramble eggs and make a peanut butter sandwich.

He preferred to stay near his room and ventured outside only to smoke. After four months he had not figured out the bus system.

Ron's childhood sweetheart was a girl named Debbie Keith. Her father was a minister who wanted his daughter to marry a minister, and Ron didn't come close. Her brother, Mickey Keith, followed his father and was the pastor at the Evangelistic Temple, Annette's new church in Ada. At Ron's request and Annette's urging, Reverend Keith drove to Norman, to the Transition House.

Ron was serious about rejoining the church and cleaning up his life. At his core was a deep belief in God and Jesus Christ. He would never forget the Scriptures he'd memorized as a child nor the gospel hymns he loved. Despite his mistakes and shortcomings, he was desperate to return to his roots. He carried a nagging sense of guilt for the way he'd lived, but he believed in Jesus's promise of divine, eternal, and complete forgiveness.

Reverend Keith talked and prayed with Ron, and discussed some paperwork. He explained that if Ron really wanted to join the church, he needed to fill out an application in which he stated that he was a born-again Christian, that he would support the church with his tithes and with his presence when able, and that he would never bring reproach upon the church. Ron was quick to fill out and sign the form. It was taken to the church board, discussed, and approved.

He was quite content for a few months. He was clean and sober, determined to kick the habit with God's help. He joined Alcoholics Anonymous and seldom missed a meeting. His medications were balanced, and his family and friends enjoyed his company. He was funny and loud, always ready with a quick retort or a humorous story. To startle strangers, he enjoyed beginning a new tale with "Back when I was on death row . . ." His family stayed as close as possible, and were often amazed at his ability to recall minute details of events that happened when he was literally out of his mind.

The Transition House was near downtown Norman, an easy walk to Mark Barrett's office, and Ron dropped in often. The lawyer and the client drank coffee, talked about music, and discussed the lawsuit. Ron's primary interest in the litigation, not surprisingly, was when it might be settled and how much money he might get. Mark invited Ron to attend his church, a Disciples of Christ congregation in Norman. Ron joined a Sunday school class with Mark's wife and became fascinated with the open and liberal discussions about the Bible and Christianity. Anything could be questioned, unlike in the Pentecostal churches, where the Word was exact and infallible and contrary views were frowned upon.

Ron spent most of his time on his music, practicing a Bob Dylan song or one from Eric Clapton until he could closely imitate it. And he got hired. He landed some gigs in coffee shops and cafés around Norman and Oklahoma City, playing for tips and taking requests from the slim crowds. He was fearless. His vocal range was limited, but he didn't care. Ron would try any song.

The Oklahoma Coalition to Abolish the Death Penalty invited him to sing and speak at a fund-raiser held at the Firehouse, a popular hangout near the OU campus. In front of two hundred people, a much larger crowd than what he normally saw, he was overwhelmed and stood too far from the microphone. He was barely heard, but appreciated nonetheless. During the evening, he met Dr. Susan Sharp, a criminology professor at OU and an active death penalty abolitionist. She invited him to visit her class, and he readily accepted.

The two became friends, though Ron soon considered Dr. Sharp his girlfriend. She worked to keep things on a friendly, professional level. She saw a deeply scarred and wounded man, and she was determined to help him. Romance was not an option, and he was not aggressive.

He progressed through phase one at Transition House, then graduated to the second phase—his own apartment. Annette and Renee prayed fervently that he would be able to live by himself. They tried not to think about a future of nursing homes, halfway houses, and mental hospitals. If he could survive in phase two, then the next step might be to find a job.

He held things together for a month or so, then he slowly fell apart. Away from structure and supervision, he began to neglect his medication. He really wanted a cold beer. His hangout became a campus bar called the Deli, the kind of place that attracted hard drinkers and kids from the counterculture.

Ron became a regular, and, as always, he was not a pleasant drunk.

ON OCTOBER 29, 2001, Ron gave his deposition in his lawsuit. The room, at the stenographer's office in Oklahoma City, was packed with lawyers, all waiting to quiz the man who'd become a celebrity in the area.

After a few preliminary questions, the first defense lawyer asked Ron: "Are you on any type of medication?"

"Yes, I am."

"And is that medication that a physician has prescribed or directed you to take?"

"A psychiatrist, yes."

"Do you have either a list, or do you have information as to what medication you are taking today?"

"I know what I'm taking."

"And what is that?"

"I'm taking Depakote, 250 milligrams, four times a day; Zyprexa, in the evening, once a day; and Wellbutrin one time a day."

"What do you understand the medication is for?"

"Well, Depakote is for mood swings, and Wellbutrin is for depression, and Zyprexa is for voices and hallucinations."

"Okay. One of the things that we're certainly interested in today is the effect that the medication may have on your ability to remember. Does it?"

"Well, I don't know. You haven't asked anything for me to remember yet."

The deposition proceeded for several hours and left him exhausted.

BILL PETERSON, as a defendant, filed a motion for summary judgment, a routine legal maneuver designed to get himself removed from the lawsuit.

The plaintiffs claimed that Peterson's immunity was dissolved when he stepped outside his role of prosecutor and began running the criminal investigation into the murder of Debbie Carter. They alleged two clear examples of evidence fabrication by Peterson.

The first came from Glen Gore's affidavit, prepared to be used in the civil suit, in which Gore stated that Bill Peterson actually came to his cell in the Pontotoc County jail and threatened him if he didn't testify against Ron Williamson. Peterson, according to the affidavit, said that Gore had better hope that his fingerprints "did not show up in Debbie Carter's apartment" and that "he just might be coming after Gore."

The second instance of creating evidence, again alleged by the plaintiffs, involved the reprinting of Debbie Carter's palm. Peterson admitted that he met with Jerry Peters, Larry Mullins, and the Ada investigators in January 1987 to discuss the palm print. Peterson expressed the opinion that he "was at the end of my rope" with regard to the investigation. Peterson suggested that a better print could be obtained some four and a half years after the burial and asked Mullins and Peters to take a second look. The body was then exhumed, the palm reprinted, and the experts suddenly had new opinions.

(Lawyers for Ron and Dennis hired their own fingerprint expert, a Mr. Bill Bailey, who determined that Mullins and Peters arrived at their new conclusions by analyzing different areas of the palm print. Bailey concluded his own analysis by stating that the source of the print on the wall was not Debbie Carter after all.)

The federal judge denied Peterson's motion for summary judgment, saying, "A legitimate question of fact exists as to whether Peterson, Peters and Mullins, as well as others, engaged in a systematic pattern of fabrication in order to obtain the conviction of Williamson and Fritz."

The judge went on to say:

In this case, the circumstantial evidence indicates a concerted pattern
by the various investigators and Peterson to deprive Plaintiffs of one
or more of their constitutional rights. The repeated omission of
exculpatory evidence by investigators while including inculpatory
evidence, inclusion of debatably fabricated evidence, failure to follow
obvious and apparent leads which implicated other individuals, and
the use of questionable forensic conclusions suggests that the involved
Defendants were acting deliberately toward the specific end result
prosecution of Williamson and Fritz without regard to the warning
signs along the way that their end result was unjust and not supported
by the facts of their investigation.

The ruling, which came on February 7, 2002, was a major blow to
the defense and changed the momentum of the lawsuit.

FOR YEARS, Renee had tried to convince Annette that she should leave
Ada. The people would always be suspicious of Ron and whisper about
his sister. Their church had rejected him. The pending lawsuit against
the town and the county would create more resentment.

Annette resisted because Ada was her home. Her brother was innocent. She had learned to ignore the whispers and stares, and she could
continue to hold her ground.

But the lawsuit worried her. After almost two years of intense pretrial discovery, Mark Barrett and Barry Scheck felt the tide was turning
in their favor. Settlement negotiations were on and off, but there was a
general feeling among the lawyers on both sides that the case would not
go to trial.

Perhaps it was time for a change. In April 2002, after sixty years,
Annette left Ada. She moved to Tulsa, where she had relatives, and soon
thereafter her brother arrived to live with her.

She was eager to get him out of Norman. Ron was drinking again,
and when drunk, he could not keep his mouth shut. He bragged about

his lawsuit, his many lawyers, the millions he would collect from those who'd unjustly sent him to death row, and so on. He was hanging around the Deli and other bars and attracting attention from the sorts of people who would quickly become his best friends when the cash arrived.

He moved in with Annette, and soon learned that her new home in Tulsa had the same rules as her old one in Ada, specifically, no drinking. He sobered up, joined her church, and became close to her pastor. There was a men's Bible-study group called Light for the Lost that raised money for mission trips to poor countries. Their favorite fund-raiser was a monthly steak-and-potato dinner, and Ron joined the crew in the kitchen. His assignment was wrapping baking potatoes in foil, a job he enjoyed.

IN THE fall of 2002, the "frivolous" lawsuit was settled for several million dollars. With careers and egos to protect, the numerous defendants insisted on a confidential settlement agreement whereby they and their insurers handed over large sums of money without admitting they had done anything wrong. The secret deal was buried in a locked file and protected with a federal court order.

Its details were soon thrashed about in the coffee shops of Ada, where the city council was forced to disclose the fact that it had forked over $500,000 from a rainy-day reserve for its portion of the total settlement. As the gossip roared around town, the amounts varied from café to café, but it was widely believed to be in the $5 million range. The *Ada Evening News*, using unnamed sources, actually printed this amount.

Because Ron and Dennis had not been cleared as suspects, many of the good folks of Ada still believed they were involved in the killing. That they were now profiting so handsomely from their crime caused even more resentment.

Mark Barrett and Barry Scheck insisted that their clients take an initial lump sum, then a monthly annuity to protect their settlement.

Dennis bought a new home in a suburb of Kansas City. He took care of his mother and Elizabeth, and buried the rest of it in the bank.

Ron was not quite so prudent.

He convinced Annette to help him buy a condo near her home and their church. They spent $60,000 on a nice two-bedroom unit, and Ron once again struck out on his own. He was stable for a few weeks. If for some reason Annette couldn't drive him, Ron happily walked to church.

But Tulsa was familiar turf, and before long he was back in the strip clubs and bars, where he bought drinks for everyone and tipped the girls thousands of dollars. The money, along with his big mouth, attracted all sorts of friends, both new and old, many of whom took advantage of him. He was generous to a fault and thoroughly clueless about managing his new fortune. Fifty thousand dollars evaporated before Annette could rein him in.

Near his condo was a neighborhood bar called the Bounty, a quiet little pub where Guy Wilhoit, Greg's father, was a regular. They met, became drinking buddies, and enjoyed hours of lively conversation about Greg and the old ghosts from death row. Guy told the bartenders and the owner of the Bounty that Ron was a special friend of his, and Greg's, and that if he ever ran into trouble, as was his custom, to call him, Guy, not the cops. They promised to protect Ron.

But Ron couldn't stay away from the strip clubs. His favorite was Lady Godiva's, and there he became infatuated with a certain dancer, only to learn that she was already spoken for. Didn't matter. When he found out she had a family and was homeless, he invited them to his place and offered the spare bedroom upstairs. The stripper, her two kids, and their alleged father all moved into Mr. Williamson's nice new condo. But there were no groceries. Ron called Annette with a long list of necessities, and she reluctantly went to the store and bought them. When she made the delivery, Ron was nowhere to be found. Upstairs, the stripper and her family were locked in the bedroom, hiding from Ron's sister, and wouldn't come out. Annette delivered the ultimatum, loudly, through the door, and threatened criminal action if they didn't leave immediately. They fled and Ron missed them greatly.

The adventures continued until Annette, as legal guardian, finally intervened with a court order. They fought again over the money, but Ron knew what was best. The condo was sold, and Ron went to another nursing home.

He was not abandoned by his true friends. Dennis Fritz knew Ron was struggling to find a stable routine. He suggested that Ron come to Kansas City and live with him. He would monitor Ron's medication and diet, make him exercise, and force him to cut back on the drinking and smoking. Dennis had discovered health foods, vitamins, supplements, herbal teas, and such and was anxious to try some products on his friend. They talked about the move for weeks, but Annette eventually vetoed it.

Greg Wilhoit, now a full-fledged Californian and raging death penalty abolitionist, begged Ronnie to move to Sacramento, where the living was easy and laid-back and the past was truly forgotten. Ron loved the idea, but it was more fun to talk about than to actually pursue.

Bruce Leba found Ron and offered him a room, something he'd done many times in the past. Annette approved, and Ron moved in with Bruce, who at the time was driving a truck. Ron rode shotgun and thoroughly enjoyed the freedom of the open highways.

Annette predicted that the arrangement would last no more than three months, which was Ron's average. Every routine and every place soon bored him, and three months later he and Bruce argued over something neither could remember. Ron moved back to Tulsa, stayed with Annette for a few weeks, then rented a small hotel suite for three months.

In 2001, two years after the release of Dennis and Ron, and almost nineteen years after the murder, the Ada police concluded the investigation. Then two more years passed before Glen Gore was moved from the prison at Lexington and put on trial.

For a host of reasons, Bill Peterson did not prosecute the case. Standing before a jury and pointing to the defendant and saying something like, "Glen Gore, you deserve to die for what you did to Debbie Carter," would have been a hard sell since he'd pointed at two other men and made the same accusation. Peterson begged off on conflict-of-interest grounds, but sent his assistant Chris Ross to sit at the state's table and take notes.

A special prosecutor was sent in from Oklahoma City, Richard Wintory, who, armed with the DNA results, got an easy conviction. After hearing the details of Gore's long and violent criminal record, the jury had no trouble recommending the death penalty.

Dennis refused to follow the trial, but Ron couldn't ignore it. He called Judge Landrith every day and said: "Tommy, you gotta get Ricky Joe Simmons.

"Tommy, forget Gore! Ricky Joe Simmons is the real killer."

ONE NURSING home led to another. Once he grew bored with a new place, or wore out his welcome, the phone calls would start, and Annette would scramble to find another facility willing to care for him. Then she would pack him up and make the move. Some of the homes reeked of disinfectant and looming death, while others were warm and welcoming.

He was in a pleasant one in the town of Howe when Dr. Susan Sharp paid him a visit. Ron had been sober for weeks and felt great. They drove to a lakeside park near the town and went for a walk. The day was cloudless, the air cool and crisp.

"He was like a little boy," Dr. Sharp said. "Happy to be outside in the sun on a beautiful day."

When he was sober and medicated, he was a delight to be with. That night they had a "date," dinner in a nearby restaurant. Ron was quite proud of himself because he was treating a nice lady to a steak dinner.

CHAPTER 17

The severe stomach pains began in the early fall of 2004. Ron felt bloated and was uncomfortable sitting or lying down. Walking helped some, but the pain was increasing. He was always tired and couldn't sleep. He roamed the halls of his latest nursing home at all hours of the night, trying to find relief from the pressure building around his stomach.

Annette was two hours away and hadn't seen him in a month, though she had heard his complaints by phone. When she picked him up for a visit to the dentist, she was shocked at the size of his stomach. "He looked ten months pregnant," she said. They vetoed the dentist and went straight to a hospital emergency room in Seminole. From there, they were sent to a hospital in Tulsa, where, the following day, Ron was diagnosed with cirrhosis of the liver. Inoperable, untreatable, no chance of a transplant. It was another death sentence, and a painful one at that. An optimistic forecast gave him six months.

He had lived fifty-one years, and at least fourteen of those had been behind bars with no opportunity to drink. Since his release five years earlier, he had certainly hit the bottle, but there had also been long periods of complete sobriety as he fought alcoholism.

Cirrhosis seemed a little premature. Annette asked the tough questions, and the answers were not easy. In addition to all the booze, there was a history of illicit drug use, though very little since his release. A likely contributing cause was the history of medications. For at least half of his life, Ron had consumed, at various times and in varying amounts, potent doses of very strong psychotropic drugs.

Perhaps he had a weak liver to begin with. It didn't matter now. Once again, Annette called Renee with news that was hard to believe.

The doctors drained off several gallons of fluid, and the hospital asked Annette to find another place for him. She was turned down by seven facilities before finding a room at the Broken Arrow Nursing Home. There, the nurses and staff welcomed Ronnie like an old member of the family.

IT WAS soon apparent to Annette and Renee that six months was an unrealistic prediction. Ron faded quickly. With the exception of his grossly swollen midsection, the rest of his body withered and shrank. He had no appetite and finally stopped smoking and drinking. As his liver rapidly shut down, the pain became excruciating. He was never comfortable, and spent hours walking slowly around his room and up and down the hallways of the nursing home.

The family circled the wagons and spent as much time with him as possible. Annette was nearby, but Renee and Gary and their children were living near Dallas. They made the five-hour drive as often as possible.

Mark Barrett visited his client several times. He was a busy lawyer, but Ron had always taken priority. They talked about death and life after it, about God and the promise of salvation through Christ. Ron was facing death with almost perfect contentment. It was something he looked forward to, and had for many years. He had no fear of dying. He was not bitter. He regretted many of the things he'd done, the mistakes he'd made, the pain he'd caused, but he had sincerely asked God for forgiveness, and it had been granted.

He carried no grudges, though Bill Peterson and Ricky Joe Simmons were strung along almost until the end. He eventually forgave them, too.

The next visit Mark brought up the subject of music, and Ron rambled for hours about his new career and how much fun he would have when he got out of the nursing home. The illness wasn't mentioned, nor was the part about dying.

Annette delivered his guitar, but he found it difficult to play. Instead, he asked her to sing their favorite hymns. Ron's last performance was at the nursing home, during a karaoke session. He somehow found the energy to sing. The nurses and many of the other patients by then knew his story and cheered him on. Afterward, with the recorded music playing in the background, he danced with both of his sisters.

Unlike most dying patients with time to think and plan, Ron did not clamor for a minister to hold his hand and hear his final confessions and prayers. He knew the Scriptures as well as any preacher. His foundation in the gospel was solid. Perhaps he'd strayed more than most, but he was sorry for that and it was forgotten.

He was ready.

There had been a few bright moments in his five years of freedom, but it had generally been unpleasant. He had moved seventeen times and had proven on several occasions that he could not live alone. What future did he have? He was a burden on Annette and Renee. He had been someone's burden for most of his life, and he was tired.

Since death row, he had told Annette many times that he wished he'd never been born and that he wanted desperately to just go ahead and die. He was ashamed of the misery he had caused, especially to their parents, and he wanted to go see them, to say he was sorry, to be with them forever. Soon after his release, she found him standing in her kitchen one day, trancelike, staring through a window. He grabbed her hand and said, "Pray with me, Annette. Pray that the Lord will just take me home, right now."

It was a prayer she couldn't complete.

When Greg Wilhoit arrived for the Thanksgiving holidays, he spent ten straight days with Ronnie. Though Ron was rapidly slipping away, and heavily sedated with morphine, they talked for hours about life on The Row, horrible as always but now the source of some belated humor.

By November 2004, Oklahoma was executing condemned men at a record pace, and many of their old neighbors had finally been laid to rest. Ron knew a few would be in heaven when he got there. Most would not.

He told Greg that he had seen the best of life, and the worst. There was nothing else he cared to see, and he was ready to go.

"He was completely at peace with the Lord," Greg said. "He had no fear of death. He just wanted to get it over with."

When Greg said good-bye, Ron was barely conscious. The morphine was being used generously, and death was only days away.

Ron's quick demise caught many of his friends off guard. Dennis Fritz passed through Tulsa but couldn't find the nursing home. He planned to return soon for a visit but didn't make it in time. Bruce Leba was working out of state and had temporarily lost contact.

Almost at the last moment, Barry Scheck paid a visit, by phone. Dan Clark, an investigator who had worked on the civil case, rigged up a speakerphone, and Barry's voice filled the room. It was a one-way conversation; Ron was heavily medicated and almost dead. Barry promised to be there soon, to catch up on the gossip, and so on. He got a smile from Ron and a laugh from the others when he said, "And, Ronnie, if you don't make it, I promise you we'll eventually get Ricky Joe Simmons."

When the visiting was over, the family was called in.

THREE years earlier, Taryn Simon, a noted photographer, traveled the country profiling exonerees for a book she planned to publish. She took pictures of Ron and Dennis and included a short summary of their case. Each was asked to write or say a few words to accompany his photograph.

Ron said:

> I hope I go to neither heaven nor hell. I wish that at the time of my death that I could go to sleep and never wake up and never have a bad dream. Eternal rest, like you've seen on some tombstones, that's what I hope for. Because I don't want to go through the Judgment. I don't want anybody judging me again. I asked myself what was the reason for my birth when I was on death row, if I was going to have to go through all that, What was even the reason for my birth? I almost cursed my mother and dad—it was so bad—for putting me on this earth. If I had it all to do over again, I wouldn't be born.
>
> —from *The Innocents* (Umbrage, 2003)

FACED with death, though, Ron retreated slightly. He very much wanted to spend eternity in heaven.

On December 4, Annette and Renee and their families gathered around his bed for the last time and said good-bye.

Three days later, a crowd assembled at the Hayhurst Funeral Home in Broken Arrow for the memorial service. Ron's pastor, the Reverend Ted Heaston, officiated the "celebration" of his life. Charles Story, Ron's chaplain from prison, spoke and recalled some warm anecdotes of their time together at McAlester. Mark Barrett delivered a moving eulogy about their special friendship. Cheryl Pilate read a letter sent in by Barry Scheck, who was occupied with not one but two exonerations elsewhere.

The casket was open, the pale, gray-haired old man was resting peacefully. His baseball jacket, glove, and bat were arranged on the casket, and beside it was his guitar.

The music included two gospel classics, "I'll Fly Away" and "He Set Me Free," hymns Ron learned as a child and sang his entire life, at revivals and church camps, at his mother's funeral with chains around his ankles, at death row during his darkest days, at Annette's the night he was set free. Toe-tapping music, the songs loosened up the crowd and made everyone smile.

The service was sad, obviously, but there was a strong sense of relief. A tragic life was over, and the one who'd lived it had now gone on to better things. This was what Ronnie had prayed for. He was finally free.

LATER that afternoon his mourners reassembled in Ada for the burial. A heartwarming number of the family's friends from the town gathered to honor his passing. Out of respect to the Carter family, Annette chose a different cemetery from the one where Debbie was buried.

It was a cold and windy day. December 7, 2004, exactly twenty-two years since Debbie was last seen alive.

The coffin was hauled into place by the pallbearers, a group that included Bruce Leba and Dennis Fritz. After a few final words from a local minister, a prayer, and some more tears, the last farewell was given.

Permanently etched on his tombstone are the words:

RONALD KEITH WILLIAMSON
Born February 3, 1953   Died December 4, 2004
Strong Survivor
Wrongly Convicted in 1988
Exonerated April 15, 1999

Two days after Ron Williamson was buried, I was flipping through *The New York Times* when I saw his obituary. The headline—"Ronald Williamson, Freed from Death Row, Dies at 51"—was compelling enough, but the lengthy obituary, written by Jim Dwyer, had the clear makings of a much longer story. There was a striking photo of Ron standing in the courtroom the day he was exonerated, looking a bit perplexed and relieved and perhaps even a little smug.

Somehow I had missed the story of his release in 1999, and I had never heard of Ron Williamson or Dennis Fritz.

I read it a second time. Not in my most creative moment could I conjure up a story as rich and as layered as Ron's. And, as I would soon learn, the obituary barely scratched the surface. Within a few hours, I had talked to his sisters, Annette and Renee, and suddenly I had a book on my hands.

Writing nonfiction has seldom crossed my mind—I've had far too much fun with the novels—and I had no idea what I was getting into.

The story, and the research and writing of it, consumed the next eighteen months. It took me to Ada many times, to the courthouse and jail and coffee shops around town, to both the old death row and the new one at McAlester, to Asher, where I sat in the bleachers for two hours and talked baseball with Murl Bowen, to the offices of the Innocence Project in New York, to a café in Seminole where I had lunch with Judge Frank Seay, to Yankee Stadium, to the prison in Lexington where I spent time with Tommy Ward, and to Norman, my base, where I hung out with Mark Barrett and talked about the story for hours. I met Dennis Fritz in Kansas City, Annette and Renee in Tulsa, and when I could convince Greg Wilhoit to come home from California, we toured Big Mac, where he saw his old cell for the first time since he left it fifteen years earlier.

With every visit and every conversation, the story took a different twist. I could've written five thousand pages.

The journey also exposed me to the world of wrongful convictions, something that I, even as a former lawyer, had never spent much time thinking about. This is not a problem peculiar to Oklahoma, far from it. Wrongful convictions occur every month in every state in this country, and the reasons are all varied and all the same—bad police work, junk science, faulty eyewitness identifications, bad defense lawyers, lazy prosecutors, arrogant prosecutors.

In the cities, the workloads of criminologists are staggering and often give rise to less than professional procedures and conduct. And in the small towns the police are often untrained and unchecked. Murders and rapes are still shocking events and people want justice, and quickly. They, citizens and jurors, trust their authorities to behave properly. When they don't, the result is Ron Williamson and Dennis Fritz.

And Tommy Ward and Karl Fontenot. Both are now serving life terms. Tommy might one day be eligible for parole, but, through a procedural quirk, Karl will never be. They cannot be saved by DNA because there is no biological evidence. The killer or killers of Denice Haraway will never be found, not by the police anyway. For more on their story, go to www.wardandfontenot.com.

While researching this book, I came across two other matters, both relevant to Ada. In 1983, a man named Calvin Lee Scott was put on trial for rape in the Pontotoc County Courthouse. The victim was a young widow who was attacked in her bed as she slept, and because the rapist kept a pillow over her face, she could not identify him. A hair expert from the OSBI testified that two crime scene pubic hairs were "microscopically consistent" with samples taken from Calvin Lee Scott, who vehemently denied any guilt. The jury felt otherwise, and he was sentenced to twenty-five years in prison. He served twenty and was released. He was out of jail when DNA testing exonerated him in 2003.

The case was investigated by Dennis Smith. Bill Peterson was the district attorney.

Also in 2001, Ada's former assistant chief of police Dennis Corvin pleaded guilty to federal charges of manufacturing and distributing methamphetamine and was sent away for six years. Corvin, as you might recall, was the Ada policeman mentioned by Glen Gore in his affidavit signed some twenty years after their alleged drug-dealing ventures.

Ada is a nice town, and the obvious question is: When will the good guys clean house?

Perhaps when they get tired of paying for bad prosecutions. Twice in the past two years, the city of Ada has raised property taxes to replenish the reserve funds used to settle the lawsuits filed by Ron and Dennis. In a cruel insult, these taxes are paid by all property owners, including many members of Debbie Carter's family.

It is impossible to calculate the total amount of money wasted. Oklahoma spends about $20,000 a year to house an inmate. Ignoring the extra cost of death row and treatment in state mental hospitals, Ron's tab was at least $250,000. Same for Dennis. Add the amounts they received in the civil suit, and the math becomes easy. It's safe to say that several million dollars were wasted because of their cases.

These sums do not begin to contemplate the thousands of hours spent by the appellate lawyers who worked so diligently to free the men, nor do they include the time wasted by the state's lawyers trying to execute them. Every dollar spent prosecuting and defending them was mailed in by the taxpayers.

But there were some savings. Barney Ward was paid a whopping $3,600 to defend Ron, and, as you remember, Judge Jones denied Barney's request for money to hire a forensic expert to evaluate the state's evidence. Greg Saunders received the same fee, $3,600. He, too, was denied access to an expert. The taxpayers had to be protected.

The financial waste was frustrating enough, but the human toll was far more damaging. Obviously, Ron's mental problems were greatly exacerbated by the wrongful conviction, and, once freed, he never recovered. Most exonerees do not. Dennis Fritz is a lucky one. He had the courage and the intelligence and, eventually, the money to put his life back together. He lives a quiet, normal, and prosperous life in Kansas City, and last year became a grandfather.

Of the other characters, Bill Peterson is still the district attorney in Ada. Two of his assistants are Nancy Shew and Chris Ross. One of his investigators is Gary Rogers. Dennis Smith retired from the Ada Police Department in 1987 and died suddenly on June 30, 2006. Barney Ward died in the summer of 2005 as I was writing the book, and I never had the chance to interview him. Judge Ron Jones was voted out of office in 1990 and left the Ada area.

Glen Gore is still housed on H Unit at McAlester. In July 2005, his conviction was overturned by the Oklahoma Court of Criminal Appeals, and a new trial was ordered. The court decided that Gore did not receive a fair trial because Judge Landrith did not allow his defense lawyer to put on proof that two other men had already been convicted of the murder.

On June 21, 2006, Gore was again found guilty. The jury deadlocked on the issue of death, and Judge Landrith, as required by law, sentenced Gore to life without parole.

I owe much to many people who helped with this book. Annette and Renee and their families gave me complete access to every aspect of Ron's life. Mark Barrett spent countless hours driving me around Oklahoma, telling me stories that I at first found hard to believe, and locating witnesses, pulling out old files, and leaning on his network of contacts. His assistant, Melissa Harris, copied a million documents and kept everything in meticulous order.

Dennis Fritz revisited his painful history with remarkable enthusiasm and answered all my questions. Greg Wilhoit did the same.

Brenda Tollett with the *Ada Evening News* dug through the archives and magically produced copies of the paper's extensive history of the two murders. Ann Kelley Weaver, now with *The Oklahoman*, was quick to recall many of the stories surrounding the exoneration.

At first, Judge Frank Seay was reluctant to talk about one of his cases. He still holds to the old-fashioned notion that judges should be heard and not seen, but he eventually came around. In one of our phone conversations I suggested that he was a "hero," a description he quickly objected to. I was overruled from twelve hundred miles away. Vicky Hildebrand still works for him and vividly remembers her first reading of Ron's petition for habeas corpus relief.

Jim Payne is now a federal judge himself and, though cooperative, showed little interest in taking credit for saving Ron's life. But he is a hero. His careful reading of Janet Chesley's brief, at home, after hours, prompted concern enough to approach Judge Seay and recommend an eleventh-hour stay of execution.

Though he entered the story in a late chapter, Judge Tom Landrith had the unique pleasure of presiding over the exoneration hearing in April 1999. Visiting his office in the Ada courthouse was always a treat. The stories, many of them probably true, flowed forth with great ease.

Barry Scheck and the warriors at the Innocence Project were gracious and open. As of this writing, they have freed 180 prisoners by DNA testing, and they have inspired at least thirty other innocence projects around the country. For a closer look, go to www.innocenceproject.org.

Tommy Ward spent three years and nine months on death row, on the old F Cellhouse, before being permanently exiled to the prison in

Lexington. We swapped many letters. Some of his stories were about Ron, and he allowed me to use them in these pages.

Regarding his nightmare, I relied heavily on *The Dreams of Ada*, by Robert Mayer. It's a fascinating book, a wonderful reminder of how good true-crime writing can be. Mr. Mayer was thoroughly cooperative during my research.

Thanks to the lawyers and staff at the Oklahoma Indigent Defense System—Janet Chesley, Bill Luker, and Kim Marks. And to Bruce Leba, Murl Bowen, Christy Shepherd, Leslie Delk, Dr. Keith Hume, Nancy Vollertsen, Dr. Susan Sharp, Michael Salem, Gail Seward, Lee Mann, David Morris, and Bert Colley. John Sherman, a third-year law student at the University of Virginia, spent a year and a half buried in the boxes of research we collected, and somehow kept it all straight.

I had the benefit of volumes of sworn testimony from most of those involved in this story. Some interviews were not needed. Some were not granted. Only the names of the alleged rape victims have been changed.

John Grisham
July 1, 2006